EcoSensory Therapy

EcoSensory Therapy addresses a growing question among practitioners in mental health, health care, social care, and education: how can the transformative and therapeutic power of nature be integrated into professional practice safely, ethically, and with confidence? This book introduces the EcoSensory Therapy Model of Practice, offering a practical, evidence-informed framework that helps practitioners move beyond the four walls and work intentionally with the therapeutic potential of natural environments.

Drawing on insights from neuroscience, psychology, sensory integration, attachment theory, trauma-informed practice, and nature-based approaches, this book presents the EcoSensory Model as a bridge between theory and practice. At the heart of the model are eight core elements, mirrored in the structure of chapters within this book, and organised within a neuro-sequential framework that translates seamlessly to practice:

- Ground
- Connect
- Rhythm
- Discover
- Attend
- Create
- Nourish
- Reflect

Together, these elements help practitioners understand how regulation, attention, learning, connection, creativity, wellbeing, and reflection can be supported through sensory experience and relationship with the natural world. Through theory, research, case examples, and professional guidance, the authors show how everyday natural spaces can become meaningful settings for therapeutic and developmental work.

An essential read for mental health practitioners, such as psychologists, occupational therapists, and psychotherapists, this book may also be of interest to practitioners, supervisors, and trainers working within related professions across health, social care, and education.

Claire Pemrick is a Consultant Occupational Therapist and co-author of *EcoSensory Therapy*. As the founder of the Jump Start Centre, an educator, and a doctoral researcher, Claire is dedicated to strengthening family systems through relational- and occupation-based interventions. Her love of the beach, forest, and garden, alongside her commitment to nature, is evident in both her therapeutic work and personal life.

Matt Slavin is a Clinical Psychologist and co-founder of EcoSensory Therapy. His work explores how modern stress and psychological challenges arise when ancient brains meet modern environments, and how reconnecting with our evolutionary roots can support healthier ways of living and performing.

Chris West is a Consultant Occupational Therapist and co-founder of EcoSensory Therapy. She works with individuals across the lifespan who have experienced developmental trauma and is passionate about working with nature to support regulation, connection, and meaningful opportunities for growth and transformation.

EcoSensory Therapy

The Transformative Power of Nature

Claire Pemrick, Matt Slavin,
and Chris West

Routledge
Taylor & Francis Group
LONDON AND NEW YORK

Designed cover image: © EcoSensory Therapy

First published 2027
by Routledge
4 Park Square, Milton Park, Abingdon, Oxon OX14 4RN

and by Routledge
605 Third Avenue, New York, NY 10158

Routledge is an imprint of the Taylor & Francis Group, an informa business

British Library Cataloguing-in-Publication Data
A catalogue record for this book is available from the British Library

ISBN: 978-1-041-31083-9 (hbk)
ISBN: 978-1-041-31082-2 (pbk)
ISBN: 978-1-003-77746-5 (ebk)

DOI: 10.4324/9781003777465

Typeset in Times New Roman
by codeMantra

ROUTLEDGE

EcoSensory Therapy

The Transformative Power of Nature

Claire Pemrick, Matt Slavin, and Chris West

Contents

Acknowledgements

To our families, without whom EcoSensory Therapy and this book would not have been possible. Thank you for every early morning and every late night we've squirrelled away to make this vision a reality.

To our mentors and teachers, thank you for your wisdom and guidance, enabling us to pass on what we share.

To our EcoSensory community, thank you for every moment of laughter and joy in the woods and for helping nurture what started life so delicately as a seedling of an idea.

To Mercedes, thank you for your clarity of thought and hard work in bringing this book to print.

To nature and to our ancestors, thank you for bringing us to this moment in time, for all the affordances you have offered us, and for laying out this path so that we may choose to take it.

Note to Readers

Clinical standards and protocols evolve over time, and there are no guarantees that any specific technique or recommendation will be universally safe and effective. This volume is intended as a general information resource for professionals practising in the fields of health care, social care, and education. It is not a substitute for training, peer review and/or clinical supervision, nor is it a substitute for training in the EcoSensory Therapy model itself, which is certification-based.

The publisher and the authors cannot ensure the absolute accuracy, effectiveness, or suitability of any specific recommendation. At the time of going to press, the URLs displayed in this book link or refer to existing sites. The publisher and authors are not responsible for any content that appears on third-party websites.

Welcome

Claire Pemrick

Millions of years of human evolution have brought you, our dear reader, to this moment in time, to read this line. Take a moment to notice. Use your senses to notice what surrounds you. Perhaps, you are sitting within nature, holding a printed copy of this book. Perhaps, you are tucked up in bed. Wherever you are, take this moment to tune into your senses. What can you hear? What can you see? What can you touch … smell … taste … sense? Perhaps, the birdsong outside, or the warmth of the wind on your skin, or an insect busy at work next to you, or your partner's snoring.

All information comes to us through our senses, and it is through our senses that we regulate our nervous system. Our senses developed over millions of years to process our environment. It has only been for the shortest of times in our evolution that we have been sitting indoors, playing on screens, and ordering take-outs. As we will show you, our senses developed to understand nature.

This thought came to me, of course outside, while sitting by the lake next to my home. I had spent a professional lifetime learning about the power of sensory integration, and how transformative sensory-rich environments were for regulating the children I worked with. I had built a clinic with swings, monkey bars, and ball pits designed to provide this sensory-rich environment, but as I sat there by the lake, it all suddenly seemed wrong. There was nowhere as sensory-rich as being in nature.

This started me on a path. How could I move my practice outdoors? How could nature join me as a therapist to support the children and families I see? What was the evidence? How could I be safe? I had no idea! However, I knew that Chris and Matt were equally passionate about nature-based therapies, and so in the coming together of our shared mind, experience, and practice … EcoSensory Therapy was born.

Initially, the plan was to learn and support each other in developing our practices outdoors. We worked together to gather the vast and disparate swathes of evidence to support applications for funding. We went on courses such as "Shinrin-Yoku", Forest Bathing, which truly inspired us, and steadily we moved our practices outdoors, developing risk assessments, equipment lists, and activities that we could use (and you can too!). We started to have our outdoor work funded, yet our commissioners wanted to know more precisely what an EcoSensory Session would

DOI: 10.4324/9781003777465-1

look like. From us trying to explain this, the EcoSensory Model germinated, a gift from nature itself, and slowly formed itself as if it were leaves budding on a tree. Originally, it was just seven elements; as we proudly showed the model to the head teacher, they pronounced, "I love it, but this is one tree, here we are a forest", and the final, although maybe the most essential element was added: "connect".

In the forest, a key way trees connect, nurture, and communicate with each other is through their roots and mycorrhizal fungi. In this symbiotic relationship, both the plant and fungi benefit, sharing nutrients and information. In this book, we similarly hope to connect, nurture, and communicate with passionate others who, like us, recognise the transformative power of nature in improving the lives of those we work with. Our aim is to support, nurture, encourage, and help grow your practice and to help build strong and deep foundations or "roots", so that your EcoSensory tree can withstand any storm.

In this book, we will guide you through the EcoSensory Model of Practice. We also encourage you to join our training community, and to let us help you "move beyond the four walls" and to move your practice into your local nature spaces. While we hope that this book will delight and excite you, the information we share should not be used in place of the practitioner training we provide. To continue to move safely and with confidence into nature, we encourage you to join our training community and onto our "Growing Roots" Online Practitioner Training and "In Leaf" Immersive Practicum Trainings. We would be delighted to welcome you.

Our hope is that you, too, discover the confidence and joy of taking your practice outdoors.

Claire

The EcoSensory Therapy Model of Practice

Claire Pemrick, Chris West, and Matt Slavin

At the very heart of EcoSensory Therapy is its model, with its eight core elements, as the trunk of the tree, and the leaves. These core elements help us to conceptualise and bring together the essential components of EcoSensory Therapy. We see them in the (neuro)sequential way that you see them represented on the model below, recognising the importance of grounding as our foundations and following the "map of the brain" to guide how we support those we work with.

When we began developing EcoSensory Therapy, we started off without a model of practice. We were using the theories and evidence of nature-based approaches with our own models and skill sets, such as Occupational Therapy, Clinical Psychology practice, Sensory Integration, and Sensory Attachment Intervention.

Bringing together research, evidence, and practice, our EcoSensory Therapy model synthesises and holds the evidence-based and known theories of change into a singular construct. At its heart, the EcoSensory model is a neurosequential and neuro-biophysiological model of practice. As you move up through the tree to its canopy, we reach practice tasks that require higher-order brain functioning (from regulation to thinking, planning, reasoning, and reflective practice).

A model is an important and helpful way to bridge the gap between theory and practice. It helps us think about not only how to help people based on underlying theories but it also helps us to map support, development, create change, and promote growth, guide our thinking, and help us to plan our interventions (Figure B.1).

Just as trees need strong roots and foundations to grow from, so too we recognise that humans have similar needs. After starting with our foundations for safety, nurture, and nourishment – "Ground", "Connect", and "Rhythm", we move up the neurosequential model and up the heights of our tree model. We find ourselves at "Attend", "Create", and "Discover", which help us to further understand individuals' sensory, motor, cognitive, and executive function systems. In our training and workbooks, we provide assessment proformas for each element and our EcoSensory model supports practitioners to assess the relevance of each element for their client/client group and to plan and sequence activities that directly meet their needs and intended goals. These three elements, "Attend", "Create", and "Discover", more than any of our elements, constitute our "doing" elements. Right

DOI: 10.4324/9781003777465-2

Figure B.1 EcoSensory Tree Model.

at the top, within the canopy, we have our higher-order cognitive piece, that of "Reflect". Within "Reflect", we consider our highest-order meta-cognitive activities that allow us to reflect upon what has happened in the day and in the session, to use metaphors, and to support top-down emotion regulation, along with planning, reasoning, and risk management.

The representation of our model as a tree, our neurosequential model, has become the cornerstone of EcoSensory Therapy. It provides a framework, approach, and method for how to consider clients' strengths, challenges, and needs. It supports reasoning to formulate "why it is" that someone is facing the challenges they do, and how we can best help them in the here and now. We believe that any intervention or practitioner, no matter how skilled, will be of most help if they can match their support to the underlying need, values and goals of whoever they support.

As practitioners, we are aware that we are given the privilege of "walking alongside" clients for a limited period of time. We do not get to walk with them for their whole journey but just a part of it. With that at the forefront of our mind, we hope that our model of practice provides you with the frame of reference to assess, formulate and plan *how* you can be most impactful and supportive in the part of the journey you walk with your client.

While we found the tree model helpful for our understanding of our client's needs and where to focus our support neurosequentially, we found it was a little bit harder to plan our sessions based on this version of our model. When the three of us sat together to discuss the shape and rhythm of our sessions, we found that, although each of us worked slightly differently, all three of us had three distinct phases to our sessions, just like the phases of the day and the seasons of the year.

From this reflection, the idea of our Leaf Mandala took shape. We found it to be an intuitive and practical way of supporting our formulation, clinical reasoning, and session planning. The mandala also reflects three phases, or focuses of support.

The first phase centres upon "Ground", "Connect", and "Rhythm". This phase is about creating the foundations of safety, stability, and relational connection. When we consciously began our sessions with these elements in mind, we found that both we and our clients settled more easily into the space, the relationship. It helped us attune more closely to what was present in that moment, allowing us to better notice our client's rhythm, their state, and what they needed that day, while also holding a wider awareness of their broader needs and journey.

Once this foundation was established, we found that both our clients and ourselves were more ready to move into the "doing" activities of the session. And into the active heart of the work, represented by Attend, Discover, and Create. These elements capture the more engaged and exploratory activities of EcoSensory practice. Depending on the client's needs, this might involve building a den, attending carefully to a tree or patch of ground, following an animal track, or engaging creatively with materials in the environment.

Towards the end of the sessions, we found that we wanted to sit down and come together and further connect. This final phase, represented by Nourish and Reflect, became a time for integration. We might sit together, share a snack or a cup of hot chocolate, and start to work with our clients on reflecting and transferring accomplishments from the session to everyday life; sharing stories, poems and laughter through being together.

Within the mandala, each "leaf" represents one element of the EcoSensory model. Looking closely at each leaf allows practitioners to focus on a specific area of need. Within each "leaf", we consider the relevance of that element for the client, identify needs or challenges, and explore possible EcoSensory practices that might support them. To support this process, we have developed assessment proformas for each leaf element, helping practitioners reflect more deeply on what a client may need in that area. These leaves also invite consideration of appropriate EcoSensory activities that might respond to those needs. For example, if we identified that a client struggled to remain grounded for any sustained period of time, we might think creatively about how the natural environment and the structure of the session could support experiences of grounding and stability.

The mandala structure also allows the same framework to be used at different levels. At one level, it offers a conceptual overview of the EcoSensory model. At another, it can be used as a detailed formulation and session planning tool, with the centre holding a summary of the client's needs and formulation, and the surrounding leaves capturing areas of focus and possible interventions (Figure B.2).

We hope that the EcoSensory model, and the ideas explored throughout this book, give you the confidence, inspiration, and practical skill set to safely move your practice outdoors and into the natural world with those you support. Our

Figure B.2 EcoSensory Mandala Model.

intention is that the model helps practitioners feel equipped to work creatively and thoughtfully in outdoor spaces, drawing upon the therapeutic potential of nature while remaining grounded in sound clinical reasoning.

We also hope that this book inspires you to draw upon the many trainings, experiences, and ways of working you already carry. Rather than replacing what you already know, our intention is that the EcoSensory model offers a framework, an approach, and a method through which the many skills in your existing toolkit can be expressed in an ecological context. In this way, we hope that EcoSensory Therapy will add to and enhance your already established skilled, sensitive, and attuned practice, enriching the experiences of those you walk alongside for this part of their journey.

Perhaps, just for now, you can consider what *you* need in this moment of time? When you "check-in" with your "Rhythm", do you need to slow down just for a moment or do you need to stand and start to move? Or do you need to "Ground" yourself, away from distracting thoughts? Or are you called to "Discover", to put down this book and explore the natural world that awaits your curiosity?… If you find a particular calling, let it speak to you and perhaps give yourself permission to be guided by what you need.

Chapter 1

Introduction and Theoretical Foundations

Matt Slavin

Who We Are and Where We Came From

Give yourself a moment to arrive. You may be reading this after a busy day or at the start of another. Wherever you find yourself right now, allow yourself to arrive at this start … At the beginning of this journey back to our ancestral past and our origins as a species. In this chapter, we will consider *who we are* and *where we come from*. For the answer to these questions gives us the foundations from which we build our practice.

All journeys have a beginning. Our journey, our story, takes us to the origins of our species, and the story of how we find ourselves here today.

This story starts in the distant past, billions of years ago with the early foundations of life: cyanobacteria taking root on a pale blue dot in the midst of a vast universe.

We are at the heart of it all, evolutionary creatures. We come from the origins of life and have developed, if nothing else, with the will and ability to survive and reproduce. A simple fact, yes, but one whose importance to human development and therapeutic practice is easily overlooked. Today, we will remember.

Diane Ackerman, an American poet and naturalist, captures just this point in her poetic insights into the natural world. Her book, *A Natural History of the Senses*, brings us back to an uncomfortable humility … that beneath our language, technology, and social complexity, we remain sensing, striving animals shaped by deep time (Ackerman, 1991). The instincts that once kept us alive still pulse through everyday moments: in conflict, in love, in ambition, and in fear. To understand human behaviour, distress, and resilience, we must remember that although modern life dresses us in the symbols of progress, our bodies remain rooted in an older story.

Our Sensory Foundations

The foundations of our lives are sensory. All information that we process is sensory because we are sensory beings. The very idea of being "sentient" comes from the Latin ***sentire***, "to feel", and the Indo-European ***sent***, "to head for or

DOI: 10.4324/9781003777465-3

go mentally". Being sentient, having consciousness, quite literally means that we have "sense perception".

As sensory beings, we are always and forever intertwined with the physical landscape we find ourselves in. We cannot step outside the world but are constantly in relationship with it through sight, sound, smell, taste, touch, physicality, and balance. Whether we approach this from philosophy or neuroscience or sensory processing, the conclusion is the same: to exist is to be immersed in an environment that is continually shaping us. This perspective shows us that "to be" is "to be in the world", with no grounds for dividing humankind from the environment we find ourselves in. We are fundamentally relational creatures, and just as development occurs in relation between infant and caregiver, so too does human life unfold in relation to the wider world that holds us from birth to death.

And just as we have a primal calling to be in our parents' arms, we also carry a deep need for connection to the world around us, whether through a home, a landscape, a community, or a place that offers orientation and familiarity. This belonging is not just a person-to-person connection but a person-to-environment connection, and as we see it, a person-to-nature connection … an EcoSensory connection.

I remember first reading Matthew Johnson's *Ideas of Landscape* (2007) as a fresh-faced undergraduate, drawn to the idea that landscapes shape us even when we are not aware of it. Johnson, a British landscape archaeologist whose work examines the deep relationship between people and place, argues that environments are not simply physical settings but lived spaces infused with memory, identity, and meaning. He asserts that "people are emotionally attached to their landscape even if they are not consciously aware of it" (Johnson, 2007), a claim that initially struck me as poetic and beautiful but entirely abstract. Years later, in my work as a Clinical Psychologist, I spend much of my time listening to people's stories and trying to understand who they are and where they have come from. It was through this process that I first began to see just how true this was, that place is not a backdrop to human life but part of the fabric of experience itself, shaping how we feel, connect, and come to know ourselves.

In this way, the world we inhabit – the streets we walk, the rooms we occupy, and the landscapes that hold our daily lives – becomes the homeland of our thoughts. Whatever we sense, feel, or imagine arises through our embodied encounter with the world around us. Phenomenologists such as Merleau-Ponty and Heidegger remind us that human existence is not something that happens inside the mind alone, as if we were detached observers, but through our lived participation in the environments we interact with. We are always "caught up in the fabric of the world" (Merleau-Ponty, 1962, p. 256), shaped by it even as we shape it in return. The landscapes that surround us are therefore not passive backdrops for human life, but living contexts that participate in our perception, regulation, identity, and sense of belonging.

Human life is, in this sense, co-created with place. We arrange spaces, build homes, plant gardens, carve paths, and design cities, and then those same spaces begin to organise us in return, guiding our movements, moods, relationships, and rhythms of living. They influence how fast we move, how loudly we speak, where we gather, and whether we linger or pass through. A quiet reading room is designed to slow voices and movement; an open-plan office encourages collaboration by limiting territorial space; a park bench facing a view invites the sitter to pause and linger, while a brightly lit corridor invites through-flow. Through light, acoustics, temperature, scent, texture, openness, and compression, environments guide behaviour and shape experience.

The relationship is reciprocal and ongoing: we shape our environments, and they shape the kinds of people we become within them.

We can probably notice this most easily in the spaces we work in every day. Think about the rooms you use, the therapy rooms, clinics, classrooms, consultation spaces. Consider the way chairs are arranged, the distance between people, the lighting, what sits between you and the person you are working with, and how all of it signals how you are meant to behave there. Rows of desks tell children to face forward and listen. A circle invites conversation. A softly lit room with comfortable seating encourages reflection, while a bright assessment room with a desk in between can create distance and formality. Sensory rooms, soft play areas and therapy gyms invite movement and exploration by their very design. We build these environments with intention, and in return they shape us. They shape how we sit, speak, wait, share, focus, or hold back.

And while maybe this feels more obvious within urban settings, where we humans, have quite obviously built and designed spaces that are not naturally found without our hands at work, the same is true of places we think of as "nature". If you have ever gone for a walk in your local countryside, you might imagine you are entering a space separate from human influence and something purely natural, something untouched. But certainly, in the UK, that is rarely the case. Much of what we call woodland or countryside has been shaped by human hands for centuries. The paths we follow, the clearings where we stop, the boundaries we rarely cross, all of these guide how we move and what we experience. Some of the woodlands that feel oldest and most untouched were once medieval royal hunting forests, deliberately laid out with long straight rides for visibility, managed clearings for assembly, and routes designed to channel the movement of people and animals alike. Even today, we still walk those same lines, pause in those same openings, and experience the landscape through patterns set in motion hundreds of years ago. Across the world, landscapes carry rules, signs, pathways, and subtle cues that suggest where to walk, where to rest, what to protect, and what to avoid.

It might be helpful right now to see this in action around you. I invite you to pause for a moment and take in your immediate world. Engage your senses – sight, hearing, smell, touch, and even taste – and notice how you are sitting, where your body has settled, what feels supported, and what does not. Notice the light, the sounds, the temperature, and the textures within reach. Pay attention to what draws your attention and what fades into the background, what invites you to stay, and what makes you want to move. Consider how this space is shaping your posture, your breathing, your pace of thought, your willingness to engage…

Written personally, I notice how the relationship between place and person becomes most visible when I travel. Moving between city and countryside – or between countries – I can feel my pace change, my thoughts speeding or slowing, my appetite shifting, and what I am drawn towards or away from, alters without conscious effort. In some places, I feel invited to speak to strangers; in others I instinctively withdraw.

Place, in other words, does not simply surround us. It enters us, and shapes perception, emotion, and behaviour long before we are aware of its influence.

The Biophilia Hypothesis

As we look to understand why nature can be so healing, restorative and reparative, Edward O. Wilson offers us the Biophilia Hypothesis (Wilson, 1984). An outdoorsy and adventurous child, Wilson was blinded in his right eye at an early age. His 20/10 vision prompted him to focus on the "little things" in life, and his way of seeing led him into a career in entomology, ecology, and sociobiology. First coined by social psychologist and psychoanalyst, Erich Fromm, the Biophilia Hypothesis refers to humankind's innate love for the natural world, living things, and natural systems. It speaks to the innate desire that human beings consciously and unconsciously have to connect with the rest of life.

By way of definition, the Biophilia Hypothesis refers to "the passionate love of life and of all that is alive; it is the wish for further growth, whether in a person, a plant, an idea or a social group" (Fromm, 1973, p. 21).

We have gained so very much since the dawn of technology, industry, and the cyber-age, with freedoms that humanity could rarely have dreamed of, just some 200 years ago. That being said, we also need to reflect on what we have lost in this process of gain.

We have come to think of nature as a luxury, that space for a holiday, the "nice" but seemingly extra. However, our love for and connection with nature is so much more profound than that. That is the central theme of the Biophilia Hypothesis.

It is clear that in our early years as a species, a love and respect for the well-being of the natural world would be an effective evolutionary adaptation, aiding survival. It makes sense that certain habitats, ones that offer natural resources in plenty, would trigger a positive response within us. When we consider what humans are often drawn to in natural spaces, the landscapes that feel most desirable, these tend to be those rich in the resources needed for survival; water to drink, food to gather or hunt, materials for shelter and warmth. I often explore this during EcoSensory trainings by inviting participants to imagine the most luxurious or ideal landscape they could find themselves in. The responses are strikingly consistent: a beach with fresh water nearby; a woodland offering shade and wood for fire; open views across land or sea; a sense of shelter at their back and visibility ahead. Without prompting, people describe environments that would have supported human survival for millennia. Trees suggest fuel, building material, and protection; water signals life and sustenance; oceans hint at fish and reliable food sources. Many imagine standing with a wall of trees or rock behind them, facing outward towards an open vista, a position that offers both refuge and the ability to detect potential threats from a distance. These choices, we contend, echo ancient survival logic as landscapes of protection and resourcing. The Biophilia Hypothesis suggests that these ancient preferences continue to influence what many of us perceive as safe, restorative, and appealing environments today.

If these preferences truly echo something ancient within us, then we might expect to see this reflected not only in story and imagination but also in empirical research. And increasingly, we do. A recent meta-analysis examining emotional responses to natural environments drew together 49 experimental studies involving more than 3,000 participants (Gaekwad et al., 2022). Across these studies, time spent in natural settings was consistently associated with meaningful increases in positive emotion and reductions in unpleasant emotional states.

Interestingly, the effect was stronger when people were physically immersed in nature – walking through it, breathing it in, sensing its textures and sounds – compared to when they merely viewed images or listened to recordings of natural scenes in laboratory conditions. It appears that something about the full, embodied, sensory experience matters.

While such findings do not, in themselves, prove an innate "love of life" in the philosophical sense proposed by Fromm and Wilson, they do suggest that our emotional systems respond reliably to natural environments in ways that support recovery from stress and unpleasant effects. The precise mechanisms remain under exploration – whether attentional, physiological, sensory, evolutionary, relational, or integration of these – but the pattern is becoming harder to ignore. The landscapes our ancestors may have intuitively recognised as supporting survival are now being shown by modern research to support emotional restoration too.

Green Mind Theory

If the Biophilia Hypothesis helps us understand why we are drawn towards nature, Green Mind Theory helps us understand what may be happening inside us as we respond to it.

From an evolutionary perspective, it is highly likely that natural selection favoured a negativity bias within the brain-mind. Our ancestors survived not because they were relaxed, but because they were vigilant. Missing a single threat could mean death. Missing a single opportunity rarely did. As a result, our amygdala, the threat-detection centre of the brain, is exquisitely tuned to cues of danger. It reacts quickly, often prior to conscious appraisal, mobilising the body before the thinking mind has caught up.

This reactivity has kept us alive for millennia, and it continues to serve us well. When we hear an unexpected knock in the middle of the night, the body reacts before thought has time to form. When a car swerves towards us, we respond in milliseconds.

This is our architecture of survival, and it is highly adaptive. These survival patterns are ancient, efficient, and deeply protective, allowing us to respond to immediate threats without the delay of conscious reasoning.

Yet the challenge in modern life is that this system can be so readily activated and so rarely given space to settle. Our amygdala is not easily persuaded that the contemporary world is truly safe. The pace of modern living, the persistent glow of artificial light, the steady stream of digital notifications, the pressures of performance and evaluation, the constant sense of urgency woven through daily life, all of this can register as "threat". And of course, the body responds, as it always has.

When such activation becomes frequent and sustained, the system designed for brief episodes of survival begins to operate as a default state. The sympathetic nervous system and the hypothalamic–pituitary–adrenal axis are engaged not for seconds, but for hours and days at a time. While this mobilisation is protective in the short term, prolonged activation carries a cost. The cumulative physiological toll of repeated stress responses can, over time, contribute to dysregulation across emotional, cognitive, and bodily systems (Cicchetti et al., 2011; Luecken & Appelhans, 2006). What evolved to protect us in moments of danger can begin to wear on us when it rarely powers down.

It is within this context that Pretty et al. (2017) proposed Green Mind Theory. Drawing on decades of research into green exercise and nature-based interventions, they suggest that contact with natural environments facilitates what they describe as a "Green Mind" state. In their words, this state is "an optimal mixed mode of mainly activated Parasympathetic Nervous System (PNS) activity, interest and excitement-associated mild Sympathetic Nervous System (SNS) stimulation, and the presence of only occasional SNS spikes for alarm response" (Pretty et al., 2017, p. 4).

Nature appears capable of shifting us out of chronic alarm and into a more regulated mode of being alert, interested, alive, but not overwhelmed.

As we said earlier, today we remember *who* we are and *where* we come from. Our arousal regulation systems were shaped in natural environments.

Homo sapiens "arrived" on this planet around 200,000–250,000 years ago. Evolved and adapted to survive in the world, our anatomy and neurophysiology comes from this ancient past. Evolution happens slowly and successively, and whilst as a species we have used our larger than average pre-frontal cortex to innovate and adapt, our neural architecture (that which gives us our survival responses, that lays the foundation of our mental and physical health) has not adapted so fast. Our stress–response system itself was founded hundreds of thousands, if not millions of years ago, and we would be at pains to forget this.

As Yoshifumi Miyazaki, a physical anthropologist and figure central to Shinrin-Yoku, discusses with Florence Williams, an American journalist and author: "throughout our evolution, we've spent 99.9 percent of our time in nature. Our physiology is still adapted to it. During everyday life, a feeling of comfort can be achieved if our rhythms are synchronized with those of the environment" (Williams, 2017, p. 23).

Our arousal regulation systems continuously organise themselves according to the cues they receive, and those cues are patterned by geography, power, and socio-economic distribution, by the neighbourhoods we inhabit, the safety we experience, the histories carried in the ground beneath our feet. The body learns its landscape. It calibrates itself to what surrounds it. And if certain environments chronically amplify vigilance, it follows that others – under the right conditions – may help to amplify comfort.

Green Mind Theory, then, is not simply the claim that nature is "nice", or that it makes people calmer. It suggests that regular, intentional contact with natural environments may help support arousal regulation systems that were designed for a different tempo of life, one characterised by periods of exertion followed by genuine rest.

Pretty et al. (2017) argue that green environments facilitate a particular pattern of neurophysiological functioning and a state in which the body is restored without being shut down; alert without being overwhelmed; engaged without being driven by chronic threat.

Green Mind Theory therefore makes a broader assertion: that the environments we repeatedly inhabit participate in shaping our regulatory baseline. If our stress–response architecture was forged in landscapes of variability and natural complexity, then regular contact with those kinds of environments may help regulate and rebalance the systems that modern life so easily keeps on edge. The theory does not romanticise nature, nor does it deny socio-political realities, but it does suggest that by reintroducing patterned, sensory-rich contact with the natural world into daily life, we may be working with, rather than against, our evolutionary design.

Blue Mind Theory

There is something about water that draws us to it, that inspires us, that invigorates us, that gives us life. Perhaps, that's no wonder. After all, we were born into a water-world. Water covers more than 70% of the Earth's surface.

And at the most practical level, our lives depend on it. On bushcraft and survival courses, I was taught the *survival rule of three*: three minutes without oxygen, three days without water, three weeks without food. We can survive far longer without food than we can without water. Our bodies are organised around it, sustained by it, and regulated by it. Perhaps our attraction to rivers, lakes, and oceans is that ancient echo once more, a deep biological signal of safety and survival. Water is not simply something we find beautiful or calming; it is something we are utterly dependent upon.

Perhaps no image captures this more powerfully than a photograph you've almost certainly seen. It's a photo that shows Earth as a tiny blue speck suspended in darkness. In 1990, as the Voyager 1 space probe was leaving the Solar System, NASA – at the request of astronomer Carl Sagan – turned the camera back towards its place of origin. From 3.7 billion miles away, it took a final image of home. What appeared in the vastness of space was what Sagan later called the "Pale Blue Dot".

Like a child depends upon its mother for survival, humans have always depended upon nature, upon water for survival. So, just as we intuitively love our parents, so are we linked to the natural world, mother nature, physically, emotionally, cognitively, and neurophysiologically.

Our love for water is rooted deep within our psyche and DNA. Our ancient ancestors came from the water and evolved from the watery deep, and we are water. Humans spend their first nine months immersed in a water-world and throughout our life, we walk around as primarily water beings. Our bodies are made of approximately 60% water, and our brains some 80% water.

Dr. Wallace J. Nichols, a marine biologist, examined our deep connectedness and preference for "blue spaces" (lakes, rivers, and oceans). Using neuroimaging, he has researched the beneficial effects of being near water and argues for a theory of "Blue Mind".

> Blue Mind, a mildly meditative state characterized by calm, peacefulness, unity, and a sense of general happiness and satisfaction with life in the moment.
>
> (Nichols, 2014, p. 6)

Building on Nichols' popularisation of "Blue Mind", academic research has increasingly explored whether proximity to, and engagement with, water environments corresponds with measurable health outcomes. We now have a growing body of evidence suggesting that blue spaces are associated with enhanced mood, greater psychosocial well-being, increased physical activity, stress reduction, cognitive restoration, social connectedness, and improved health indicators across adulthood and later life (Britton et al., 2020; Gascon et al., 2015; Guan et al., 2025; Maund et al., 2019; Wang & Md Sani, 2024; Wang et al., 2016).

In a recent umbrella review on blue space, health, and well-being, Han and Zhang (2026) examined six meta-analyses comprising over three million participants to evaluate the strength and certainty of this evidence. Importantly, they found that proximity alone, how close someone lives to the coast, the percentage of visible water in satellite imagery, indices of "blueness", did not consistently predict health outcomes. What appeared to matter more was interaction, immersion and engagement, actual contact with coasts, rivers, and lakes.

So, if you live *near* the ocean, *near* rivers and lakes, the recommendation is to make contact, and engage with these water worlds. Walk along the coastline, and dip your toes in. Listen to the break of the waves and watch them lap the shore. Watch the leaves dance on the stream. Find ways to meet and *connect* with the blue spaces.

Nature Connectedness

We can sit in a park scrolling on a phone and remain psychologically distant. We can walk along a coastline while preoccupied with deadlines. Proximity alone does not guarantee relationship.

Over the past two decades, researchers at the University of Derby, most notably Professor Miles Richardson and colleagues, have helped formalise a deceptively simple idea: it is not only time in nature that matters but also the relationship we experience with it. It is our *connection* that matters.

Rather than assuming connection simply emerges from exposure, the Derby research group asked a crucial question: how does nature connection actually develop? What differentiates someone who merely passes through a natural landscape from someone who feels connected to it?

In their work, nature connectedness is described as a measurable psychological construct reflecting the strength of an individual's relationship with the natural world, involving cognitive beliefs, emotional bonds, and experiential engagement (Richardson et al., 2017). It concerns how we think about, feel towards, and relate to nature. It is not simply about being outdoors. It is about how we connect, and to what degree we feel connected, *part* of nature.

In 2017, Lumber, Richardson, and Sheffield proposed five "pathways to nature connectedness": namely contact, emotion, meaning, compassion, and beauty (Lumber et al., 2017). More recently, the language has evolved, reframing "contact" explicitly as "*senses*", tuning in to nature, actively perceiving it, receiving it, and allowing it to register in the body, through our senses.

The five pathways are now commonly articulated as follows.

Senses: Tuning in to Nature through the Senses

Listening to birdsong. Feeling bark beneath the hand. Noticing the temperature of the air, the scent of damp earth, the rhythm of waves, and the weight of wind on skin.

Emotion: Feeling Alive through the Emotions and Feelings Nature Brings

Allowing oneself to feel awe, calm, joy, wonder, tenderness, and even grief, in response to the living world.

Beauty: Noticing Nature's Beauty

Light shifting across water. Fractal patterns in leaves. The geometry of branches against the sky.

Meaning: Nature Bringing Meaning to Our Lives

Recognising personal and cultural significance. Using nature as metaphor. Marking seasons. Seeing landscapes as part of one's own story.

Compassion: Caring and Taking Action for Nature

Extending care beyond the self. Acting with concern for ecosystems, species, and future generations.

Together, these pathways describe *qualities* of engagement. They suggest that what deepens connection is not exposure alone, but visceral, embodied engagement in the more-than-human world.

When researchers pooled findings across dozens of studies, they found that individuals who report a stronger sense of connection to nature also tend to report higher levels of well-being. Pritchard, Richardson, Sheffield, and McEwan's meta-analysis (2020), synthesising data across multiple populations, found reliable associations between nature connectedness and both hedonic well-being (the experience of feeling good) and eudaimonic well-being (the experience of living well). Notably, the strongest association within eudaimonic well-being was with personal growth, suggesting that feeling connected to the natural world may be particularly linked with a sense of development and psychological flourishing.

And perhaps what is most reassuring of all, is that nature connectedness is not reserved for the already attuned. It can be nurtured. McEwan et al. (2023) looked at programmes that invited people back into relationship, through sensory noticing, emotional openness, aesthetic appreciation, and compassionate action. When people were guided to meet the natural world in these ways, their sense of connection strengthened. And as that connection strengthened, so too did their well-being.

The more people begin to feel connected to nature, it would seem the more they naturally start to care for it. A large meta-analysis looking at 37 studies and over 13,000 people found a clear and consistent pattern: people who felt a stronger sense of connection to nature were far more likely to reduce waste, conserve resources, and act in ways that protect ecosystems and future generations (Whitburn et al., 2020). Perhaps the most telling insight is that people cared for the environment not because they knew more, but because they felt part of it.

It would seem, then, that nature connection isn't simply about spending more time outdoors. It is about allowing a relationship with the living world to re-emerge.

The benefits do not come from adding nature onto an already busy life like another item on a checklist. They arise from encounter, from sensory experience, emotional resonance, and the embodied remembering we have explored throughout this chapter: that we are not separate from the living world, but part of it.

Stress Reduction Theory and Attention Restoration Theory

Ulrich et al. (1991) argued for and developed extensive research into the stress-reducing quality of time in nature. Ulrich argues that one of the primary processes underlying beneficial change is a "Stress Reduction Theory" or SRT. Based on clinical populations, Ulrich argued that natural spaces not only have a restorative effect more generally but also reduce our stress levels following a stressful situation. In other words, nature can restore us following a stressful situation and act as a stress buffer, allowing us to be more stress-resilient to the inevitable stresses of modern life. Demonstrated in research, a systematic review by Antonelli et al. (2019) shows that conscious time in forest environments can significantly lower levels of stress (as measured through salivary or serum cortisol – a direct stress biomarker). More on this in our "Attend" element.

Kaplan and Kaplan (1989) propose Attention Restoration Theory, or ART, as a theoretical model to understand the beneficial effects of nature on our attentional capacity. Where SRT speaks to emotional and physiological recovery, ART focuses on cognitive recovery, and our ability to think clearly, concentrate, and direct attention. As the pace of life has increased with our urban and modern living, we are increasingly disconnected from the natural world. It is estimated that young people spend on average 50 hours or more each week staring at some form of screen. The environment and way we live our life taxes our ability to think and drains our attention. Whilst our lives have been sped up, the price is that our body, in particular our attentional capacity, is taxed to no end.

Whilst born (in an evolutionary sense) into a natural world with a cocktail of ingredients evolutionarily designed to calm us, restore us, and activate our parasympathetic nervous system "rest and digest" response, the majority of the world now live within urban environments (Kaplan, 1995).

In this way, researchers and clinicians have begun to question how some of the difficulties observed in children and young people might be understood in the context of the environments we have created, environments that differ dramatically from those in which we have evolved and adapted to. Some writers have sought to "fight fire with fire" by introducing language that highlights ecological disconnection itself as the problem.

The term *Nature Deficit Disorder* was popularised by American journalist and author Richard Louv in his book *Last Child in the Woods* (2005). Louv did not propose a formal psychiatric diagnosis, but rather a cultural descriptor, "a way to describe the psychological, physical and cognitive costs of human alienation from nature, particularly for children in their vulnerable developing years" (Louv, 2009). His intention was to draw public attention to the rapid reduction in children's outdoor play and unstructured engagement with the natural world.

While the phrase has been influential in public discourse, and evocative in its impact, it is not a clinical diagnosis, nor is it without criticism. Labelling disconnection as a "disorder" risks medicalising what instead we see as a relational, societal, and environmental issue. But perhaps, Louv's passionate discourse reminds us that there is a cost to our disconnection with the natural world.

A Smidgen of the Evidence

As the research and academic literature continues to grow, both in volume and in weight of evidence, it felt only right to share a small smidgen of it with you here.

This is neither the time nor the place for an exhaustive review, but we present a compact and digestible glimpse into what is now emerging across disciplines.

If this sparks your curiosity, we strongly encourage you to explore the original studies in more depth. What follows are some of the key findings that continue to shape the field.

One small point though, to keep in mind as you read this table, is that this is not about scaling mountains or disappearing into the wild, but about stepping into the natural spaces close to home. Whilst there is growing evidence demonstrating the beneficial effects of wilderness experiences (Russell & Phillips-Miller, 2002), adventure experiences in nature (Autry, 2001; Gass, 1995), and spending time deeply immersed in remote and undisturbed pockets of nature, it is equally clear that the benefits of nature can be found in any space where you can be fully present with the natural world around you.

We hope that Table 1.1 gives you a clear, grounded sense of just how wide-reaching these effects can be.

Table 1.1 A Smidgen of the Evidence

Area of Benefit	*Key Findings*	*Sources*
Immune function	Time in nature boosts immune system functioning. Natural killer (NK) cells (white blood cells that destroy tumour and virus-infected cells) increased by ~40% after three days of forest walking. Effects lasted seven days, and remained ~15% above baseline after one month. Equivalent urban walking showed no change.	Li et al., 2009
Physical health	Increased greenspace exposure associated with decreases in blood pressure, cholesterol, cardiovascular mortality, stroke risk, asthma, coronary heart disease, and improved respiratory and cancer outcomes across the lifespan.	Twohig-Bennett & Jones, 2018
Stress physiology	Forest exposure significantly lowers salivary cortisol (stress biomarker) compared with urban environments before and after intervention.	Antonelli et al., 2019
Autonomic regulation	Reductions in adrenaline, noradrenaline, and blood pressure persist throughout the day following a nature walk, indicating increased parasympathetic activity and physiological restoration.	Gladwell et al., 2016
Cardiovascular regulation	Forest bathing associated with improvements in cardiovascular functioning and reductions in blood pressure.	Li, 2012; Ochiai et al., 2015
Mood and emotional well-being	Nature therapy and Shinrin-Yoku reduce depression, anxiety, stress, and anger in clinical and non-clinical populations; anxiety reductions particularly robust.	Kotera et al., 2022

(*Continued*)

Table 1.1 (Continued)

Area of Benefit	*Key Findings*	*Sources*
Depression and anxiety treatment	Forest therapy significantly improves symptoms and ratings of depression and anxiety, offering preventative and non-pharmacological approaches.	Rajoo et al., 2020; Yeon et al., 2021
Self-esteem and mood	Short-term green exercise improves self-esteem and mood across ages, genders, health status, duration, and intensity. Largest effects seen in younger participants; strongest benefits near water.	Barton & Pretty, 2010
Sleep quality	As little as two hours walking in forest environments associated with improvements in sleep duration and quality.	Li, 2018; Morita et al., 2011
Cognitive and developmental outcomes	Exposure to nature associated with improved cognitive functioning, brain activity, physical activity levels, sleep quality, and reduced mental health symptoms in children and youth.	Jimenez et al., 2021
Long-term health protection	Evidence suggests protective effects on mental health outcomes, cognitive functioning, and chronic disease over time.	Jimenez et al., 2021
Population mental health	Access to green spaces associated with improved mental health and vitality across regions and nationalities.	de Vries et al., 2003; Gascon et al., 2015; Maas et al., 2009; van den Berg et al., 2016
Dose–response relationship	Greater availability and use of green spaces associated with higher mental well-being.	Wood et al., 2017
Socioeconomic buffering	Proximity to natural spaces buffers stress particularly in socioeconomically deprived populations.	Harrison et al., 2023; Mitchell & Popham, 2008; Wheeler et al., 2012
Multi-system regulation	Forest medicine research demonstrates effects across the psycho-neuro-endocrino-immune network, indicating integrated regulation across bodily systems.	Li, 2023

An EcoSensory Model of Practice

If this chapter has one purpose, it is to help us remember. That beneath our plans and pressures and professional language, we remain sensory beings shaped by nature and deep time. We hope it gives you the beginnings of knowledge, understanding, legitimacy, evidence, and *permission* to step beyond the four walls and into a different way of working.

But remembering alone is not enough. Understanding is only helpful if it changes what we do.

So, as we move forward, we shift from foundations into practice. The chapters that follow will guide you through the EcoSensory Model of Practice, element by element, translating theory into ways of working that support regulation, reconnection, and therapeutic change through intentional contact with the natural world.

As you continue, we invite you to read not only with your professional mind but also with your sensory awareness, noticing how these ideas resonate with your own experience of place, practice, and personhood.

Just as the Earth is built upon successive layers (or strata) and the brain can be understood as having evolutionary layers, so too we follow this layered approach with our neurosequential model of practice.

We begin at our foundations of safety, stability, orientation, and support. We begin with "Ground".

References

Ackerman, D. (1991). *The natural history of the senses*. Vintage Books.

Antonelli, M., Barbieri, G., & Donelli, D. (2019). Effects of forest bathing (shinrin-yoku) on levels of cortisol as a stress biomarker: A systematic review and meta-analysis. *International Journal of Biometeorology*, *63*(8), 1117–1134.

Autry, C. E. (2001). Adventure therapy with girls at-risk: Responses to outdoor experiential activities. *Therapeutic Recreation Journal*, *35*(4), 289–306.

Barton, J., & Pretty, J. (2010). What is the best dose of nature and green exercise for improving mental health? A multi-study analysis. *Environmental Science & Technology*, *44*(10), 3947–3955.

Britton, E., Kindermann, G., Domegan, C., & Carlin, C. (2020). Blue care: A systematic review of blue space interventions for health and wellbeing. *Health Promotion International*, *35*(1), 50–69.

Cicchetti, D., Rogosch, F. A., Toth, S. L., & Sturge-Apple, M. L. (2011). Normalizing the development of cortisol regulation in maltreated infants through preventive interventions. *Development and Psychopathology*, *23*, 789–800.

de Vries, S., Verheij, R. A., Groenewegen, P. P., & Spreeuwenberg, P. (2003). Natural environments—Healthy environments? An exploratory analysis of the relationship between greenspace and health. *Environment and Planning A*, *35*(10), 1717–1731.

Fromm, E. (1973). *The anatomy of human destructiveness*. Holt, Rinehart and Winston.

Gaekwad, J. S., Molsehain, A. S., Roos, P. B., & Walker, A. (2022). A meta-analysis of emotional evidence for the Biophilia Hypothesis and implications for biophilic design. *Frontiers in Psychology*, *13*, 750245.

Gascon, M., Triguero-Mas, M., Martínez, D., Dadvand, P., Forns, J., Plasència, A., & Nieuwenhuijsen, M. J. (2015). Mental health benefits of long-term exposure to residential green and blue spaces: A systematic review. *International Journal of Environmental Research and Public Health, 12*(4), 4354–4379.

Gass, M. (1995). Adventure family therapy: An innovative approach answering the question of lasting change with adjudicated youth. *Monograph on Youth in the 1990s, 4*, 103–118.

Gladwell, V. E., Kuoppa, P., Tarvainen, M. P., & Rogerson, M. (2016). A lunchtime walk in nature enhances restoration of autonomic control during night-time sleep: Results from a preliminary study. *International Journal of Environmental Research and Public Health, 13*(3), 1–9.

Guan, H., Okely, A. D., Aguilar-Farias, N., Draper, C. E., & Hamlin, M. J. (2025). Associations between blue space exposure and health outcomes: A systematic review and meta-analysis. *Environmental Research, 243*, 117605.

Han, K. T., & Zhang, T. (2026). Blue space and human health: An umbrella review of meta-analyses examining associations between aquatic environments and wellbeing outcomes. *Environmental Research, 254*, 118421.

Harrison, H., Burns, M., Darko, N., & Jones, C. (2023). Exploring the benefits of nature-based interventions in socio-economically deprived communities: A narrative review of the evidence to date. *Perspectives in Public Health, 143*(3), 156–172.

Jimenez, M. P., DeVille, N. V., Elliott, E. G., Schiff, J. E., Wilt, G. E., Hart, J. E., & James, P. (2021). Associations between nature exposure and health: A review of the evidence. *International Journal of Environmental Research and Public Health, 18*(9), 4790.

Johnson, M. H. (2007). *Ideas of landscape*. Blackwell Publishing.

Kaplan, R., & Kaplan, S. (1989). *The experience of nature: A psychological perspective*. Cambridge University Press.

Kaplan, S. (1995). The restorative benefits of nature: Toward an integrative framework. *Journal of Environmental Psychology, 15*(3), 169–82.

Kotera, Y., Richardson, M., & Sheffield, D. (2022). Effects of Shinrin-Yoku (forest bathing) and nature therapy on mental health: A systematic review and meta-analysis. *International Journal of Mental Health and Addiction, 20*, 337–361.

Li, Q. (2012). *Forest medicine (Public health in the 21st century)*. Nova Science Publishers.

Li, Q. (2018). *Shinrin-Yoku: The art and science of forest bathing*. Penguin.

Li, Q. (2023). New concept of forest medicine. *Forests, 14*(5), 1024.

Li, Q., Kobayashi, M., Wakayama, Y., Inagaki, H., Katsumata, M., Hirata, Y., Hirata, K., Shimizu, T., Kawada, T., Park, B. J., Ohira, T., Kagawa, T., & Miyazaki, Y. (2009). Effect of phytoncide from trees on human natural killer cell function. *International Journal of Immunopathology and Pharmacology, 22*(4), pp. 951–959.

Louv, R. (2005). *Last child in the woods: Saving our children from nature-deficit disorder*. Algonquin Books.

Louv, R. (2009, January 28). No more "nature-deficit disorder." *Psychology Today*. https://www.psychologytoday.com/us/blog/people-in-nature/200901/no-more-nature-deficit-disorder

Luecken, L. J., & Appelhans, B. M. (2006). Early parental loss and salivary cortisol in young adulthood: The moderating role of family environment. *Development and Psychopathology, 18*(1), 295–308.

Lumber, R., Richardson, M., & Sheffield, D. (2017). Beyond knowing nature: Contact, emotion, compassion, meaning, and beauty are pathways to nature connection. *PLoS One, 12*(5), e0177186.

Maas, J., Verheij, R. A., de Vries, S., Spreeuwenberg, P., Schellevis, F. G., & Groenewegen, P. P. (2009). Morbidity is related to a green living environment. *Journal of Epidemiology and Community Health*, *63*(12), 967–973.

Maund, P. R., Irvine, K. N., Lawson, B., Steadman, J., Risely, K., Cunningham, A. A., & Davies, Z. G. (2019). What motivates the public to engage with nature? A systematic review of nature-based interventions. *Environmental Research*, *179*, 108845.

McEwan, K., Richardson, M., Sheffield, D., Ferguson, F. J., Brindley, P., & Wood, C. J. (2023). A nature connectedness intervention to improve wellbeing: A systematic review and meta-analysis. *Journal of Environmental Psychology*, *85*, 101921.

Merleau-Ponty, M. (1962). *Phenomenology of perception*. Routledge.

Mitchell, R., & Popham, F. (2008). Effect of exposure to natural environment on health inequalities: An observational population study. *The Lancet*, *372*(9650), 1655–1660.

Morita, E., Imai, M., Okawa, M., Miyaura, T., & Miyazaki, S. (2011). A before and after comparison of the effects of forest walking on the sleep of a community-based sample of people with sleep complaints. *BioPsychoSocial Medicine*, *5*, 13.

Nichols, W. J. (2014). *Blue mind: How water makes you happier, more connected and better at what you do*. Hachette.

Ochiai, H., Ikei, H., Song, C., Kobayashi, M., Miura, T., Kagawa, T., Li, Q., Kumeda, S., Imai, M., & Miyazaki, Y. (2015). Physiological and psychological effects of a forest therapy program on middle-aged females. *International Journal of Environmental Research and Public Health*, *12*(12), 15222–15232.

Pretty, J., Rogerson, M., & Barton, J. (2017). Green mind theory: How brain-body-behaviour links into natural and social environments for healthy habits. *International Journal of Environmental Research and Public Health*, *14*(7), 706.

Pritchard, A., Richardson, M., Sheffield, D., & McEwan, K. (2020). The relationship between nature connectedness and eudaimonic well-being: A meta-analysis. *Journal of Happiness Studies*, *21*, 1145–1167.

Rajoo, K., Karam, D., & Abdullah, M. Z. (2020). The physiological and psychosocial effects of forest therapy: A systematic review. *Urban Forestry & Urban Greening*, *54*, 126744.

Richardson, M., Passmore, H. A., Barbett, L., Lumber, R., Thomas, R., & Hunt, A. (2017). The green care code: How nature connectedness and simple activities help explain pro-nature conservation behaviours. *People and Nature*, *1*(2), 186–198.

Russell, K. C., & Phillips-Miller, D. (2002). Perspectives on the wilderness therapy process and its relation to outcomes. *Child & Youth Care Forum*, *31*, 415–437.

Twohig-Bennett, C., & Jones, A. (2018). The health benefits of the great outdoors: A systematic review and meta-analysis of greenspace exposure and health outcomes. *Environmental Research*, *166*, 628–637.

Ulrich, R. S., Simons, R. F., Losito, B. D., Fiorito, E., Miles, M. A., & Zelson, M. (1991). Stress recovery during exposure to natural and urban environments. *Journal of Environmental Psychology*, *11*(3), 201–230.

van den Berg, M., van Poppel, M., van Kamp, I., Andrusaityte, S., Balseviciene, B., Cirach, M., Danileviciute, A., Ellis, N., Hurst, G., Masterson, D., Smith, G., Triguero-Mas, M., Uzdanaviciute, I., de Wit, P., van Mechelen, W., Gidlow, C., Grazuleviciene, R., Nieuwenhuijsen, M. J., Kruize, H., & Maas, J. (2016). Visiting green space is associated with mental health and vitality: A cross-sectional study in four European cities. *Health & Place*, *38*, 8–15.

Wang, R., Zhao, J., Meitner, M., Hu, Y., & Xu, B. (2016). Characteristics of urban green spaces and their relationship with health outcomes: A systematic review. *Landscape and Urban Planning*, *154*, 1–10.

Wang, Y., & Md Sani, M. N. (2024). Blue spaces and human health: A systematic review of environmental and health outcomes. *Urban Forestry & Urban Greening*, *94*, 128142.

Wheeler, B. W., White, M., Stahl-Timmins, W., & Depledge, M. H. (2012). Does living by the coast improve health and wellbeing? *Health & Place*, *18*(5), 1198–1201.

Whitburn, J., Linklater, W., & Abrahamse, W. (2020). Meta-analysis of human connection to nature and pro-environmental behaviour. *Conservation Biology*, *34*(1), 180–193.

Williams, F. (2017). *The nature fix: Why nature makes us happier, healthier and more creative*. W. W. Norton & Company.

Wilson, E. O. (1984). *Biophilia*. Harvard University Press.

Wood, L., Hooper, P., Foster, S., & Bull, F. (2017). Public green spaces and positive mental health – Investigating the relationship between access, quantity and types of parks and mental wellbeing. *Health & Place*, *48*, 63–71.

Yeon, P. S., Jeon, J. Y., Jung, M. S., Min, G. M., Kim, G. Y., Han, K. M., Shin, M. J., Jo, S. H., Kim, J. G., & Shin, W. S. (2021). Effect of forest therapy on depression and anxiety: A systematic review and meta-analysis. *International Journal of Environmental Research and Public Health*, *18*(23), 12685.

Chapter 2

Ground

Matt Slavin

We start our journey with "Ground". We start all our journeys, walk all our paths and return to earth, all from our own place in the world. As Jon Kabat-Zinn, a student of Zen Buddhism, Professor Emeritus of Medicine, and founder of Mindfulness-Based Stress Reduction, famously reminded Western audiences when introducing the health-promoting potential of meditation, "Wherever you go, there you are" (Kabat-Zinn, 2004, 2009). It's something that is often overlooked, but perhaps that is why we want to start by looking straight at it and seeing what we commonly forget to notice. How we see, how we notice, always comes from our place in the world, the place which we inhabit each and every day, our corner of the universe ... our physical body (Jager, 1985).

I wonder if you know where the centre of the observable universe is. Well, you're in it. You're living it. You are it. You're seeing from it. It's hard not to be ego-centric about this, because well, it speaks to the existence of an ego, but nevertheless, here you are.

Here you find yourself at the centre of the observable universe. Of course, I also am writing this from my centre of the universe, and Claire and Chris also see from their cosy and comfortable centre of the universe.

As human beings, we experience the world from where we are. To live is to live *in Place*. And that place, our home, is our bodies. As Heidegger (1951) writes, "It is only as inhabiting, embodied beings that we find access to a world". As sensory beings, we live in "the paradigm of embodiment" (Csordas, 1990).

So, we start with "ground", in recognising, noticing, and coming *back* to our bodies and the here and now. If we are to say that we experience the world from our own corner of the universe, then it's worth spending some time connecting with *that* place. We just need *intention* to do so.

The body is immediately present to us, because we *are* our body. So, let's come back to it. Plant your feet on the ground. Feel the sensation of the earth beneath your feet. Notice how you feel held by the earth beneath you. Experience what it is like to feel "grounded".

DOI: 10.4324/9781003777465-4

What Is Grounding and Why Start with It

> Grounding Refers to the ability to have not only our feet on the ground but our minds on the ground.
>
> Fisher (1999)

If we are to *ground* ourselves, it is worth reflecting on what that actually means and why it matters. Janina Fisher, PhD, a clinical psychologist, former instructor at Harvard Medical School, and internationally recognised expert in trauma treatment, uses this phrase to highlight that grounding is the capacity for body and mind to arrive in the same place at the same time.

But of course, so much of our lives are spent with our minds anywhere but in the *here* and *now.*

This is just the nature of the mind itself.

As Professor Paul Gilbert, clinical psychologist and founder of Compassion Focused Therapy (Gilbert, 2009), has written, the human mind or as he often writes, our "tricky mind", did not evolve primarily to make us happy or peaceful, but to detect threat, solve problems, and anticipate danger. In many ways, our minds are time travellers, constantly scanning the past for lessons and the future for risks. It can pull us into places that feel vividly real, even when we are physically safe in the present. Where the mind goes, the body follows. If we *imagine* a personal crisis or *mentally rehearse* a professional problem, our autonomic nervous system responds as though it is happening now, preparing us to "fight", "flee", and "feign" in familiar crisis-driven ways. However, nothing has *actually* changed in the world around us. Tricky, indeed.

For many people, this is simply the background hum of modern life: a mind that rarely rests and a body that struggles to keep up. But for those living with anxiety or trauma, the pull is stronger. The mind becomes a place of alarm rather than reflection, replaying what has happened or bracing for what might. The body, in turn, can remain caught in states of readiness, prepared to fight, flee, freeze, or submit long after the original danger has passed.

As Semple and Lee (2008, p. 65) explain, "attention that is overly focused on past and future events is also characteristic of most childhood [and adult] anxiety disorders".

Grounding is the process of interrupting this loop. It is a way of signalling to the nervous system that the threat is not here, not now. Rather than trying to control thoughts directly, a task that often proves frustratingly ineffective, grounding works through the body, through sensation, through contact with the present moment. It brings attention back to what can be seen, heard, touched, and felt, allowing the mind to settle because the body has found something tangible (and safe) to orient around.

This is why grounding sits at the foundation of trauma-informed practice and anxiety work. Before insight, before processing, before meaning-making, there must first be stability. Before we venture into the "murky waters" of another's distress, it is *essential* that whoever you are working with, and you as their guide, feel that it is *safe* to do so. It would be dangerous and unethical to lead someone into deep waters before they knew how to swim to safety.

We also know that our neurophysiology is organised as a hierarchical system. Dr Bruce Perry, a child psychiatrist, neuroscientist, and founder of the Neurosequential Network, widely known for his work on trauma and brain development, has emphasised the importance of following the brain's sequence when supporting healing and change. His Neurosequential Model of Therapeutics highlights that to access thinking, reflection, and reasoning (Reflect in Our EcoSensory Model), the lower systems of the brain must first feel safe and regulated (Perry, 2006). In other words, regulation precedes reflection.

A helpful way of understanding what this looks like in practice is through the concept of the *Window of Tolerance*, originally described by psychiatrist Dan Siegel (1999) within his work on interpersonal neurobiology, referring to the optimal zone of arousal in which a person can remain regulated, present, and able to think and relate effectively. Within this window, the person can think and feel comfortably, with the capacity to act in ways that they consciously intend. Outside it, people are reacting from hyper-arousal (anxious, agitated, and reactive states) or hypo-arousal (shut down, numb, and disconnected states).

Although now widely used across trauma-informed disciplines, the underlying message is universal. Our ability to learn, relate, reflect, and function depends on our level of physiological regulation. One of the most reliable ways to help someone move back towards this zone, and remain there for longer, is through connection to the here and now, and developing the skills to do so. Through grounding.

So, as you read this, take a deep breath or sigh. Move and shuffle to make contact with the physical world around you. Perhaps take off your shoes and socks and feel the ground beneath you. Look around and notice what you sense.

Grounding literally relies on connection. Connection to the immediate world around us, *through* our many senses. And there's no better environment to do this in than our natural environment and evolutionary home, *nature* (Gladwell et al., 2013; Li et al., 2011; Park et al., 2010).

It is suggested that time in nature affects the two main stress systems, namely the sympathoadrenal medullary and the hypothalamus–pituitary–adrenal axis (Li, 2010; Park et al., 2010). These two systems are responsible for regulating cortisol, adrenaline, noradrenaline, and dopamine amongst other key hormones involved in our stress response system. These studies help us understand the relaxing and stress-reducing properties of time in nature, as observed by reductions in physiological markers of stress. It would seem that nature, in all its glory, provides us with a sensory-rich environment in which to ground.

As we will explain further, much of human suffering – and the foundation of many mental health difficulties – is associated with a *disconnection from* the present moment. Across experiences such as trauma, dissociation, anxiety, depression or obsessive-rumination, there is a common thread: the mind is pulled away from the here and now – into the past or into imagined futures – into *there and then* instead of *here and now*.

Bessel van der Kolk (2015), a psychiatrist, trauma researcher, and author of *The Body Keeps the Score*, has been central in demonstrating how trauma is held not only in memory but also in the body itself. His work highlights that change does not come solely from thinking differently, but from reconnecting with our physical experience, becoming aware of sensation, movement, breath, and how we relate to the world around us. As he describes it, this process begins to support the "releasing [of] the tyranny of the past".

Trauma is not just something we remember, but something we continue to live through, carried in the body as an imprint of past experience long after the danger itself has passed. Recovery begins when we can return to the body, noticing sensations, orienting to the present, and gradually rediscovering a sense of safety within ourselves and in the world around us. As this happens, the brain updates its understanding of what is happening now, recognising when we are safe, and allowing us, over time, to settle more fully into the present moment with greater ease, back into the immediacy of our lived, sensory experience.

As physical, sensory beings, we can use our very existence to ground back to our place, our centre of the universe, our home. You might pause for a moment and notice: what can you see? what can you hear? What can you touch … smell … taste…?

And if you are to help anyone access higher-order thinking, to reflect and make use of our wonderful prefrontal cortex, in your supportive work within the outdoors (or any support setting for that matter) then we must first start with grounding. If we return to the work of Janina Fisher, she contends that your support session, whatever your discipline, is rarely going to be useful if the client (young person or adult) is less than 60% present in their body (Fisher, 1999). The natural world provides a sensory-rich landscape of sights, smells, sounds and sensations. It is this abundance of natural stimuli that provides excellent foci of attention for grounding (more of this later in "Attend").

A word of caution. The first principle of support work is "do no harm". Always work within the limits of your professional competency. Well-meaning practices can inadvertently do more harm than good. Inviting someone to pay attention to their body (such as in a grounding technique) can be alerting, uncomfortable, or even triggering for people whose past experiences have made bodily awareness feel unsafe. If you are working with individuals who may carry trauma, which includes far more people than we might assume, appropriate trauma-informed knowledge and supervision are essential. When we do work with people who have experienced trauma, we begin grounding through "external cues" of attention. So, we're now back to nature, and the endless possibilities of things to be "mindful" of in grounding techniques. Whether someone has had trauma in their past or not, the practice of starting with external stimuli before gradually turning people's attention inwardly, towards their body, is good practice. So for grounding … step out into the natural world and witness the abundance of resources to pay attention to, to be mindful of, and to ground with.

So, that is where we must begin – by connecting to the here and now, by grounding in the present moment. Like a lightning bolt in a storm, we can help people to "touch down" and connect with the "here and now" through connecting with the world around them.

And the bonus here is that the natural world, the home we have found ourselves in for hundreds of thousands of years, is the ideal sensory environment in which to ground. Our senses have been developed in our natural ecology, and our natural ecology is perfectly designed to ground us through our senses. As our mission statement reminds us:

EcoSensory Therapy: Working with Nature to Regulate through Our Senses

The Evolution of Our Survival Strategies

So, in order to understand the present, we need to understand our past. We'd like to take you back beyond what you remember, your parents remember, beyond recorded history and to the origins of our species, approximately 200,000–250,000 years ago. The world would look quite different back then, but *we* wouldn't. If we look at our evolution, we can trace how our bodies have come to be as they are today.

One thing is true for evolution: change happens slowly. Very slowly. So, when we look back at our ancestors, the first *Homo sapiens* who lived on our beautiful planet, they are remarkably similar to you and me today (except, of course, for smartphones, synthetic clothing and well the extra "store" of fats many of us carry with us).

And we are all remarkably similar to *each other*. In 2003, a team of scientists completed their final analysis of the Human Genome Project (International Human Genome Sequencing Consortium, 2004). The project was a mammoth task to understand our DNA, our genetic code, which makes us who we are. They found that the three billion base pairs of genetic letters in human beings were 99.9% identical in every person. The other way to make sense of that is that, on average, we are only 0.01% genetically different from every other person who lives with us on this pale blue dot. So, we as a collective are similar in our genetics and anatomy to our ancestors and our brothers and sisters across the world.

So, we can say with some confidence that your body, at a genetic level – this place you find yourself experiencing the world from – is 99.9% similar to those you work with and to your distant ancestors. What we also know about evolution is that we have evolved to effectively manage the world we find ourselves in, or better said, the world we *found* ourselves in 250,000 years ago.

The world back then looked quite different – life was survival, and it was not a clear call that we *were* the fittest. So, many of our ancestors did not survive the fight. Life was tough, and our ancestors spent much of their time protecting their kith and kin and nurturing future generations. Weekends were not yet invented; days on the couch were not yet invented; instead, we had to develop an incredible ability to survive. And that story is the one that needs to be told to understand why we might find it so hard to "ground" in our modern-day world, and why we spend so much of our time caught up in our thoughts and "tricky minds".

Perhaps, one way in which to make sense of this is through the lens of humans as problem-solvers. We are excellent at prediction and abstract reasoning, and better than any other species on this planet. But ... when many of us are privileged enough to not have "the problem" of survival to solve day-to-day, we can be drawn to "solve" problems in life that have no solution.

First, let's go back ... way back.
So, how did we evolve?

Well, that story is bigger than we have time for just here, but in future elements, such as Attend, we will show you how our senses have evolved. After all, we are sensory beings and just as our human story is about how we have shaped and impacted the world, it is also true that the world has shaped and moulded us and our senses.

At the very basics, we have evolved to be equipped to survive and reproduce. We have learned how to fight off the dangers we can, run away from the fights we cannot win, hunt and forage for food and procreate, nurture and keep our families safe.

Our brain's anatomy and physiology were designed and fine-tuned to *identify* and *adaptively manage* threats in the outside world. And these threats came in all shapes and sizes, so our survival strategies developed in kind.

You may know the usual two: *fight or flight*, but we developed a whole lot more for different situations. We developed "fight" to ward off dangers and to hunt for food. "Flight" to flee when the danger was too formidable. "Freeze" to stay perfectly still for animals that track their prey by movement, remaining poised and ready to react when the moment presents itself. "Flop" when "playing dead" felt like the only answer. We learned too to "flirt" or seduce, to reproduce and to ensure that our DNA is passed on and that in a way we live on, even if we are to succumb to the inevitability of mortality. "Feed", to fatten up and to store whilst the harvest is good, just in case the next may not be so abundant. And "Fart", yes, your mind may go to toilet humour, and it may be embarrassing to reflect upon, but we have also learned that in times of stress (our physiological response to perceived threats), we let go and vacate what we have been holding in. Just consider, if you had to run away from a sabre-toothed tiger or escape a forest fire, you would want all your energy devoted to pumping those legs and arms, keeping your heart rate elevated, your muscles full of oxygen, and you would not want to be expending energy on digestion. Right then, at that moment in time, it's a matter of energy conservation, and digestion is not high on the priority list. And if a predator is in search of a tasty morsel, perhaps releasing a foul-smelling odour may make them look elsewhere for their next meal.

We have learned the need for multiple survival strategies to manage the many dangers and threats of the big bad world. And because the matter of our survival cannot wait for meetings to be arranged next Tuesday and for a board of directors to consensually agree on the best way to move forward to manage any given threat, these survival strategies work quickly, without or before "thinking". You hear a loud bang, you jump. You see a scary movie, and you curl up into a ball or flee behind the couch. We don't have time to think these things through, so knowing this, our evolution has developed our brain and nervous system to respond to threats accordingly.

Neuroscience: The Autonomic Nervous System, Polyvagal Theory, and Our Adaptive Brain

As animals, born in nature, we have developed our "autonomic nervous system" as our personal surveillance system. Our survival was too important to be based on how "concentrated" we were on threats around us because, let's face it, as humans, we can be incredibly distracted by anything bright and shiny.

Instead, we evolved our autonomic nervous system to run even when we are not paying attention. If it had a tagline, it would surely be "Your safety is our priority" and it works around the clock to get a five-star rating.

So, beyond "conscious" awareness, which is when we "pay attention", this system has developed to work like an autopilot, hence, the word "autonomic". Stephen Porges, founder of polyvagal theory, has coined the term "Neuroception" to describe how neural circuits distinguish whether situations or people are safe, dangerous or life-threatening. Neuroception takes place without our conscious awareness; our autonomic nervous system consistently and uninterruptedly, involuntarily, searches for "threats" in the world. Porges argues that the detection of a person as safe or dangerous triggers neurobiologically determined prosocial or defensive behaviours. Even though we may not be aware of danger on a cognitive level, on a neurophysiological level, our body has already started a sequence of neural processes that would facilitate adaptive defence behaviours such as fight, flight or freeze (Porges, 2004). It can often pay in these moments to trust our "gut" and listen to the cues of danger our sensory systems are registering (Porges, 2011).

We can further make sense of our survival strategies through a dive into neuroscience and polyvagal theory. Research into this area shows us that our autonomic nervous system is made up of two main branches, the "sympathetic" and "parasympathetic" branches. Adding to a functional and evolutionary perspective on our survival strategies, polyvagal theory helps identify the processes that take place in our neurophysiology that have enabled us to survive and thrive as a species.

If we start with the sympathetic branch, we can see how this branch of the autonomic nervous system is activated to respond to cues of danger by preparing us to "fight" or "flight". It releases adrenaline and ensures that our bodies are prepared to manage the dangers out there by battling the immediate danger or fleeing if we perceive it to be too formidable.

If the sympathetic branch is our "up-regulating" branch, then we can understand our parasympathetic branch as our "down-regulating" branch. This branch manages the Vagus Nerve and two important pathways, that of the "Ventral Vagal" and

"Dorsal Vagal" pathways. The "Dorsal Vagal" pathway is responsible for the other side of the survival coin. It responds to extreme cues of danger and is responsible for the "flop" response – of "shutting down". It helps us understand the adaptive reason for dissociation. Consider a child who cannot run away from or fight off dangers. The one ability they can do is to dissociate, to "space out", for their bodies to remain in place but their minds to go somewhere else. It is the escape strategy when escape simply is not possible. The Dorsal Vagal in this case is responsible for down-regulating our systems and, in the extremes, slowing our regulatory systems down to such an extent that we can feel "numb".

The other pathway here is the "Ventral Vagal" pathway, which responds to cues of safety and connection. It is the social engagement part of our system that has allowed mammals and humans to flourish. It allows for and provides enjoyment, feelings of relaxation and warmth within the company of cherished others, and it is the part of our autonomic nervous system where we feel calm, safe, connected, and social. If we understand the "sympathetic" branch of our autonomic nervous system as our "fight or flight" response, then the ventral vagal pathway of our parasympathetic branch can be understood as our "rest-and-digest" response.

And for individuals who have grown up in threat, whose home and relationships were not a place of safety, we can see how our autonomic nervous system works over time to identify and respond to threats. We might talk of a child being "hypervigilant", and from a survival point of view, we can perhaps see why this is so adaptive. Their neurophysiology has learned to keep them safe by being hyper-alert to signs of danger and responding in kind. There may be few experiences of "ventral vagal" engagement, and in order to help access higher-order thinking, we need to prioritise "grounding", "stabilisation", and providing experiences of safety, which can activate the "ventral vagal" and provide reparative experiences of what it is like to feel calm, centred and grounded. Here we come back to nature and its role as a co-facilitator of change.

> Whereas we'd once believed that the symptoms and behavior exhibited by our clients primarily rejected their psychological defenses, a view that attributed a degree of intentionality, no matter how unconscious, now, we better understood the symptoms as manifestations of instinctive brain and bodily survival responses. We understood that sympathetic activation fuels anxiety and rage, parasympathetic dominance causes shutdown and passive-aggressive behavior, flight responses spur fleeing the therapist's office, and fight responses lead to verbal or physical aggression or violence turned against the self. When clients self-harm, for example, these days, we understand their actions to be instinctive, rather than thought out-an effort to regulate or relieve, rather than punish.
>
> Fisher (2014)

Interoception: Body Awareness and Sense of Self

Interoception is one of our eight key body senses (alongside vision, hearing, touch, taste, smell, balance, and body position). It involves the sensory process of receiving, accessing and interpreting *internal* bodily signals. It has a critical role in survival, supporting our regulated response to sensations related to bodily integrity (e.g., sensations of hunger, temperature and pain) – in this way its importance cannot be overestimated – but it also plays a critical role in autonomic nervous system activity related to emotions. We need to be able to *detect* and *evaluate* our body's reactions to stress, and then use effective regulation strategies to settle ourselves and manage the emotional response.

Many of the individuals we work with have reduced or disrupted interoceptive awareness, often because they have learned, sometimes at great personal cost, to turn away from internal signals and rely instead on thinking or external cues to feel safe. From the perspective of the Dynamic-Maturational Model of Attachment and Adaptation (Crittenden, 2008), this can be understood as a protective strategy. Attending too closely to one's internal experience may once have felt overwhelming, unsafe, or impossible to act upon. Over time, the mind adapts by prioritising cognition, action, or the other's emotional states, while the body's messages become quieter or easier to ignore. When connection to interoceptive cues is limited, it can become harder to recognise one's own emotions, how one truly feels, or what the body is signalling in the moment.

This pattern is often reflected not only in emotional awareness but also in sensory registration more broadly, for instance, noticing hunger, thirst, fatigue, temperature, or discomfort. The outside world continuously provides information that helps us regulate, but if internal signals are muted, these cues can be missed or misinterpreted.

When I take people into the woods, these moments of noticing – and the cues they give about someone's interoception – become especially visible. I find myself paying attention to whether someone recognises they are thirsty, whether they add or remove layers as the temperature changes, whether they sense when their energy is dropping, or when they need to rest. A person may arrive underprepared for the conditions, not out of carelessness, but because those internal prompts did not register clearly enough to guide action. The natural environment, with its shifting weather, terrain, and physical demands, tends to bring these things into clearer view.

Seen in this way, the outdoors becomes a place where awareness can be rebuilt. Hunger, fatigue, warmth, cold, comfort, and discomfort all become opportunities to help someone reconnect with their internal experience and listen to what is happening beneath the surface. And making marshmallows over a campfire or cinnamon apple tarts (my clients are far better cooks than I am) is a worthwhile activity regardless … more of this when you reach the chapter on *Nourish*.

There are important links between understanding our emotions and our interoception. So, bear with me as we dip briefly into neuroscience. Primates have a specialised "interoceptive cortex" (the parieto-insular region) that helps us identify *where* in the body an internal sensation or pain is located. The insula provides this topographical and homeostatic information, the distinct physical sensation itself. We also process interoceptive signals in the anterior cingulate cortex, which contributes to the emotional meaning of that experience.

Together, these systems help us answer two questions: *where do I feel this?* and *what does this feeling mean to me?* That second question is shaped by memory and past experience. A racing heart might be interpreted as excitement, fear, or danger depending on what we have previously learned about that sensation.

Before we can make sense of our feelings, we first need to recognise and register the somatic markers that make up the sensory experience of having an emotion. For fear, we might notice our hands shake. For anger, we might notice our breath quicken and our heart race. For shame, we might notice nausea in our belly.

There are three steps towards emotional regulation that highlight why "interoception" is so key. These three steps are *"registration"*, *"interpretation"*, and *"modulation"*. So, let's go through this process, which starts in early life.

As we repeatedly have an emotion, we begin to "register" the experience. Over time, we start to "interpret" "where" it is, and what it might mean. Again and again, by direct visceral (sensory) experience, we come to notice what this "sensation" might mean. We learn "how" that sensation makes us feel, and these feelings increasingly become the basis for our knowledge about ourselves, our consciousness, and our identity.

Through this "interpretation", learning and increased interoceptive awareness, our bodies and, in turn, our feelings become understandable. Once they become understandable, they also become manageable. So, after registration and interpretation, comes "modulation", where we can put in place effective emotional regulation strategies based on an accurate sense of what feeling we need to manage.

In our busy urban lives, many of us, and the people we work with, can feel "out of touch" with our bodies. Grounding provides an avenue through which to become conscious of what is mostly unconscious. With grounding and getting "in touch" with our bodies, we can help our clients become increasingly aware of their inner sensations so that "interoceptive awareness" is increasingly available (Price et al., 2018). Of course, a thorough understanding of an individual's history and presenting problems is key here. It is important to remember that what is right for one person may not be right for another. Many young people and adults use strategies to consciously or unconsciously stay out of touch with their bodies. With trauma and histories of adversity in particular, it is important to consider why someone may struggle with interoception and what survival function being out of touch with the body may serve. If this applies to the client group you work with, it may be helpful to explore trauma-informed approaches to body awareness and regulation, including the work of Bessel van der Kolk, Pat Ogden's sensorimotor psychotherapy, Janina Fisher's stabilisation work, and Stephen Porges' polyvagal theory, which all offer frameworks for understanding the protective role of disconnection from bodily experience.

Just as we consider how EcoSensory sessions can use the external stimuli of nature to regulate us – the movement of leaves on the trees, the sounds of water, the feel of the ground beneath our feet – we also want you to consider how nature can provide the right environment in which to eventually turn attention inward. Simple practices might include mindful noticing of the senses, slow barefoot walking on different textures, listening for distant and nearby sounds, feeling the temperature of the air on the skin, or holding natural objects such as stones, bark, or leaves. All of these have graded variations and invite attention through the senses before gently building awareness of the body's internal responses.

In this way, the natural world becomes both anchor and pathway: first helping to settle the nervous system through external sensory input, and then supporting a gradual shift towards interoceptive awareness. After all, interoceptive awareness is central to regulation, an integrated sense of self, and ultimately our health and well-being.

In our training, we demonstrate activities that support this progression, beginning within *Ground* and extending into later elements such as *Discover* and *Create*, which highlight the benefits of climbing, carrying heavy objects, and building dens to increase body awareness and interoception. For now, it is worth just remembering that where we start from, our bodies, are the centre from which we sense the world, and also how we make sense of ourselves.

Our Brains Have Evolved to Be Adaptive to Threats

To understand why grounding works, we also need to understand what it is working *with* … an ancient brain designed first and foremost for survival.

Our brains, rather than develop layer upon successive layer, have a more complex story. This story is again all about "adaptation, survival, and reproduction", and our evolutionary history helps us understand that our interdependent brain networks have evolved to increase adaptation to be able to survive and reproduce. Emerging evidence also suggests new horizons for just how adaptive we truly are. It is suggested that "the brain uses interoceptive [within our body] and exteroceptive [external to our body] information to predict future conditions and needs to enable optimal adaptation to continuously changing internal and external environments" (Steffen et al., 2022, p. 2). In other words, our brains adapt to the needs placed on us at any moment in time, with different brain networks being differentially activated based upon need. If we need to respond to an immediate danger, our brain and nervous system will respond to keep us safe. If we need to respond to another person's distress, then our brain and nervous system will respond to regulate ourselves to tolerate their distress, mentalise, empathise, and to attune with them … *Of course, that's when things are going well…*

It's also important to say that we learn from experience too. Neurobiology highlights the "transactional" and use-dependent characteristics of the developing brain. Remember too, we are always in this process of development – it's not something purely restricted to early life. We learn and continue to adapt throughout our lives.

Developmental Psychology and Neuroscience have helped us to understand that environmental conditions adapt our brain *over time* (Rutter & Rutter, 1993; Sroufe et al., 2010). Early adaptations become the starting point for subsequent adaptations, and our brain "adapts" to predictions of the "probable" world and eventualities we will face. If in early life, there are repeated experiences of fear, threat and loss, then the brain is likely to be wired more ready for expectation of further fear, threat and loss. This brain, and indeed this person, is more likely to perceive others and the world as threatening, and their responses to the world and others would develop "in kind". A "sensitive-fight response", i.e., being hypervigilant to danger and quick to react to defend oneself, is an entirely understandable (and helpful) adaptation if the world in which you have developed is one where being vigilant to dangers and standing up for yourself is the basis of survival.

In this conceptualisation, we refer to "The Adaptive Brain" (Steffen et al., 2022), with the term emphasising the interdependence and plasticity of brain regions and the brain's ability to predict and adapt to future needs and conditions.

Language, Representation, and Internal Threats

Human beings, because of our relatively large cortex (compared to other animals), can do something that most animals cannot. It's something that we love at times and despair with at others. Humans, beyond any other animals, have the capacity for language and symbolic representation.

This means that we can hold in mind fears and dangers that are not right here and right now. In this way, we have the incredible ability to time-travel and to teleport. From the comfort of our beds, we can think ourselves back to our place of work and imagine we are back in that difficult meeting.

While this is a hugely favourable thing, it means we can learn from our mistakes, adapt for the future and build ideas and concepts over time; our brains are not able to distinguish what is a "real" threat in the outside world and what is a "scary" thought in our minds. Our autonomic nervous system will work just the same and respond just the same if we were standing in front of a sabre-tooth tiger or strongly imagining that we were. Of course, the same is true for "safe space" imagery, and the positive effect of visualising "safe", "happy", "calming", and "beautiful" spaces in our mind.

So, what does that really mean? Humans, more than any other animal, have the capacity to fear that which is outside of the here and now. A book you might want to read is *Why Zebras Don't Get Ulcers* (Sapolsky, 2004). It argues that we as human beings can worry, stress, become low in mood, and experience pain and suffering for things that are not happening in our immediate external world. While we pride ourselves on this ability – we are expert problem-solvers after all – it can be the very foundation of our suffering. It can also lead us to disconnect from the world around us, and into an internal landscape shaped by memory and anticipation.

Animals, too, experience fear, attachment, and loss, particularly in more social species where bonds are strong. Whales have been observed carrying deceased calves for extended periods, birds may grieve lost partners, and primates can show prolonged distress after separation. Their responses remind us that emotional life is not uniquely human. What differs is the human capacity for language, symbolic representation, and extended mental time travel, which allows threat to persist long after the danger has passed.

Zebras, like many prey animals, respond intensely to immediate danger. If a lion were to give chase to their herd, their autonomic nervous system would activate rapidly, mobilising the body for survival. The result is an immediate flight response, with the herd running as fast as possible towards safety. Inevitably, some days, the lion would catch its prey and a member of the zebra herd would lose its life. Once the threat has passed, however, their physiology often returns to baseline, and they resume grazing, their bodies shifting back towards a rest-and-digest state.

Humans, on the other hand, carry an additional burden. Even when the body is safe, the mind can continue to replay the event or anticipate future danger. We call this *rumination*, from the Latin *ruminare*, meaning "to chew over". Grazing animals do this literally, chewing the cud again and again. Humans do it metaphorically, repeatedly chewing over past threats and imagined futures in the mind. Our capacity to reflect, remember, and project forward is profoundly adaptive, allowing us to learn from experience and plan ahead, but it can also sustain distress long after the original danger has passed.

While zebras return to grazing once safety is restored, humans may remain mentally tethered to what has happened or what might happen next. Our ability to think, to revisit our history, and to anticipate the future can become a source of ongoing pain and suffering, even in the absence of immediate danger.

Understanding this gives rise to the ability to notice, become aware of, and consciously attend to the here and now, as well as the need to "Ground". Within the present moment, the "nowness" of experience, we can reconnect with the safety of our immediate place in the world. No longer caught in past adversity, nor pulled towards future uncertainty, grounding invites us to return to what is real and available now. By paying attention on purpose to the present moment, we create the opportunity to loosen the grip of past and future suffering.

Groundlessness

"The ground is always shifting", writes the Buddhist nun Pema Chodron in her book *Living Beautifully with Uncertainty and Change* (2012), "whether we like it or not". Nature shows us in no uncertain terms that the only constant is change. Seasons come and go. Summers pass and sunny days move onto cloudy skies. Life and nature itself are forever in process of change.

One theory of suffering is that change is not necessarily the cause of distress, but rather, our resistance to that change is. We may feel pain in the face of denial and strive for things to remain *just as they are*, only to fight a losing battle. In "groundlessness", we look to accept and embrace the fragility, impermanence and changing nature of reality. In groundlessness, nothing is solid, nothing is fixed.

Chodron suggests that much of our discomfort comes from the effort to create solid ground beneath our feet, and a desire for life to feel stable, certain, and consistently okay. Yet in trying to hold things in place, we often create the very tension we are seeking to avoid. When we soften that grip and begin to meet change without resistance, we open ourselves to a different way of being, one that allows us to move with the shifting ground beneath us, rather than struggle against it (Chodron, 2012).

Nature teaches us this again and again. Nothing in the natural world is fixed, yet everything belongs. Trees bend with the wind. Tides rise and fall. Seasons transition without resistance. "Groundlessness" is not something to overcome, but something to learn from. It's a way of relating to life that invites flexibility, trust, and a deeper connection to the present moment. It is a lesson available to us, if we are willing to notice and to lean into it.

More on the nature of change in our chapter on "Rhythm".

Grounding in Nature

So, we start with "Ground". Consider how you can ground through your senses in your immediate sensory-rich nature space. Step into a natural setting, and spend some time "noticing". Pay attention to your surroundings and notice:

- five things you see
- four things you can hear
- three things you can touch
- two things you can smell
- one thing you can taste (that's safe to do so!)

Or perhaps, you step into nature, and you take off your shoes. Remove the barrier that separates you from the earth and place your bare feet on the ground to play with "barefoot walking".

But before you do, you might begin exactly as you are.

Shoes still firmly on your feet, simply bring your attention downwards. Notice the ground beneath you. As you walk, feel the subtle conversation between your feet and the earth, notice the firmness or softness, the stability or slight give. Even through your shoes, there is information to play with.

You might notice the difference between surfaces: the resistance of tarmac, the cushioning of grass, the uneven, unpredictable texture of a woodland path. And as you move, allow your awareness to travel upwards. Notice what happens not just in your feet, but in your ankles, your calves, your knees. Perhaps even your hips and lower back. How does your body organise itself to meet the ground beneath you?

From here, there are many points of entry, with no single "right" way in, only what feels manageable for you (or who it is you're supporting).

You might begin by shifting to a lighter, thinner-soled pair of shoes, allowing more of the ground to be felt beneath you. When that feels comfortable, you could remove your shoes and keep a layer of protection, thick socks, or even waterproof socks if that helps you feel more at ease.

And eventually, if and when it feels right, you may choose to remove all barriers and place your bare feet directly onto the earth.

Even here, you can choose your starting point. Grass may feel softer and more forgiving than mud. Sand or the shoreline may feel more predictable than the uneven floor of the woods.

The invitation is simple: go just one step further than you have before.

And importantly, tend to yourself afterwards and tend to those you support. Warmth and comfort matter, especially with our hands and feet. Cold feet are rarely enjoyable. Bring a soft towel, dry your feet, and have a clean pair of socks ready.

This is not about pushing through discomfort. It is about building a relationship with yourself and the ground, slowly and safely, and with care.

Remember, it's as much about *how* you do these activities as *what* you do in the process. We encourage you to consider how you can use "grounding" elements of your practice in nature and how you might adapt some of your routine practice into the natural world.

Summary

If we are to help our clients engage with sessions in the outdoors (or any support session for that matter), then we must first start with grounding. So that is where we encourage you to start; in your assessment and practice of "grounding".

References

Chodron, P. (2012). *Living Beautifully with Uncertainty and Change*. Shambhala Publications.

Crittenden, P. M. (2008). *Raising Parents: Attachment, Parenting and Child Safety*. Willan Publishing.

Csordas, T. J. (1990). Embodiment as a paradigm for anthropology. *Ethos*, *18*(1), 5–47.

Fisher, J. (1999). Stabilization in trauma treatment. *Psychotherapy Networker*, *23*(3), 1–6.

Fisher, J. (2014). *Healing the fragmented selves of trauma survivors: Overcoming internal self-alienation*. Routledge.

Gilbert, P. (2009). *The compassionate mind: A new approach to life's challenges*. Constable & Robinson.

Gladwell, V. F., Brown, D. K., Wood, C., Sandercock, G. R., & Barton, J. L. (2013). The great outdoors: How a green exercise environment can benefit all. *Extreme Physiology & Medicine*, *2*(1), 3.

Heidegger, M. (1951). Building dwelling thinking. In A. Hofsdater (Ed.) *Poetry, language, thought* (pp. 143–162). Harper & Row.

International Human Genome Sequencing Consortium. (2004). Finishing the euchromatic sequence of the human genome. *Nature*, *431*(7011), 931–945.

Jäger, W. (1985). *The way of contemplation: Christian meditation and zen*. Image Books.
Kabat-Zinn, J. (2004). *Wherever you go, there you are: Mindfulness meditation in everyday life*. Hyperion.
Kabat-Zinn, J. (2009). *Wherever you go, there you are: Mindfulness meditation in everyday life* (10th anniversary ed.). Hyperion.
Li, Q. (2010). Effect of forest bathing trips on human immune function. *Environmental Health and Preventive Medicine*, *15*(1), 9–17.
Li, Q., Morimoto, K., Kobayashi, M., Inagaki, H., Katsumata, M., Hirata, Y., Hirata, K., Suzuki, H., Li, Y. J., Wakayama, Y., Kawada, T., Ohira, T., Matsui, N., Kagawa, T., Miyazaki, Y., Krensky, A. M., & Kawada, T. (2011). A forest bathing trip increases human natural killer activity and expression of anti-cancer proteins in female subjects. *Journal of Biological Regulators and Homeostatic Agents*, *25*(3), 317–324.
Park, B. J., Tsunetsugu, Y., Kasetani, T., Kagawa, T., & Miyazaki, Y. (2010). The physiological effects of Shinrin-yoku (taking in the forest atmosphere or forest bathing): Evidence from field experiments in 24 forests across Japan. *Environmental Health and Preventive Medicine*, *15*(1), 18–26.
Perry, B. D. (2006). Applying principles of neurodevelopment to clinical work with maltreated and traumatized children. In N. B. Webb (Ed.), *Working with traumatized youth in child welfare* (pp. 27–52). Guilford Press.
Porges, S. W. (2004). Neuroception: A subconscious system for detecting threats and safety. *Zero to Three*, *24*(5), 19–24.
Porges, S. W. (2011). *The polyvagal theory: Neurophysiological foundations of emotions, attachment, communication, and self-regulation*. W.W. Norton & Company.
Price, C. J., Hooven, C., & Thompson, E. A. (2018). Interoceptive awareness skills for emotion regulation: Theory and approach of mindful awareness in body-oriented therapy (MABT). *Frontiers in Psychology*, *9*, 798.
Rutter, M., & Rutter, M. (1993). *Developing minds: Challenge and continuity across the life span*. Penguin Books.
Sapolsky, R. M. (2004). *Why Zebras don't get ulcers: The acclaimed guide to stress, stress-related diseases, and coping* (3rd ed.). Henry Holt.
Semple, R. J., & Lee, J. (2008). *Mindfulness-based cognitive therapy for anxious children: A manual for treating childhood anxiety*. New Harbinger Publications.
Siegel, D. J. (1999). *The developing mind: Toward a neurobiology of interpersonal experience*. Guilford Press.
Sroufe, L. A., Egeland, B., Carlson, E. A., & Collins, W. A. (2010). *The development of the person: The Minnesota study of risk and adaptation from birth to adulthood*. Guilford Press.
Steffen, P. R., Austin, T., DeBarros, A., & Brown, T. (2022). The adaptive brain: Interoception, prediction and survival. *Neuroscience & Biobehavioral Reviews*, *138*, 104715.
van der Kolk, B. A. (2015). *The body keeps the score: Mind, brain and body in the transformation of trauma*. Viking.

Chapter 3

Connect

Chris West

Connecting with Ourselves, Others, and Nature

This is our attachment element, all about our connections and attachment to ourselves, those around us, and with nature. In this chapter, we will explore the concepts of regulation, how nature supports and facilitates this, the secure base, and how crucial nature is in our well-being and protection. We will find out about how nature senses us, and how we sense it.

We are going to think about activities that support connection with others, ourselves, and the natural environment, and how you can utilise the concepts of connection from an EcoSensory Therapy Model of practice.

We invite you to immerse yourself in and connect with, and explore how powerful nature can be in supporting our connections, in so many rich and meaningful ways.

"Connect" for Regulation

More than ever, we are recognising the crucial importance of our connection with nature, as well as how our health as humans, and the health of the planet, is so interconnected and interdependent on one another. We cannot separate our human selves, as other than nature. We are nature. We are animals. As Harper, Rose, and Segal put it so clearly, "We are embedded and inextricably linked with nature and occupy animal bodies" (Harper et al., 2019, p. 101). It is no surprise then that our connection with the natural world is so fundamental to our health. The recognition of this powerful connection goes way back in our evolutionary history, as well as relatively more recently, where psychiatrists at a US Congress meeting in 1959, Karl Menninger, stated, "Another Psychological Need is for the maintenance of contact with Non-human Nature" (Selhub & Logan, 2012, p. 211).

When we think about the concept of connection, where does our mind take us, what does it mean to us personally, what do we see in our mind's eye? In our introduction piece, we were reminded that we spend so much of our lives now connected to devices, the internet and technology, and that has led to us losing a sense of connection to that which has been so important to us since time immemorial.

DOI: 10.4324/9781003777465-5

Mobile devices enable us to be connected to others more than ever before; however, with that comes a risk that we are not in touch with ourselves, including our bodies, and to the universe of sensations through which we sense. It is these that provide our primary connection to our own interiority (known as the quality of being interior or inward). The importance of counterbalancing our nervous system in this way of connecting, with the calming, restorative, and enriching world of nature spaces, has never been more crucial to our well-being and survival. Being and connecting to nature is more aligned with our nervous systems and helps counterbalance the endless demands for technological connection.

In their book, *Escaping the Modern Predicament: Nature as Refuge and Community in Contemporary Health Practices in Wales, Sweden, and Finland* (2023), Lord et al. suggest that our modern technological society could be seen as "pathological", in other words, unhealthy for us. They argue that nature provides "an escape" and allows engagement with a "complex community of life represented by nature".

Along with counterbalancing the negative effects of our modern lives, a strong connection to nature is associated with increased eudaimonic well-being and, notably, higher levels of self-reported personal growth (Pritchard et al., 2020). In *Cementing the Bond between Children and Nature*, Szczytko et al. (2020) found a correlation between children who are *connected* to nature and the amount of time they spend outside. More time outside led to benefits in mental and physical health, the children's attention span and their relationships with adults. As the children grew more connected to nature, they also cared more about nature and did more to conserve it (more on this in our Nourish element). Outdoor social activities, like camping, were observed to be particularly effective in strengthening the bonds among children and nature. Perhaps surprisingly, what they also found was that a "Key starting point was being outside, in a more solitary activity". This study highlights the importance of giving children time to be more contemplative in nature, which could include them finding their own "Sit Spot", a place from which children can look and observe on their own, with adults stepping back and providing space for this (whilst ensuring their safety).

The Art of Regulation

Harper et al. (2019) remind us we are mammals, with mammalian nervous systems, and therefore nature is the ideal mammalian environment, as "engaging in practices that awaken and align with our mammalian nervous system will have the most profound impact" (2019, p. 101). Natural environments therefore are the preferred therapeutic environment to support the development of connection between individuals, along with opportunities for play, regulation of arousal states, and deepening of relationships.

Nature spaces have a powerful role to play in calming the nervous system, providing balanced sensory input to support feeling "just right". Sensory pathways have direct connections to the emotional parts of the brain. Activating these in regulating ways strengthens pathways that are more organising for us. The natural sensory-rich opportunities of outdoor spaces provide endless ways in which to do this. Lyons reminds us of the importance of activating both internal (our body-centred senses of movement, body awareness, and touch) and external (hearing, seeing, tasting, and smelling) senses to support the activation and organising of the senses to support enhanced sensory integration.

Using the concepts of polyvagal theory within nature (this is briefly described below, see the "Ground" element for further information) helps us to understand the importance of self-regulation and co-regulation, supporting individuals to find and use ways that help them in relation to this, so that they can socially engage with others in meaningful ways. It also helps us to really appreciate how "socially engaged play can produce transformative learning experiences" (Harper et al., 2019, p. 97). There is nowhere better to do this than outdoors, where so many possibilities and opportunities exist.

Thinking about this, I am reminded of a session with our young people in the secure children's home where I work. Throughout the year, we have days together where we explore what well-being means for them. For one of these sessions, we spent time as a group in our forest school, lighting a fire, drinking hot chocolate, and exploring different foods. For so many young people who have experienced early adversity, being with others in ways that feel safe can feel so out of reach. The experience of connecting with each other in an outdoor space brought such a sense of connection and community, with the opportunity for them to learn about engaging with their peers in more regulating ways. I recall this time with them with great fondness, and it is a session that, as a well-being team, we often comment on. This case example also highlights how group work, as well as seeing people individually, can have a powerful impact on both self- and co-regulation.

Polyvagal theory, developed by researcher Stephen Porges, provides us with an understanding of the hierarchical nature of regulation, in which newer circuits of the autonomic nervous system (ANS) inhibit older circuits. According to the theory, the ANS regulates three fundamental physiological states: focused (calm/alert), frantic (flight/fight), and collapse (freeze/dissociation). The ventral vagus complex (VVC) supports a calm-alert state and is the newer, more highly evolved self-calming part of the ANS that fosters early caregiver–infant interactions. It enables shutting out irrelevant sounds and facilitates attention, e.g., the human voice. In the face of threat, it is deactivated to facilitate a sympathetic system response (fight/flight). The VVC part of the nervous system is key to our ability to connect with others in deep and meaningful ways that support our growth, development, and well-being (Porges, 2011).

When this part of the nervous system runs the show, we feel safe and connected, calm, and social … we smile. It sends signals down to our heart and lungs, slowing down our heart rate, helping us to feel calm and relaxed, centred or aroused. It controls sucking, swallowing, facial expressions, and sounds produced by the larynx. It fosters a sense of pleasure and connection, from the infant/child and parent, and to the later relationships and connections we develop.

Dana (2020) tells us that connecting with nature is a restorative experience that helps to bring the ANS in a state of ventral vagal regulation. Evidence demonstrates that ecotherapy activities help to improve the function of the ANS, including increased vitality and reduced negative emotions. An ongoing connection with nature acts as a preventative experience and an autonomic exercise that shapes the system towards well-being (Torng & Lin, 2023).

For individuals who have experienced early adversity and trauma, feeling safe and knowing that our attachment figures will help us with this has been severely disrupted. They are unable to trust that this will happen, as their early experiences have shaped a nervous system that tells them this isn't possible, and it is common to respond to everyday life with hypervigilance, stuck in fear states of fight/flight/freeze/dissociation, and shutdown.

Heginworth & Nash (2020) describe how, for individuals who find it difficult to feel safe in intimate human relationships, this can be lessened by the additional holding that the environment offers. Being in therapeutic nature spaces provides unique opportunities for the nervous system to feel calmer, less overwhelmed, and more organised, which helps the individual to move from a place of hypervigilance to a place of quiet calm, where they can experience a greater sense of safety and connection with significant others in their lives.

It is important to note that fear-based hypervigilance, such as being raised in an unsafe environment, may mean that unfamiliar and unpredictable environments do not feel safe for some individuals and may lead to a miscalibration of their perception systems (Kain & Terrell, 2018). They may feel they need to listen for predators, visually scan and assess their environment, rather than connect with it and experience pleasure. Observing this and supporting cues of safety for them will be a key role we help practitioners understand and respond to as EcoSensory Therapy Practitioners. The buffering and restorative components of nature can offset and regulate the nervous system, supporting greater regulation and a sense of safety, but only when the environment feels safe. Taking an individual who has experienced trauma in a forest is likely not to find forested areas restorative. Likewise, dangerous weather conditions or challenging physical environments, although in nature, may indeed increase fear-based hypervigilance. As practitioners, it is essential to tune in to how our clients' nervous systems respond to the environments around them.

Working with nature can provide a therapeutic environment that is truly enriching (Bhreathnach, 2017), feeding and nourishing all our senses, and providing opportunities to create a sense of safety and nurture, fostering engagement with the physical environment and those around us. Activities such as foraging and looking for plants, smelling them, looking at them, and gardening, such as growing edible plants and then cooking with them, create the potential for joint attention, engagement, and co-regulation, as well as bonding experiences through the use of the powerful nurturing senses of taste and smell.

It provides the opportunity to take risks, take on challenges, to co-regulate intense affective states with the support of nature, to stand tall, to maintain their own balance, and to allow their nervous systems to regulate itself, and with others. The importance of safety in the co-regulation process is key here, as individuals will take risks, and thus increase their window of tolerance and resilience, when they feel safe, both physically and emotionally.

Attachment, Regulation, & Nature

"Attachment is an integral part of human nature … and we are biologically predisposed to connect to others" (Bettmann et al., 2013, p. 219). A child's capacity to self-regulate is dependent on the parents' capacity to regulate themselves, and therefore co-regulate their child. Many factors influence the ability to self-regulate, including our early childhood experiences, our experiences of co-regulation, neurodevelopmental issues, and sensory processing difficulties, to name but a few.

The infant's primary attachment figure is the source of the infant's stress regulation and sense of safety. The attachment relationship is the fundamental environmental influence on the development of the limbic system, and severe disruption of this leads to regulatory failure of the limbic system structures and impaired autonomic homeostasis, producing extreme and rapid alterations and impairments in ANS arousal and exposure to intensive and traumatic arousal states.

When danger emanates from the attachment figure, it has short- and long-term consequences on the developing psyche and soma (our bodies); this includes the developing limbic-autonomic circuits, as their maturation is experience-dependent/highly vulnerable to relational trauma.

The dysregulating events of abuse create severe and chronic alterations in the infant's brain, including excessive pruning of cortical, subcortical, limbic, and ANS circuits, affecting the infant's ability to cope with intense states (Schore, 2001).

Linking to the soma, we know from the work of Bhreathnach (2017) and Van Der Kolk (2015) that developmental trauma severely disrupts the attachment connection, and the body is directly and adversely affected by this, which affects our ability to regulate our arousal states. Working in nature is working alongside the physical world, and therefore engaging the body, with all its senses connecting and engaging. Heginworth & Nash (2020, p. 65) remind us, "Nature is Physical" and thus provides us with a physical, embodied experience which is truly sensory regulating in nature.

Hugging a tree is a great way to experience this! One session that comes to mind is of a father and his adopted son. In the part of the forest we were in, there were trees of so many different diameters, which fascinated the little boy. There was such a sense of joy and pleasure for them in finding out which trees could they put their arms around, and be able to clasp each other's hands. For this dad, letting go of what they "needed to do" vs what brought them a sense of connectedness was transformational in their relationship going forwards.

The Sensory Attachment Intervention approach, pioneered and developed by Consultant Occupational Therapist, Éadaoin Bhreathnach, helps to consider how we might use our understanding of polyvagal theory to consider states of ANS arousal, alongside nature spaces, to support greater co- and self-regulation.

Her work has helped us to understand how we can consider activities that support those who are in a parasympathetic nervous state (freeze/dissociation), such as those of movement, for instance, swinging in a tree swing, versus those who are in a sympathetic nervous state (fight/flight) where we would consider activities such as climbing, hanging from a tree or digging, and the importance of doing this *alongside* the attachment figure. There is ever-emerging and growing research demonstrating the benefits of nature spaces as a therapeutic medium in the treatment of supporting relationships and connection, particularly for client groups with attachment disruptions, who require trauma-informed care. This enables us to think more about the opportunities and lens that this offers to us as therapists, and the ability to engage the physiological, affective, sensory and cognitive abilities of the individual to further enhance self-regulation and co-regulation, with Norton et al. (2017, p. 3) describing it as a "unique, experiential tool to facilitate change".

Bettmann et al. (2008, 2017) carried out research with adopted adolescents using nature-based environments, and found that these spaces can challenge the individual's long-held (negative) relational beliefs, and provide opportunities to have different relational experiences, due to the change in environment, and the way that nature supports this. They also found that participants who engaged in nature-based therapies not only experienced notable reductions in mental health issues and improved interpersonal relationships but they also showed a greater sense of trust in others, a crucial piece in co-regulation and trusting others.

Other research also confirms how nature-based therapies have supported better relationships, such as continued relationship improvements, a better understanding of each other, reduced trauma symptoms, and improved family functioning (Liermann & Norton 2016).

Huff et al. (2003) found that challenging activities in nature spaces encouraged families with adolescents to work together and grow closer, illustrating the positive relationship between challenging outdoor family activity and communication. They stated that "Nature is a unique resource to help strengthen families and provide therapeutic benefits" (p. 30).

Schore (2001) helps us to understand the importance of shared joy and pleasure between the individual and their primary attachment figure. It is during these experiences that the nervous systems of both release endorphins as well as oxytocin, which positively impacts the development of the nervous system (i.e., making "positive" neural connections), and positively influences the maximum potential of the genes, leading to increased positive outcomes. It also provides an antidote to trauma, supporting increased social bonds and a sense of safety (Porges, 2011). Nature spaces provide countless opportunities that support these kinds of rich experiences.

We must remember as practitioners the importance of the primary attachment figure in playing a key role in this, and how we as practitioners can promote, facilitate and support this, through the powerful medium of nature. This could be paddling in a stream, climbing a tree and nestling in it, or swinging from a rope. For one mother and her son, the experience of creating and building a "photograph frame" from sticks and other forest gifts, and then making a picture of themselves, brought a sense of connectedness they had previously found so hard to feel.

As one participant from a nature-based programme shared (Stevens et al., 2004, p. 281),

> Nature awakens your senses so that you can connect deeply with yourself ... the adventure in the other end develops in people the love for each other, the need of each other, and the sense of collaboration ... at the same time you realize that other people need and respect you, and that brings together your self-confidence, self-respect, and finally you realize you are important and you can make great things happen.

This incredible quote reminds us that nature is also our co-therapist, becoming an "active partner in the therapeutic relationship" (Pfeifer, 2017, p. 187).

Our regulation as practitioners is also very important. We need to know what regulates (and dysregulates) us, so that when we are with individuals in therapeutic nature spaces, we are able to be fully present, in a truly regulated way, to ensure we are attuned to our client's needs, and thus support the co-/self-regulation process. In order to be as aware of this as we can be, we need to be regulated, grounded and "connected" to ourselves in the present.

As EcoSensory Therapy Practitioners, we also need to be actively and regularly engaging in self and co- regulation activities, as part of our everyday lives, for our own well-being, and that of those we work with. As part of this, we encourage you to think about what regulates you, how often you do these things, with whom, when and where, ensuring that you do them regularly, as this is so key to supporting the therapeutic process with those we are working alongside.

The importance of emotional intelligence in achieving success is widely recognised. Most successful individuals, families, teams, and communities have a high level. However, it's often overlooked that this intelligence is fundamentally rooted in the capacity to manage emotions, both one's own and those of others.

By connecting, engaging, and attending to the senses in the natural environment, nature provides a calming environment through which individuals can connect together, helping to calm the nervous system and offer co-regulating experiences. It is through our interactions with the natural world, including discovering, playing, and exploring, that we get into our animal bodies and senses.

Connecting to Develop a Secure Base

> The deeper we delve into our natural world, the deeper our connections grow. Our natural world is the most incredible gift - not only for our health and wellbeing, but also in reconnecting with ourselves. By doing so we can discover what really makes our hearts sing.
>
> (Douglas, 2020, p. 54)

Douglas highlights the importance of our connection to both the natural world and ourselves. Going back further in time, the concept of a secure base was first described by Bowlby (1958), who proposed that attachment can be understood within an evolutionary context in that the primary caregiver provides safety and security for the infant. A secure base enables us to be curious, to go out and explore, to take on challenges in everyday life, and know that we can come back to the safety and security of our secure base, and that it will be there for us, helping us to feel nurtured and protected.

It is this sense of safety and security that is crucial to helping us to know that we are safe, and it is the outside, natural environment that can help us to explore this, within the context of our safest relationships. It is from this secure base that we can begin to take risks, take on challenges, knowing that we can come back to the safety of our attachment relationship, and the nurture and comfort that this provides us with.

We looked at this earlier from the perspective of the neurosequential model in our "Ground" element, recognising the importance of a strong foundation, a secure base to support the growth and development of our physical and emotional well-being. As we read in "Ground", nature itself provides us with a secure base, with its solid foundations beneath our feet, always there, providing a firm, stable footing for us. Connecting with our bodies can be essential in creating safety, which can allow us to support the processing of trauma (Haines, 2019).

Siegel (2012) talks about the triangle of well-being as the foundation of health, with the points being: a healthy mind, a healthy brain, and healthy relationships. He goes on to say that our minds emerge from our relationships with others and with our planet, thus highlighting the crucial importance of the environment to our well-being. Being outside in nature combines these central concepts, providing opportunities to connect, explore, and be curious and playful within the healing space of nature. "Resources are anything that supports health. They are fundamental to healing. Creating safety involves finding resources and reconnecting to experiences of health" (Haines, 2019). As we have already recognised, we have evolved alongside nature and have a deep connection with it, spanning millions of years. It provides us with so many opportunities and resources to connect with our bodies in rich, meaningful ways that have been lost in the busyness of everyday life. Going into nature provides a myriad of opportunities to explore natural resources that support physical and emotional health and well-being.

Bowlby helps us to understand that as practitioners, we have some key roles in supporting those we work with. Two of these are that of being a secure base and supporting them in their explorations (more of the latter in our "Discover" and "Create" chapters). As practitioners, we provide a further secure base by ensuring that the environments we use with them are safe and that the activities we support them in engaging in provide this, along with opportunities for nurture and challenge. For instance, in the form of sustenance, such as a drink and snack (maybe making your own trail mix in the forest), and challenges, such as climbing a tree, exploring a woodland together, and listening to the wildlife around.

When we look at nature, we can see how the research tells us, in compelling depth and detail, that there is no doubt about the way that it supports the development of a secure base, our "Triangle of Well-Being".

In our EcoSensory Therapy sessions, we create both a physical and psychological triangle of well-being. An example of this is when we are going to light a stove: we create a triangle by placing the stove. We do this using sticks, which provide a boundary for safety. Nature offers us an abundance of ways to create a secure base, both physically and psychologically. Often, we find that our participants will want to create a secure base from which to explore. This can be in many forms; they typically create some sense of containment, whether it is gathering sticks and logs to create a boundary to sit in, such as a circle around a fire, or building some form of shelter with a tarp or a den. These spaces take a life of their own, and we will frequently return to the same spot in future sessions, adding that element of ritual and return.

In his systematic literature review on the benefits of children's engagement with nature, Tim Gill (2014) suggests that spending time in nature is an essential component of a "balanced diet" of experiences that foster healthy development, overall well-being, and positive attitudes towards the environment. The review specifically emphasised the importance of child-led, playful engagement with nature, such as free play, exploration, and leisure. We also know that "visiting therapeutic nature can constitute an effective and affordable supplement to depression treatment for patients as well as function as a self-care intervention for the healthy population to maintain their mental health" (Olszewska-Guizzo et al., 2022).

Gill (2014) highlighted several key benefits linked to children's participation in outdoor, nature-based activities:

- **Environmental and Personal Connection:** early nature experiences are linked to developing a deeper connection to nature, stronger environmental values, and an enhanced sense of place and belonging in adulthood.
- **Physical Health:** living near green spaces is associated with increased physical activity.
- **Mental and Emotional Health:** access to natural areas supports improved mental health and emotional regulation in children generally, and particularly for specific groups like those with ADHD.
- **Cognitive and Behavioural Skills:** school gardening projects have been shown to boost scientific understanding and promote healthier eating habits.
- **Motor and Social Development:** play in natural settings enhances motor skills in preschool-aged children.
- **Social Skills:** engagement in forest school and gardening programmes is associated with stronger social skills, with forest school fostering self-control and gardening projects encouraging greater self-awareness.

Nature Spaces and Development of the Vagal Brake

From the perspective of "Polyvagal Theory" (Porges, 2011), the *vagal brake* is a key mechanism that regulates your heart rate by influencing vagal tone. For the individual, the vagal brake is the ability to experience fear and excitement (i.e., the upper ends of the emotional window) while keeping the heart regulated. When the vagal brake is engaged, vagal tone increases. This slows the heart rate, promoting a state that supports relaxation, self-soothing, physical repair, and growth. When the vagal brake is released, the sympathetic nervous system (SNS) becomes dominant, increasing heart rate to prepare the body for a quick response to external demands or perceived threats.

Critics of the polyvagal Theory, like Paul Grossman, argue that Respiratory Sinus Arrhythmia – the common measure used for the vagal brake – is heavily influenced by breathing patterns, not just vagal tone. Furthermore, the "vagal brake" concept oversimplifies the ANS by focusing too heavily on a single mechanism, ignoring the complex, bidirectional, and integrated nature of sympathetic and parasympathetic interactions. However, even critics agree that the vagus nerve (especially the parasympathetic branch) exerts an inhibitory influence on the heart (Grossman et al., 2026). Given the level of debate on the actual neurophysiological complexity and the involvement of other processes, such as breathing, in our physiological regulation, it is easy to get lost in the complexity of the systems. However, as practitioners, we recognise that this level of discussion does not alter the fundamental understanding that there are inhibitory regulatory mechanisms we can tap into to support our clients' regulation.

The vagal brake, according to Porges, is essential for developing healthy social skills, as its ability to quickly adjust SNS activation allows for flexible and adaptive social interactions (engagement and disengagement) with others. Securely attached children and adults are likely to have a good baseline autonomic tone and be able to tolerate high-intensity emotional states (Siegel, 2012).

Natural spaces provide opportunities for individuals to take risks, take on challenges, practice exercising the vagal brake, co-regulate intense affective states with the support of nature, stand tall, maintain their own balance, and allow their nervous system to regulate itself, both with and without others (see more in *Discover*).

It is within safe, secure relationships that we can take risks and develop a "vagal brake". The play that parents have with their young children, such as peek-a-boo, trains the heart not to flip into SNS/parasympathetic nervous system and builds the capacity to remain regulated in the face of challenge. The parent is therefore training the child to cope with challenges and remain regulated. In this dance, the nervous system practices being activated, aroused, and then regulated, via neural exercises to develop the vagal brake (re: fear/excitement/anticipation within the social engagement system). For individuals with a poor vagal brake, engaging in these kinds of activities, which in the context of nature spaces might include walking along a log or swinging in a tree, literally exercises and supports the development of the vagal brake.

A project entitled "Fathers and Sons in the Trees" (Lyytinen, 2018) outlines how the combination of stress and perception of risk, in an activity such as abseiling, causes worry and activates the parents' need to protect their child. This causes a state of alarm in the parent and prompts them to consider the need to comfort or rescue the child. It is this that supports the mentalising process (i.e., for the parent to consider the experiences and emotions of the child and reflect on them), and the parents' potential to use reflective functioning. This helps the child to feel safe and that the parent will help them. In this intersubjective state, the parent and child are able to experience attuned interactions, to further enhance their connection and co-regulation.

Positive changes were noted in the father–son relationships and quality of their interactions, enhancement in the child's self-regulation abilities, and experiences of nature. Additional findings were that neuropsychiatric symptoms were ameliorated by them engaging in adventure weekends together, along with engaging in activities regularly within the home environment. They found that "shared experiences of success ... [had] brought them together, carrying out challenging tasks together" and fathers were able to bear these successes, this attunement and this connection in mind when returning to everyday life. In reflecting upon their experiences "in the trees", they shared meaningful shifts in perspective, saying "if we managed this [forest-based father-son tasks] we can get through that [everyday challenges in home life and their relationship]".

Resilience and opportunities to develop resilience (i.e., the vagal brake) are rich in nature spaces. Underpinning resilience are safety and security, and it is important that we consider these in both physical and relational terms when we are out in nature spaces. Whilst stress can lead to being aversive to exploration and social contact (Music, 2019), supporting engagement and connection within nature spaces can enhance and support greater emotional and physical resilience, confidence, and sense of self. For one little boy, who was so hypervigilant and fearful, working on increasing resilience and confidence in himself was supported in his search for bugs, which he was fascinated by! The sense of curiosity and excitement he felt, through the lifting of logs and looking at the bugs through his magnifying glass alongside his mum, enabled him to shift his arousal from one of hypervigilance to a sense of feeling absorbed and captivated in the magic of how many legs they had, and where their home was.

Activities in nature spaces provide opportunities to experience new and novel ways of being and interacting together, to notice positive qualities, experience fear, and grapple with unfamiliar challenges. It is the doing of the challenges together that can help disrupt the "homeostatic patterns that maintain problem behaviour" and develop more positive connections with each other (Mulholland & Williams, 1998). In their study, family members reported more positive feelings towards each other, less conflict, greater physical competence, and enhanced communication.

The importance of safety in the co-regulation process with their key attachment figure is crucial here, as individuals may be more likely to take risks with them present, and thus increase their window of tolerance and resilience, when they feel safe, both physically and emotionally.

The powerful research outlined in this element really illustrates how we can blend natural spaces and attachment theory to support the attachment figure and child to build strong, lasting bonds of connection with each other. The different physical and emotional experiences that these offer, time spent together without external distractions, provide the opportunity to enhance their emotional connection and a greater sense of togetherness.

Play as a Way of Connecting with Outside Spaces

The core elements of play, which are fundamental to a child's development, are relative internal control, intrinsic motivation, and the freedom to suspend reality (Bundy & Lane, 2019). It is our intrinsic motivation, the very essence of free play, that drives engagement and supports the individual to engage and connect in the world around them, and to develop fully. The outside environment invites them to engage in ways that support the development of the key elements of play: freedom to suspend reality, to have an internal locus of control, and to be in an environment that invites the individual to become an explorer running through the forest, wading through the stream, building a sandcastle, and creating a den.

Sensing Nature and Being Sensed by It

Remember the sensation of walking barefoot in the "Ground" chapter. We feel, see, smell, and hear nature when we are out in it. We feel the wind on our skin and are enveloped by it; we see trees, fields, and flowers, taste the fresh air, and hear the birds. Our senses are "on" all the time, perceiving and experiencing the world around us. But how much do we connect to this myriad of sensations and experiences, to the way that nature is sharing its world with us, and us with it?

As we have explored, when we are in nature, we are sensing it through our range of senses (smelling, hearing, touching, etc.), but have you considered that when, for instance, we are touching the tree, we are also being touched by it? This concept, suggested by Abram (2010), talks about this in the context of reciprocity, that whenever we are touching an entity, we are also being touched by that entity. This sensory perception isn't limited to just our tactile system; it is an ongoing interweaving. However, this only happens to the extent that we are open to, and allow ourselves to be part of this.

Consider how our feet, being on the ground, are also *felt* by the ground, met by the ground. David Abram, in his book *Becoming Animal,* describes how our feet have an ancient ancestral connection to the ground, and when we step outside and take our shoes off and place our feet on the ground, we reestablish this connection (Abram, 2010).

In the same way that we taste the world around us, by eating the fruits of nature, so too are we tasted; for instance, when an insect lands on us, a cycle of exchanges, if you like, takes place. Abram describes this "gifting" as part of the cycle of life, in which all beings both give parts of themselves and take from others.

How Nature Connects

Any time you are out in a natural space, you will be inadvertently communicated with by the plants, animals and more-than-human world around us. Communication is the transmission of information between a sender and a receiver. Plants, fungi, other animals, insects, and microbes share information both underground and in the air. The forest, in particular, is a place rich in communication, as Wohlleben coined the "Wood Wide Web". Underground, mycorrhizal fungal networks allow water and nutrients to be shared among trees, so they can nurture one another (Wohlleben, 2017). Arvay (2018) suggests that we imagine the tree crowns as radio stations broadcasting their messages through the air, where the messages are received by the plants and animals in the forest, and indeed by us when we are in it. This intricate communication system uses chemical signals, including clicking and crackling sounds created by roots. When they are doing this, they are releasing substances that contain messages for other plants around them, warning of potential dangers, such as being eaten by an animal. If they are under attack, they warn nearby plants, prompting them to adapt by producing bitterness or even by emitting attractive chemicals to attract the pest's enemies. The Acacia tree, for example, will notice its leaves being eaten by a giraffe and send chemical messages (in the form of ethylene) to nearby trees, which will respond by making their leaves more bitter. The poor giraffe then has to travel much farther, usually upwind, to find a tasty one.

Likewise, that lovely robin singing to its heart's content, that you are enjoying listening to, is probably warning its mates about you, or telling you to get lost. The more-than-human life in the forest knows you are there and is responding accordingly. Some of those communications, such as the terpenes that trees release, are actually good for us; they support our immune system (see nourish for more on this). Some might be protective of territories that we have inadvertently wandered into. Some might be resource seeking, like the friendly dog, wanting to know what you are cooking. Being outdoors will be full of these interactions.

In our sessions, it is helpful to take moments to notice how the more-than-human world responds to your presence. In your planning, be mindful of the environment you are entering. Is your presence there damaging to the ecology of that place? Can you be in harmony with those who share the space with you?

Natural spaces, in particular those that are healthy and thriving, provide opportunities to connect with our own internal landscape whilst exploring the external world. As we have already learnt, being in healthy natural environments supported by a "real biochemical ally" soothes the nervous system. Heginworth & Nash speak eloquently of this, stating, "Mother Nature can offer a profound experience of unconditional acceptance of emotion, providing synchronistic natural mirroring of the client's emotional experience just as it is needed" (p. 68).

As we offer ourselves to the universe, we are at the same time drawing the world into ourselves, a continual cycle of sensory perception. A truly open and reciprocal relationship with the earth and all that it offers. Recognising and thinking in this way helps open us up to the possibility of rich, meaningful interactions and exchanges, facilitating reciprocity between our bodies and the breathing earth.

We are, however, reminded that the earth is not simply an object to be used and at our disposal. As Abrams reminds us, it is through our connection and relationship with the earth, with each other, with the more-than-human, and with the environments that provide for us that we can wake up to how we use or misuse nature. We must shift our attention away from digital screens and reconnect with the world (Abram, 2012).

Summary

There can be no doubt that the environment we are in can have a powerful influence on us, those we are in relationships with, as well as with each other. Working in and with nature-based spaces to support and promote growth and change provides a way of connecting individuals within their relational world that supports physiological, sensory, and affective processes, for greater regulation, connection, and engagement in everyday activities. Our connection with nature, once such a central part of how we lived our lives, is becoming increasingly rare, and yet we need it more than ever. As humans, we share 50% of our DNA with trees, 70% with slugs (gross), 44% with honey bees, and even 25% with daffodils (Kovacs, n.d.), and it is thought that genetic material from plants passed through our ancestral DNA via bacteria.

The Biophilia hypothesis (Kellert & Wilson, 1993) helps us to understand that humans have an innate tendency to connect with life and life-like processes. This natural desire to connect with nature is an inherited instinct, part of our genetic make-up, and it enhances our well-being, mental health, and personal fulfilment.

Engaging physically in outdoor spaces helps us to build a strong foundation, a stable base which positively influences our emotional, physical, and cognitive skills and abilities. It enhances our sense of self, gives us a sense of mastery, builds our relationships with others, and the world around us. Connecting with our natural sensory world offers the potential for inexhaustible new discoveries, about ourselves and the world around us, that provide the richest opportunities to feed our mind, body, and soul.

It is within the context of a sensory-rich environment, one which feeds all of our senses with rich and diverse information, that we can truly create and develop strong, solid foundations that support our regulation, health, and well-being. It is the dynamic interaction of all of our senses that helps us to fully participate and engage in everyday activities. Nature is the place to connect and use all our senses, and to truly learn by doing.

References

Abram, D. (2010). *Becoming animal: An earthly cosmology*. Pantheon Books.

Abram, D. (2012). *The spell of the sensuous: Perception and language in a more-than-human world*. Vintage.

Arvay, C. G. (2018). *The biophilia effect: A scientific and spiritual exploration of the healing bond between humans and nature*. St. Martin's Essentials.

Bettmann, J. E., Demong, E., & Jasperson, R. A. (2008). Treating adolescents with adoption and attachment issues in wilderness settings. *Journal of Therapeutic Schools & Programs*, *8*, 117–138.

Bettmann, J. E., & Karikair, I. (2013). Attachment processes in wilderness therapy. In J. E. Bettmann & D. D. Friedman (Eds.), *Attachment based clinical work in children and adolescents*. Essential Social Work Series. Springer.

Bettmann, J. E., Tucker., A., Behrens, E. (2017). Changes in late adolescents and young adults' attachment, separation, and mental health during wilderness therapy. *Journal of Child and Family Studies*, *26*, 511–522.

Bhreathnach, E. (2017). *Sensory attachment intervention Level 1 training manual: Paediatrics, CAMHS (Children) and learning disabilities*. Aldertree Press.
Bowlby, J. (1958). The nature of the child's tie to his mother. *The International Journal of Psychoanalysis*, *39*, 350–373.
Bundy, A., & Lane, S. L. (2019). *Sensory integration theory and practice*. F.A Davis.
Dana, D. A. (2020). *Polyvagal exercises for safety and connection*. Sheridan Books.
Douglas, F. (2020). *The nature remedy*. Harper Collins Publishers Ltd.
Gill, T. (2014). The benefits of children's engagement with nature: A systematic literature review. *Children, Youth and Environments*, *24*(2), Greening Early Childhood Education, 10–34 (25 pages). https://doi.org/10.7721/chilyoutenvi.24.2.0010
Grossman, P., Ackland, G. L., Allen, A. M., Berntson, G. G., Booth, L. C., Burghardt, G. M., Buron, J., Dinets, V., Doody, J. S., Dutschmann, M., Farmer, D. G. S., Fisher, J. P., Gourine, A. V., Joyner, M. J., Karemaker, J. M., Khalsa, S. S., Lakatta, E. G., Leite, C. A. C., Macefield, V. G., … Zucker, I. H. (2026). Why the polyvagal theory is untenable: An international expert evaluation of the polyvagal theory and commentary upon Porges, SW (2025). Polyvagal theory: Current status, clinical applications, and future directions. *Clinical Neuropsychiatry*, *22*(3), 169–184, *23*(1), 100. https://doi.org/10.1016/j.biopsycho.2023.108589
Haines, S. (2019). Finding safety via embodiment. www.BodyCollege.net
Harper, N. J., Rose, K., & Segal, D. (2019). *Nature-based therapy: A practitioner's guide to working outdoors with children, youth, and families*. New Society Publishers.
Heginworth, I., & Nash, G. (Eds). (2020). *Environmental arts therapy. The wild frontiers of the heart*. Routledge.
Huff, C., Widmer, M., & McCoy, K. (2003). *The influence of challenging outdoor recreation on parent- adolescent communication*. Brigham Young University.
Kain, K. L., & Terrell, S. (2018). *Nurturing resilience: Helping clients move forward from developmental trauma*. North Atlantic Books.
Kellert, S. R., & Wilson, E. O. (1993). *The biophilia hypothesis* (p. 484). Island Press. ISBN:1–55963-148-1.
Kovacs, A. (n.d.). How much DNA do humans share with other animals and plants? Retrieved May 3, 2023, from https://www.scribbr.com/apa-examples/website/
Leirmann, K., & Norton, C. L. (2016). Enhancing family communication: Examining the impact of a therapeutic wilderness program for struggling teens and parents. *Contemporary Family Therapy*, *38*, 14–22. https://doi.org/10.1007/s10591-015-9371-5
Lyytinen, P. (2018). Fathers, sons, trees, and attuned interaction – Reflections on concepts [Paper presentation]. *8th International Adventure Therapy Conference, Sydney, Australia*.
Mulholland, R., & Williams, A. (1998). Exploring together outdoors: A family therapy approach based in the outdoors for troubled mother/daughter relationships. *Journal of Outdoor and Environmental Education*, *3*, 21–31.
Music, G. (2019). *Nurturing children. From trauma to growth using attachment theory, psychoanalysis and neurobiology*. Routledge.
Norton, C. L., Tucker, A., Farnham-Stratton, M., Borroel, F., & Pelletier, A. (2017). Family enrichment adventure therapy: A mixed methods study examining the impact of trauma-informed adventure therapy on children and families affected by abuse. *Journal of Child & Adolescent Trauma*, *12*(1), 85–95.
Olszewska-Guizzo, A., Fogel, A., Escoffier, N., Sia, A., Nakazawa, K., Kumagai, A., Dan, I., & Ho, R. (2022, April 7). Therapeutic garden with contemplative features induces desirable changes in mood and brain activity in depressed adults. *Front Psychiatry*, *13*, 757056. https://doi.org/10.3389/fpsyt.2022.757056

Pfeifer, E. (2017). Music-nature-therapy: Outdoor music therapy and other nature related approaches in music therapy. In A. Kopytin & M. Rugh, (Eds), *Environmental expressives therapies: Nature assisted therapy and practice* (pp. 107–203). New York and Oxon.
Porges, S. W. (2011). *The polyvagal theory: Neurophysiological foundations of emotions, attachment, communication, and self-regulation* (Norton Series on Interpersonal Neurobiology). W. W. Norton & Company.
Pritchard, A., Richardson, M., Sheffield, D., & McEwan, K. (2020). The relationship between nature connectedness and eudaimonic well-being: A meta-analysis. *Journal of Happiness Studies*, *21*, 1145–1167. https://doi.org/10.1007/s10902-019-00118-6
Schore, A. N. (2001). The effects of early relational trauma on right brain development, affect regulation, and infant mental health. *Infant Mental Health Journal*, *22*(1–2), 201–269.
Selhub, E. M., & Logan, A. C. (2012). *Your brain on nature. The science of nature's influence on your health, happiness, and vitality*. John Wiley and Sons.
Siegel, D. J. (2012). *The developing mind. How relationships and the brain interact to shape who we are*. (2nd ed.). The Guilford Press.
Stevens, B., Kagan, S., Yamada, J., Epstein, I., Beamer, M., Bilodeau, M., & Baruchel, S. (2004). Adventure therapy for adolescents with cancer. *Pediatric Blood & Cancer*, *43*, 278–284. https://doi.org/10.1002/pbc.20060
Szczytko, R., Tate Stevenson, K., Nils Peterson, N., & Bondell, H. (2020). How combinations of recreational activities predict connection to nature among youth. *The Journal of Environmental Education*, *51*(6), 462–476. https://doi.org/10.1080/00958964.2020.1787313
Torng, C.-S. and Lin, P.-C. (2023). Impacts of ecotherapy on physiological and psychological benefits. In AIP Conference Proceedings. *Applied physics of condensed matter* (APCOM 2022), AIP Publishing, p. 060008.
Van der Kolk, B. A. (2015). *The body keeps the score: Brain, mind, and body in the healing of trauma*. Penguin Books.
Wohlleben, P. (2017). *The hidden life of trees. What they feel, how they communicate: Discoveries from a secret world*. Williams Collins.

Chapter 4

Rhythm

Claire Pemrick and Matt Slavin

The Rhythm element is our temporal element and is all about time, cycles, changes, adaptation, and planning. We have this element early in the process as we use this element to help you guide your sessions and plan how you are going to run them. Just as we check the weather in the morning to decide what to wear, we check in with those we support to see where they are too, and clinically reason how we are going to structure the current and future sessions. We also discuss the use of our proformas and assessment tools, and other tools that you might use to try and clinically reason where your participants are in terms of their health and well-being and their nature-connectedness.

In this chapter, we are going to think about the cycles of life, nature's rhythms, phases, and seasons. As part of nature, we will look at our own natural rhythms. In particular, we will look at our circadian rhythms and other internal rhythms that let us know when it is day or night or time to eat. We will look at how these rhythms develop and how entrainment helps put us into synchrony with the rhythms in the natural world and people around us.

We will introduce the concepts of the Just Right Time and the Art of Allowing – how these are important considerations in planning our sessions, and how we can use resonance to amplify the impact of our work.

We will look at trauma and how this changes our perception of time, and how we can use these concepts to plan and deliver a session using the EcoSensory model.

Nature's Rhythms

No matter where you look in nature, you will find rhythms. Whether it be the ebb and flow of the sea, the sun rising and falling, the moon waxing and waning, or the sunflower opening and turning to face the sun. Even in the forms and patterns we see in nature, we can see rhythmic growth, time passing, etched into the trunk of a tree as rings, the grooves in a ram's horn, or the stripes on a shell. If we dig deep, we will find this rhythmic history through the strata of the earth. Wherever you look at form in nature, you will see rhythm (Flannery, 1990).

The natural world is governed by circles, cycles, and repeated patterns, and the modern world by straight lines. Whether it is at the microcellular level, with the

DOI: 10.4324/9781003777465-6

oscillations of enzymes, or at the macro level, with the cycles of nitrogen and carbon in the biosphere, the natural world is full of cycles within cycles.

Our calendar is set by nature's rhythms; the day and night equate to the rising and setting of the sun. A month started as a moon's cycle; the year, as a navigation through the seasons. The human drive to have some mastery over time means us being guided by calendars, stop-watches, and numbers, what the Greeks termed "Chronos", nature reminds us of the cyclic nature of life itself. Beyond chronological time, we can appreciate "moments" in time, and their unhurried nature. If "chronos" refers to a specific unit or amount of time (seconds, minutes, days, and weeks), then the Greek term "Kairos" can help us appreciate the "moments", "seasons", "phases", and even "epochs" of nature and life.

Assessment Using Chronos and Kairos as Principles

In a similar way, as clinicians, teachers, coaches, or facilitators of EcoSensory Therapy, we need to be mindful of both the "chronos" and the "kairos". As health professionals, many of our assessments of our clients' needs are based on "statistics", "numbers", and "measurements" – the chronos. These quantitative tools are vital in evidencing what we may feel we know from "intuition" and "gut-feelings", without them, assessments would be more supposition. Frequently, as occupational therapists, we use standardised or norm-referenced tools to assess motor skills, sensory processing, mood, executive functioning; as a clinical psychologist, you may use trauma scales; and as a teacher, reading scores. At EcoSensory Therapy, we wholeheartedly continue to encourage you to use the tools you are skilled and trained in to gather the data you need. Likewise, the use of standardised and normed assessments is often paramount to showing change in sessions, carrying out research or evidencing for funding. These can be tools that have attained a high level of validity and reliability, but you can also create simple quantitative measures. Over a campfire in Wales, Claire chatted to the lovely and prolific nature-based researcher from the University of Derby, Kirstin McEwan, on how she draws three circles on the ground at the beginning and end of a Forest Bathing session and asks the participants to put a stone in the one that represents how they are feeling. These are related to Paul Gilbert's: threat, drive, and sooth systems. You could equally create simple Likert scales based on goals your clients have noted as important, and take a photo at the beginning and end of each session. We use Goal-Based Outcomes (Law, 2013), as we find that our clients directing the goals helps us as facilitators focus on what is meaningful for them.

In the nature-based world, there are assessments and outcome measurements that you might find very helpful in your practice. There are those that measure well-being. We mostly use the Profile of Mood scores, but there is also the Warwick-Edinburgh Mental Well-being Scale (NHS Health Scotland et al., 2006) and others. There are tools that look at connection to nature: The Nature-Connectedness Parental Self Efficacy Scale (Barnes et al., 2021); The Environmental Benefits from Nature (England, n.d.); Connectedness to Nature Scale (Frantz & Mayer, 2014); and perceived restorativeness scales (Hartig et al., 1997, 2011).

Alongside the chronos, or measurements, that give us numbers, the qualitative information, or the "kairos", is vital too. As much as we can look at our weather app and get a number for how much it will rain or the temperature, only going outside and seeing how the rain is falling – whether it is driving or spitting, whether the wind is howling or there is a breeze – will tell us what to wear. In our sessions, this is an ongoing dialogue about knowing our participants, how they are feeling compared with the last week, what events have happened, and what changes are afoot. Knowing this allows us to adapt our sessions in meaningful ways. Use the elements to find out more, use "connect" to ask about their connectedness to their body, family, and friends. Use "rhythm" to ask about their sleep, or activities, and so on and so forth. Some changes are small, quick, and changeable like the weather, and some last for longer like the seasons.

The Seasons

Our natural world is constantly in a process of change. The life cycle and seasons in nature show us that it is ever-changing, yet always familiar. The more time we spend in nature, the more we are able to attune to the patterns of life, and those patterns are quite different from those of the modern world.

We rise, and we fall. We come from stardust and return to stardust. Whether you understand this from a spiritual vantage or from astrophysics, both disciplines understand the cyclic nature of life itself. The very matter we are made from, the elements and chemicals that shape our bodily existence, come from the natural world and so too will return. Life itself is a matter of seasons.

So, just for a moment, consider the mirrored experience of nature and our human lives. Consider that just as nature has seasons, so we too live our lives through seasons.

Spring is for life and new beginnings; summer is the time for productivity and development; autumn is the time for harvest, a mark of change from the summer sun; and winter is the time for dormancy, reflection, and perseverance.

As you read this passage, perhaps you can reflect upon which season you find yourself in today, this week, this month, or this year? Just as we can be drawn to consider why we experience hardship, perhaps we can consider why nature and life itself need seasons. What do seasons serve in nature? How do seasons serve your life? If we are to have rich and bountiful summers, so too do we not need cold and blustery winters?

We also experience much of life through contrast. We understand light when confronted with darkness. We appreciate life because we know of death. In order to live a full and enriched life, consider why we might need all four seasons and how, for you, the four seasons give meaning to times of joy and also to times of suffering.

When you meet your clients in the natural world, its seasonality is an ever-constant companion to add to your therapeutic toolkit, both for understanding them more fully and for avenues of support. Where is your client when you meet them for the first time? If we are to take a functional approach to health, rather than a pathological approach, we can begin to appreciate the reasons why someone might find themselves in the space and season they inhabit. You only need to step outside to see the beauty in a falling leaf, or a newly budding flower, or the needle of grass growing through a bed of snow. Life continues through, and needs all of its seasons. When we look at more transitory natural phenomena, like weather, we can also appreciate the transitory nature of much of our existence. Just as the weather will change moment to moment, so too our thoughts, feelings, bodies, sensations, and experiences change moment to moment.

And there can be great relief in acknowledging that experience is transitory and changing. We can help those we support to remember that thoughts, feelings, and sensations are often fleeting experiences, and we can help them to untangle from the idea that the current internal hurricane will last a lifetime. When we look beyond the day-to-day, to the seasons, we can begin to appreciate the need and necessity for stretches of darkness and winter, for feverous heat, for raging seas, times of growth and beginnings, and times of decay. The seasons and observable rhythms in nature become powerful metaphors that can support and guide those we help in times of great hardship.

Trauma and Time

Connecting to seasons, connecting to nature, brings us back to the here and now. Intentional immersion in our natural world promotes a sense of nowness, a reminder of where we are in time and space. One of the main "symptoms" of trauma is the dislocation and disorganisation of time and space. Nature and our beneficial relationship with it provide opportunities in which to step out of the darkness of timelessness and walk into the light of nowness.

Family Life Cycles

As our lives have transitions, phases, and cycles, so do our relationships. Carter and McGoldrick (1988) talk about the Family Life Cycle when looking at family systems. They discuss the ever-changing nature of families. Individuals age and develop, and so in turn, their roles and responsibilities change and develop. Just like the swallows, there are periods of great endeavour, periods of nest-building and nurturing young, and times to fledge. A major task for individuals and the family system is to negotiate these transition points. We often meet our clients at these transition points, where each generation in the family is negotiating what it means to be entering a new phase of life.

At these times, our rhythm may move from synchrony to dyssynchrony; the tide has changed direction, and we must work harder. Problems can sometimes freeze the system at a particular change; for example, an unwell child may freeze the system to see that young person as a vulnerable infant, the child as dependent and the parents as all-encompassing figures. As the child develops and is more independent, the family may struggle to negotiate this new transition. At the other end of life's cycle, having parents age and become frail, often requires a shift in the roles, as they become more dependent and the routines and patterns that have developed need to adapt to the changing circumstances. It is hard when we swim against the tide, and at times, it takes a helping hand, a helpful guide to help us see when we are struggling against. Nature, as ever-changing, can serve to help us through these different life cycle transitions, through the many mirrored experiences and metaphors that abound.

Entrainment

We also have our own rhythms. We are born with internal rhythms. Our heart rate, pulse, and breathing provide a constant rhythm to our lives that may accelerate and slow, but don't stop until we do.

Do you march to the beat of your own drum? Well, perhaps you and your clients do. That being said, research about "entrainment" shows us that we also can't help but march to the beat of the drums that surround us.

Entrainment is a principle in the physical sciences in which independent rhythmical systems interact with each other. It is a universal phenomenon where one system's motion or signal frequency synchronises with, or "entrains", that of another system. This phenomenon can be observed when independent metronomes are brought together on a shared platform. At the beginning, they have their own independent rhythm. However, over a period of time, they start to synchronise with each other. Christiaan Huygens was the first to notice this entrainment in pendulum clocks in 1665 when he placed them on or suspended them from a common support (Pikovsky et al., 2003).

Numerous other mechanical instances of this phenomenon have been identified, but entrainment also extends to the biological world, where examples include synchronising fireflies (Thaut, 2013) and the resetting of body clocks by sunlight (circadian entrainment; Clayton, 2012).

Entrainment is also seen in human behaviour, with both internal entrainment, where our body systems entrain with one another, and external entrainment, where we entrain with the natural world. Chronobiology concerns the way our bodies synchronise with the natural world, such as how our menstrual cycles may be linked to lunar cycles, or our wake/sleep cycles with the sun. In sessions, we can notice how a windy day may require a client to talk louder, walk faster, encourage less eye contact, and allow moments of reflection, whereas a summer's day may encourage more openness and a slower pace.

Circadian Rhythm

One of the great synchronies of nature and our bodies is "Circadian Rhythms". Our circadian rhythm gives us the daily rise and fall that influences our sleep–wake cycle, hormone release, body temperature, and other important bodily functions, and it also determines when we are hungry and able to digest.

Our circadian rhythm happens at a cellular level. Virtually all cells in the universe have some form of circadian rhythm. They are metabolic cycles that rely on key rhythms of feeding and fasting, light and dark, hot and cold, and movement (for those organisms that move).

Our circadian rhythm is influenced by our immediate environment. Just like the sunflowers turning to face the light, we are also entrained by the world around us. The sun rises and sets, and it entrains our melatonin levels in relation to patterns of light and darkness. We feel sleepy as the sun sets and naturally feel more awake as the sun rises the next morning.

Circadian rhythmicity is evident in numerous aspects of our behaviour and bodily functions, such as sleep patterns, alertness, physical activity, hormone levels, body temperature, immune system activity, and digestion.

Our circadian rhythm helps the functioning of many of our bodily processes. Light is detected by specific melatonin receptors and signals the suprachiasmatic nucleus (SCN). The SCN is a tiny region of the hypothalamus responsible for the circadian rhythm. It processes this information and triggers neurotransmitters and hormonal responses around the body. It also triggers other body clocks:

- Our feeding clock
- Our exercise clock
- Our temperature clock
- Our reproductive clock (linked to phases of the moon!)

A loss of synchrony between the internal circadian rhythm and the environment causes things like jet lag or seasonal affective disorder.

With advances in technology, more time spent indoors, with bright lights on until long after sunset, and blue light emitting from all the digital devices we use, our circadian rhythms can become "out of sync" with the diurnal rhythm of nature. Perhaps, that's right for your job or for the lifestyle of your client, but perhaps, too, it is making life more of a challenge. With not only sleep affected but also our hormone levels, such as our daily production of cortisol, the natural "peaks" and "troughs" of our energy can become less and disorganised through irregular sleep–wake cycles and entrainment with a digital, "the city that never sleeps" way of living. With our cortisol levels out of sync with the waking day, evidence suggests that people will feel more prone to the stressors of the day, less able to manage stress effectively and more easily overwhelmed. Here again, nature provides an opportunity and environment in which to entrain our circadian rhythm. Time spent outdoors, with natural light, will help our bodies to regulate our circadian rhythm in line with the diurnal day/night rhythm. Likewise, nourishing ourselves at the right time will help our cell cycles. Sleep deprivation in adolescents is also associated with poor decision-making, impulsivity, and risky behaviours, and is thought to predispose individuals to psychiatric disorders such as mood disorders, depression, substance use, and schizophrenia.

Lunar Cycles

Popular culture abounds with moon-related intention setting, but do the lunar cycles influence human rhythms? Is there any research that backs up these claims? Having a good look at the literature, it seems the consensus was probably not; however, a recent longitudinal study by researchers in America and Germany states that there is, in fact, synchrony with menstrual, sleep–wake, and manic-depressive cycles. However, these can be temporary and can occur with more than one time of lunar cycle (who knew there was more than one type), more than one phase, and more than one resonant frequency (more about resonance later in this chapter) (Wehr & Helfrich-Förster, 2021).

Hormonal changes that correlate with menstrual cycles and the change in emotional states are areas that practitioners may have some trepidation in supporting; however, helping our clients understand their own cycles and rhythms can be invaluable in thinking about timings and predicting their needs. Apps abound for tracking these cycles, which, in my practice working with teenage girls with mental health needs, we have anecdotally found that the phase of the cycle can impact their emotional well-being. Also, the activities that they are keen on doing change based on where they are in their cycle.

Further to our circadian rhythms, we also have "circatidal harmonics", a 12-hour biological clock that is thought to be linked to our marine past, where the prominent time cues (zeitgebers) would have been lunar-driven and included tidal cues (Zhu & Liu, 2023). This rhythm allows us to ramp up our activity during busy times of dawn and dusk. The loss of this rhythm has been researched to be missing in people with schizophrenia (Scott et al., 2023). In our practice, we often notice differences between engagement, energy, and focus at different times of the day, and thinking of these rhythms will help you plan or adjust your session accordingly.

Development of Entrainment

Entrainment starts early. In the womb, we are entrained to our mother's cycles, and become entrained to the rhythms of maternal feeding, body temperature, and melatonin, her heartbeat and breathing rate, and her movements, either walking, rocking, or swaying.

While our circadian rhythms after birth are triggered mostly by phases of light and darkness, in the womb our ear apparatus, both early hearing and the vestibular system, pick up our mother's rhythms. We hear the beating of her heart, and her breathing. We even hear her voice, in particular, the tone and prosody of it. At birth, we prefer when we hear the same speech sequences and rhythms.

Vestibular System and Rhythm

Gravity is one of the earth's most powerful physical forces, keeping the planets in orbit around the sun. Our bodies are in constant, active relationship with gravity.

One of the first senses to develop in utero is our vestibular system. The vestibular system detects gravity and movement. It allows us to know which way is up, our position in the world, starting with our position in the womb. We have been able to see how entrained we are with gravity by observing how astronauts cope without it! It turns out, not only well, with prolonged time in space with low gravity impacting bone density, muscle, sight, and even the immune system (Guzman, 2023).

The vestibular system not only keeps us in connection with the spinning earth but also, in utero, connects us to the movement of our mother. It connects us to her walking, rocking, swaying, acceleration, and deceleration. Mostly we are calmed and soothed by these movements. Many studies have concluded that the vestibular system is primal to rhythm perception. Phillips-Silver and Trainor (2005) noted that babies who were bounced to a rhythm preferred that rhythm when played later (Trainor et al., 2009). The latest advances in neuroanatomical imaging have shown an overlap in the brain areas associated with both rhythm and vestibular processing. Furthermore, strong musical rhythms have been shown to evoke the same brain area associated with motor timing, even when there is no explicit movement (Todd & Lee, 2015).

Dancing could be described as a type of entrainment. The sensory integration of the sound, vibrations, and movement can be helpful for learning or developing new tasks; for example, the rhythmic sound of music can aid motor control (Krasovsky et al., 2010). Within sensory integration, "entrainment" has been used to help shift arousal states, such as the use of rhythmic music to be either calming or arousing (Champagne, 2008).

Movement and rhythmic entrainment are often observed between humans, for example, dancing or walking in time, or cooperative tasks such as sawing together, or pounding grain, or rowers rowing in sync. We can watch this synchrony in the natural world, for example, when birds flock together, fish school together, or locusts swarm.

When we see many people moving together in synchrony, the power is amplified. Watching the All Black rugby team doing the Haka, is designed to provoke fear in the opposing tribe or team, which is partly due to the resonance of them moving and chanting in sync. There is also thought to be a regulating effect on the people doing the Kapa Haka (Hollands et al., 2015)

Resonance

We have all heard people say, "that really resonated with me", when they felt that something matched their own feelings, views, or ideas. In the natural world, resonance is when we match the natural frequency of an object. For example, a spider uses resonance to catch prey; the radial silk threads of a web have a frequency that the spider can tune. When the frequency is matched, it is amplified. Resonance is really about timing. If we get the timing just right, we are able to put energy into the system that adds to the energy that is already there. In our sessions, we must be alert to how we fine-tune, or as occupational therapists often refer to "grade" so that our sessions meet the frequency, energy, arousal, and ideas of our participants. The activity we planned may just not be at the right frequency; I often find myself shelving my plans to meet my client where they are.

Just Right Time

"Timing is everything", so the saying goes, and if we take the theories of resonance and entrainment, we can see the importance of the "Just Right Time" in our sessions. As practitioners, we may be skilled in considering the "just right challenge"; however, we often neglect to consider the "Just Right Time". Nature is all about timing, gardening, and foraging, and the weather teaches us that we need to get our timing right.

All things, certainly all things in nature, entail rising and falling timing. Timing is observed in universal order and the seasons which arrive and recede. The ocean tides are influenced according to the moon's gravity and the planets' orbits in accordance with the sun's gravity. The global COVID-19 pandemic showed us that nature at any point can disrupt our plans, just as an expected rainstorm or a flooded road might. Timing is that force apparent when chance and coincidence collide. Our "Growing Roots" Online Practitioner Training at EcoSensory Therapy came about because of the coincidence of having to do things online, and us being ready to do that.

Working with the Natural Order of Things

What would it mean to give space for things to happen at the right time, which does not mean simply leaving things to chance but working with the natural order of things, in synchronicity? How do we allow for the infinite possibilities of how a session may go, and be "unmarried" to your own agenda or session plans? Allow events to unfold as they do, unhurried by your watch or pre-arranged plan.

Here, working with your client's rhythms and nature's rhythms creates possibilities for arriving at the "Just Right Time". We need to be aware of these, allow them to rise, and use our intuition to create meaningful events that happen at the "Just Right Time".

Rather than this being unplanned chaos, we pay attention to the rhythm of the seasons, the day, the state of mind of the client, their learning level, their nervous system, and allow for the sessions to unfold. What might work with one client in one season, at one time of day, might not work for the next. We adjust and work with the forces, not against them. We don't push against the forces to meet our own agenda.

Having EcoSensory sessions in all weather, in all seasons, will require us to be adaptable and flexible. In doing so, we gather a whole new skill set at being mindful of timing.

While we may have ideas and plans abound for our sessions, we quickly learn that while we might be able to do anything, we might not be able to do everything, certainly not at the same time. The priority within EcoSensory sessions is not the activities you do, but when you do them. Having them up your sleeve is the skill; the art is knowing when the right time is.

It is important to understand that thoughts are also subject to timing. For our clients, it may be difficult to grasp ideas at a certain time, while at another time, things are understood with little effort. The greatest moments in an EcoSensory session will happen when you least expect it. The moment a deer stops in the path ahead or a client makes a connection. Let go and allow these events to happen … Carl Jung describes them as a "meaningful coincidence" when chance and coincidence collide (Jung, 2013).

Entrainment with Nature

Entrainment might then give us some clues into the regulating effects of being within nature and being "in sync" with nature, or "on nature time". One's system cannot help but coordinate or "entrain" to a stronger external pulse or rhythm.

Consider then, the effect of sitting by the ocean's shore and listening to the lapping of the sea against the water's edge. Witness the wave crests rise and collapse, as dark blues turn to a mass of white water or consider the gentle pitter-patter of raindrops on a tree canopy or canvas of a tent. As sensory beings, immersed in the sensory world, we cannot help but be entrained by the greater forces and rhythms that surround us, entraining our autonomic nervous system to slow our heart rate and our breathing. Many of my sessions happen at my beach hut, which gets cut off at periods of high tide! Not only do I need to plan sessions based on these natural rhythms but I also quickly notice how the sounds of the waves and the movement of the tide regulate and allow for deeper conversations. Just being able to watch the sea, entrain the breath, and take the visual gaze out to the horizon, rather than having to look at the therapist, allows for more expansiveness.

The opposite, of course, is also true. Consider standing on a busy road, cars whizzing past, loud music thumping from a shop behind you, people cycling past, flashing images on billboards, and multiple conversations being had at raised voices to compete with the noise of the urban space. Just as our bodies entrain to dance the six steps of a waltz, so too our bodies are entrained to synchronise with the frequency of this urban system. Our heart rate quickens, our breath shortens, and our rhythm is entrained by the business of the urban world.

Timing and Hidden Growth

When we consider timing and growth, nature again provides us with lessons we can learn. Within 21st-century life, there can be an expectation for fast-paced growth and the constant attainment of achievement. In nature, there are instances of remarkable fast-paced growth. Take asparagus as an example. Out of seemingly nowhere, asparagus can burst through the earth and grow at a phenomenal rate – up to 25 centimetres within a 24-hour period. In life, many of us and those we support feel pressured to "grow" … to make therapeutic change … to learn and attain educational goals … to realise excellence in a career. The messages we receive in popular culture and social media can encourage us to look for "overnight success" and "life-hacks" or short-cuts to get there. Nature here reminds us that healthy and sustainable growth takes time and nurture. Asparagus, which seemingly grows "overnight", has in fact taken three years to mature and for its network of roots to take hold. Achievement and goal-attainment in life, like asparagus growth or bamboo growth, take years of "hidden" growth and nurture. Often the hard work lies below the surface and is out of sight to others and often to ourselves. In EcoSensory sessions, it may take time for roots of trust and therapeutic alliance to develop, some progresses may be slow initially, but may be preparing the ground for future growth. Using natural phenomena as metaphor can often support our clients to appreciate their process of change, even when it means that it will take time to witness the fruits of their labour.

Summary

In your sessions too, we encourage you to use the power of entrainment. What is your rhythm today? Is it in synchrony with your client? Are you in sync with nature? Has your client hurried to a session, stressed with the business of their day?

EcoSensory sessions happen at their own pace. Practitioners need to be aware of the pace and rhythm of their clients, join them where they are, and guide them within nature to support their rhythms. A client in an activated state may need to walk fast and work hard to help regulate. So, we join them there. We might take a longer route than usual, or lift heavier logs. As they start to entrain to nature, the session may slow down, and we may be able to engage in the more focused, "voluntary attention", here and now activities, or creative endeavours. EcoSensory sessions should never feel like a checklist of activities achieved. Take time, slow down, and do not hurry. Whatever needs to be accomplished will happen best with flexibility and allowance, at the "Just Right Time".

References

Barnes, C., Harvey, C., Holland, F., & Wall, S. (2021). Development and testing of the Nature Connectedness Parental Self-Efficacy (NCPSE) scale. *Urban Forestry & Urban Greening*, *65*(127343), 127343.

Carter, B., & McGoldrick, M. (Eds.). (1988). *The changing family life cycle: A framework for family therapy* (2nd ed.). Gardner Press.

Champagne, T. (2008). Sensory Modulation & Environment: Essential Elements of Occupation (3rd ed.). Southampton, MA: Champagne Conferences & Consultation.

Clayton, M. (2012). *What is entrainment? Definition and applications in musical research.* Available at: https://kb.osu.edu/handle/1811/52979.

England, N. (n.d.). *The environmental benefits from nature tool - Beta test version - JP038.* Natural England - Access to Evidence. Retrieved March 13, 2026, from https://publications.naturalengland.org.uk/publication/6414097026646016

Flannery, M. C. (1990). Rhythm & form in nature. *The American Biology Teacher*, *52*(2), 118–121.

Frantz, C. M., & Mayer, F. S. (2014). The importance of connection to nature in assessing environmental education programs. *Studies in Educational Evaluation*, *41*, 85–89.

Guzman, A. (2023, December 1). Counteracting bone and muscle loss in microgravity. *NASA*. https://www.nasa.gov/missions/station/iss-research/counteracting-bone-and-muscle-loss-in-microgravity/

Hartig, T., Korpela, K., Evans, G. W., & Gärling, T. (1997). A measure of restorative quality in environments. *Scandinavian Housing and Planning Research*, *14*(4), 175–194.

Hartig, T., van den Berg, A. E., Hagerhall, C. M., Tomalak, M., Bauer, N., Hansmann, R., Ojala, A., Syngollitou, E., Carrus, G., van Herzele, A., Bell, S., Podesta, M. T. C., & Waaseth, G. (2011). Health benefits of nature experience: Psychological, social and cultural processes. In K. Nilsson, M. Sangster, C. Gallis, T. Hartig, S. de Vries, K. Seeland, & J. Schipperijn (Eds.), *Forests, trees and human health* (pp. 127–168). Springer Netherlands.

Hollands, T., Sutton, D., Clair, V., & Hall, R. (2015). Māori mental health consumers' sensory experience of kapa haka and its utility to occupational therapy practice. *New Zealand Journal of Occupational Therapy*, *62*, 3–11.

Jung, C. G. (1955). Synchronicity: An acausal connecting principle. In C. G. Jung & W. Pauli, *The interpretation of nature and the psyche* (R. F. C. Hull, Trans.). London: Routledge & Kegan Paul.

Krasovsky, T., Berman, S., & Liebermann, D. G. (2010). Kinematic features of continuous hand reaching movements under simple and complex rhythmical constraints. *Journal of Electromyography and Kinesiology: Official Journal of the International Society of Electrophysiological Kinesiology*, *20*(4), 636–641.

Law, D. (2013). *Goals and goal based outcomes (GBOs).* Evidence Based Practice Unit (EBPU). CAMHS Press.

NHS Health Scotland, University of Warwick, & University of Edinburgh. (2006). *Warwick–Edinburgh mental well-being scale (wemwbs)*. https://www2.uwe.ac.uk/services/Marketing/students/pdf/Wellbeing-resources/well-being-scale-wemwbs.pdf

Phillips-Silver, J., & Trainor, L. J. (2005). Feeling the beat: Movement influences infant rhythm perception. *Science*, *308*(5727), 1430.

Pikovsky, A. et al. (2003). *Synchronization: A universal concept in nonlinear sciences*. Cambridge University Press.

Scott, M. R., Zong, W., Ketchesin, K. D., Seney, M. L., Tseng, G. C., Zhu, B., & McClung, C. A. (2023). Twelve-hour rhythms in transcript expression within the human dorsolateral prefrontal cortex are altered in schizophrenia. *PLoS Biology*, *21*(1), e3001688.

Thaut, M.H. (2013). Entrainment and the motor system. *Music Therapy Perspectives*, *31*(1), 31–34.

Todd, N. P. M., & Lee, C. S. (2015). Source analysis of electrophysiological correlates of beat induction as sensory-guided action. *Frontiers in psychology*, *6*. https://doi.org/10.3389/fpsyg.2015.01178

Trainor, L. J., Gao, X., Lei, J. -J., Lehtovaara, K., & Harris, L. R. (2009). The primal role of the vestibular system in determining musical rhythm. *Cortex; A Journal Devoted to the Study of the Nervous System and Behavior*, *45*(1), 35–43.

Wehr, T. A., & Helfrich-Förster, C. (2021). Longitudinal observations call into question the scientific consensus that humans are unaffected by lunar cycles. *BioEssays*, *43*(7), 2100054.

Zhu, B., & Liu, S. (2023). Preservation of ~12-hour ultradian rhythms of gene expression of mRNA and protein metabolism in the absence of canonical circadian clock. *bioRxivorg*, 2023.05.01.538977. https://doi.org/10.1101/2023.05.01.538977

Chapter 5

Discover

Claire Pemrick

In the "Discover" element, we invite our participants to explore, discover, and navigate, thereby challenging themselves and developing their self-agency and self-actualisation. Sessions should offer the participants new experiences, whether it is the challenge of finding a new route, discovering bugs under a log, or the awe of a view at the top of the hill. "Discover" is the first of our three *doing* elements, along with "Attend" and "Create".

When we think about the element "Discover", we start to think about our direction of travel. Leaving the safe harbour of the earlier elements (Ground and Connect), we tentatively throw off the bowlines, as it is from our secure base that we can branch out to discover the world.

When the first explorers set off to find new lands, they did not have maps, but instead had a compass. Likewise, in EcoSensory, we encourage practitioners to have a compass. This book and our training serve as a map, a map to how you can become an EcoSensory practitioner. However, a map can only get you so far. Setting the bowlines free for practitioners will involve an element of adventure and a lack of certainty, with uncertain outcomes. This is likely to be scary, and we suggest that you have a compass! A compass will give you a direction of travel, from wherever you find yourself. Using a compass allows us to consider our intentions, goals, and values. Take your time to consider your direction of travel. What are your core principles? What are your values? Are you heading towards them? Are you where you thought you would be? Part of discovery is our discovery of ourselves.

Discovery means "to uncover", and in this element, we help participants reach new understandings of themselves and the world around them. Just as we may lift a log to look at the ecosystem below, we can help our participants look inside to discover what is happening in their lives. Much of this discovery is done through exploration and curiosity, in which the individual searches out new ways, new paths, and new insights. Exploration requires praxis (the ability to act on the world), and in this chapter, we will look in more depth at praxis, inner drive and how we learn to explore ourselves and our environment. Exploration involves taking risks, and in this chapter, we will look carefully at risk and how to manage, assess, and understand risk in your sessions. Finally, we will look at navigation and how we support participants in planning and steering a course in their sessions and in their wider lives.

DOI: 10.4324/9781003777465-7

Humans as Explorers

The essence of the human experience is the desire to explore, seek new knowledge, discover and navigate unknown territories. Originating on the plains of Africa, *Homo sapiens* migrated to cover all parts of the globe. This curiosity to discover has led humankind to reach the highest peaks, the farthest poles, the deepest trenches, and we continue our expansion towards our solar system and the universe beyond.

Originally, *Homo sapiens* were nomadic; they travelled in search of better hunting grounds or where they could discover and gather food. A pivotal development occurred approximately 10,000–15,000 years ago, enabling people to settle down and engage in farming (raising and storing crops) and animal domestication. Wheat in particular required tending, and this rooted us to a place to tend our crops. Today, most humans live in homes, communities, and countries, and very few still lead a nomadic, transient life. However, the urge to explore, discover, and experience new things has never been lost. While very few of us want to spend our lives on the road, most people still have a great desire to discover something, somewhere, or someone new.

Exploration–Exploitation Dilemma

So why do humans feel the need to explore?

Some evolutionary anthropologists argue that we explore to improve our lot. In the same way, a foraging animal, such as a fox, might choose between searching near its warren or straying into town. The dilemma is to stay close and stick with what you know, such as rabbits, or take the risk of searching farther away for a tasty meal, such as an "urban fox", for a potentially better dinner. With the chance of reward, so too, there is the chance of coming home hungry.

This is an example of the "exploration–exploitation dilemma" (Wilson et al., 2013). We are all likely to be familiar with it when we arrive at our favourite restaurant. Do we stick with our trusted favourite or branch out to something new? When you have found something that works, should you stay and exploit it? Do we dare to risk trying something new, with the promise of something even better?

Where safety is a concern, we may stick with what we know. Many people who have experienced trauma, have neurological differences, or sensory sensitivities will stick with what they know, feel safe with, and can control, rather than exploring novel situations. We may find our participants wanting sessions to feel and look very similar to their first session.

However, as a species, humans, it seems, are often driven to choose the option to explore. It is this willingness to explore that is fundamental to our success and is essential to our learning. In fact, some evolutionary anthropologists argue that the urge to explore is an inherent human trait, as no other mammal moves around the way that humans do (Krings et al., 1997).

In fact, researchers have identified an "explorer" gene variant, *DRD4* 7R, which helps regulate dopamine (a neurotransmitter important in learning and reward) and has been linked to curiosity, restlessness and migration. We get a buzz out of discovering new things! Having lived in four different countries and three continents, I am pretty sure that I have this gene!

This "explorer" gene was once a rare genetic mutation, which increased to high frequency in human populations through positive selection. Pioneers had more offspring; therefore, genes that favoured curiosity, innovation, restlessness and risk-taking were spread. The social cachet of having travelled increased mating opportunities and commanded social and economic support (Dobbs & Nichols, 2013).

As anthropologist Wade Davis describes, those who left the tribe and went in search of new lands became mythologised, regardless of whether they returned (Davis, 2009). Now the 7R gene is in 20% of the human population, and has been linked to increased exploration. This is both a positive and risky exploration. If you have a 7R variant, you are more likely to try new foods, go to new places, try out drugs, and explore new relationships. You are also likely to act on innovative ideas and take more risks. As humans, we are unique in our drive to cross boundaries and settle new areas, even when our current resources are sufficient. This behaviour is not mirrored in other animal species, or even in other human relatives. For example, Neanderthals existed for hundreds of thousands of years without ever dispersing globally. Yet, humans have spread everywhere, even to the moon, and onwards with our sights set on Mars. We are relentless (Zeberg et al., 2024).

Inner Drive

Could our desire to reach out, discover and explore be innate? Pavlov reported that dogs had a "What is it?" reflex, which made them curious about novel stimuli. This curiosity has even been observed in worms, where they initially explore locally and then more widely, yielding a better long-term payoff. Harlow felt that this curiosity was a basic drive in and of itself, in which animals and humans alike are driven to engage in puzzle-solving behaviour that in itself involved no tangible reward (Harlow, 1950; Harlow et al., 1950, 1956).

Dr. A. Jean Ayres, who developed the theory and therapy of Sensory Integration, believed that children are born with an inner drive to seek out what they need, to be curious, and to actively explore their environments. Modern theorists such as Loewenstein (1994) have argued that this basic inner drive creates curiosity, functioning to motivate learning. Once we notice a gap in our knowledge or understanding, we experience a sense of knowledge deprivation, and, like hunger, we seek to satisfy it by learning until we reach satiation. This has been referred to as the approach/avoid strategy (Barrett, 2024) and was described as far back as 1899. William James theorised that humans have an "impulse towards better learning" and described this curiosity drive in his book, *The Principles of Psychology*, arguing that animals have an instinctual response to new things: they approach it to explore it, then retreat, and then approach again. This approach-retreat pattern, based on curiosity, allows exploration; it also increases anxiety, as the object of exploration may be dangerous (James, 1910).

In today's busy world, with a glut of knowledge, AI, 24-hour news, and social media, our appetite for uncertainty and novelty can never be satiated. As a neuroscientist, Lisa Feldman Barrett explains that this can be metabolically expensive, as our brains are constantly releasing chemicals to up our arousal, which, depending on our appetite for uncertainty, we label as excitement or anxiety (Barrett, 2024).

In nature, our discoveries can be slower, without the metabolic expenditure. Returning to the "Green Mind" theory in the "Introduction and Theoretical Foundations" chapter, we can see how, in favourable natural environments, it allows for moments of "soft fascination" (Kaplan, 1995) which provide mild sympathetic activation, rather than a threat response (Pretty et al., 2009).

Zones of Proximal Development

This drive for development and learning was integrated into Vygotsky's model of "Zones of Proximal Development" (Chaiklin, 2003). Vygotsky describes the constant push of development (or inner drive) as one for ever more complex skills or knowledge, from comfort to challenge. Moving from a position of skill or the "comfort zone" to one of challenge, the "Challenge Zone", where we need some help, to the "Fear, Panic, Danger Zone" that is too much of a challenge, where we might need rescue. Curiosity, while beneficial, can also be seen as dangerous; hence the old adage "Curiosity killed the cat".

There is a balance to be found between the absence of curiosity and excessive curiosity. Day highlights this balance in the model "Zones of Curiosity" (Day, 1971). Arguing that activities that are not stimulating enough are unmotivating, whereas activities that give us the most pleasure can be understood as falling within the "Zone of Curiosity".

It is important to note that activities that are too challenging or dangerous fall within the "zone of anxiety". According to the psychologist Daniel Berlyne in his seminal book, *Conflict, Arousal, and Curiosity* (Berlyne, 1960), curiosity is stimulated by external factors characterised by novelty, complexity, uncertainty, and conflict. The intensity of this stimulation is crucial: insufficient stimulation fails to motivate exploration; excessive stimulation induces anxiety; and an optimal level drives exploratory behaviour. Prior to Berlyne's work, most psychologists believed that our behaviour was internally driven to reduce drives, such as hunger, rather than to increase stimulation.

Michael J. Ellis (1973) furthered Berlyne's theory of optimal arousal and argued that "play" was in itself an arousal-seeking behaviour. Play has the just-right level of arousal that allows optimal performance. He argues that we like to perform at our best and therefore seek out activities that promote a just-right state of arousal.

In Sensory Integration, Ayres described activities that met the right level of challenge for the child's development as the *"Just right challenge"* (Jean Ayres & Robbins, 2005), discussed in the Rhythm element. Activities that provide the *"Just right challenge"* at the *"Just right time"* will have the most impact on our participants (and provide that dopamine hit!).

The concept of the *"Just right challenge"* is crucial in supporting children *and* adults to engage in the world around them. The natural environment invites the individual to engage playfully in ways that are motivating and match their interests, enabling them to master them. We learn to work out, "how can I climb that tree?" or "how can I jump from this rock to that?" or "how can I find the river?" These crucial experiences help individuals to experience their own *"Just right challenge"*, one that supports a sense of accomplishment, mastery, and self-agency.

Praxis

This inner drive is a crucial foundation for our development, and one which we are driven to do, to gain mastery over our bodies and the world around us. Exploration builds stronger connections in our nervous system and broadens our knowledge of the world around us. Too little exploration reduces our chances of learning. In studies where initial exploration was reduced, opportunities for learning were impeded. Active exploration, as opposed to passive observation, allows for more in-depth learning (Stahl & Feigenson, 2015).

In Sensory Integration theory, the concept of praxis is often used to explain "the ability to interact successfully with the physical environment, to plan, organise and carry out a sequence of unfamiliar actions and to do what one needs and wants to do" (Fisher et al., 1991, p. 141).

Praxis is the ability to process the information (through the senses) from a situation and use that information to have an idea of what to do. "Praxis" is central to planning how best to carry out an idea, to execute the plan, and to adapt to any changes in the situation. For example, when a child climbs a tree, they need to process information from their bodies and the environment. How high is that branch? (depth perception). Where is my body? (body schema). Can I get my leg that high? (proprioceptive awareness).

Selhub et al. (2014) describe children's inner drive to climb trees as an evolutionary inner drive. They describe how our childhood desire to do this may be written into our DNA, and how, before we had ladders and mechanical ways of reaching fruit in trees, our communion with nature depended on our tree-climbing skills.

In our sessions, we may at times be a leader; however, participant-led activities are essential for harnessing this inner drive and maximising the learning opportunities that come with it. Activities in the outdoors are evidenced to promote personal growth and an ability to self-actualise (Yaffey, 1991, 1992). Outdoor pursuits and adventure activities, according to Yaffey (1991), facilitate Maslow's concept of self-actualisation. When we are outside exploring new environments, we can't help but offer our participants the opportunity to take risks and develop competence. Are we going the right way? How do we get over this fallen log? Is the ground too boggy to walk through? In one of my sessions, our usual route was very boggy, and my client lost her boot in the mud. It was a challenge to retrieve it without falling face-first. We were imagining we were on a reality survival TV show and had only a few yards to the extraction point, where we would be safe. Arriving there was hailed as a great success, full of humour, and was relived through frequent retellings. Through the challenge and play, she developed a sense of accomplishment, resilience, and a narrative around her success. Sometimes it is only with some challenge that we can "transcend the trap" of low self-esteem, which Yaffey identifies as a barrier to personal growth and personality maturation.

Exploration in the outdoor environment abounds with opportunities for unstructured play, independence, a sense of freedom, and the development of inner strength, which support our physical and emotional development and can be drawn upon during future times of stress.

Adaptive Play

Gill (2014) found in his systematic review of the benefits of children's engagement with nature that the most important finding was the significance of playfulness as an engagement style. Gill suggests that practitioners and policymakers should prioritise not only structured educational interventions but also initiatives that facilitate open-ended, child-directed, and playful experiences in natural environments.

The natural environment provides a myriad of opportunities to support the development and engagement of the senses: to move, see, hear, touch, smell, and taste. Forests, meadows, beaches, and parks all offer spaces to explore and connect with nature in ways crucial to our physical and emotional well-being. These natural outdoor spaces invite children and adults alike to play in ways that are richer, more diverse, and more exciting, providing opportunities for them to challenge themselves and grow.

Adaptive Responses

Adaptive behaviour is founded upon the adequate processing and integration of sensory information, according to Ayres' Sensory Integration theory. Increasingly complex behaviours are built upon the interactions of various sensory systems. For instance, the combination of vestibular and proprioceptive input is fundamental for developing adequate posture, balance, and the coordination of eye, head, and body movements. This foundation then integrates with the tactile system, which is crucial for body awareness, bilateral coordination, and praxis.

At the very heart of adaptive responses is "neuroplasticity", which allows our nervous system to change in response to experiences. This concept, along with that of repetition, is key to fostering stronger connections in the brain, which enhance development and lead to improved skills and abilities. Our brains form new connections with each experience, and environmental enrichment is fundamental to this process.

From an Ayres Sensory Integration perspective, an environment rich in tactile, proprioceptive, and vestibular opportunities fosters physical engagement that promotes adaptive responses to the world around us. It also allows us to assess risk. In the same way, climbing the tree improves our praxis skills. It is through exploration that we develop our risk mastery. It is through this active participation that individuals learn how to assess and master risk, "Will that branch break?" "What happens if I fall?" They will likely feel aroused, alive, fearful, or excited, as Barrett suggests that the brain releases chemicals that can be interpreted in different ways based on our previous experiences (Barrett, 2024). The practitioner's role is to ensure that the challenge is just right. If their footing seems unsteady, they will receive feedback (their foot slides, and their brain processes the slip). They will be required to adapt and be flexible. They need to make moment-to-moment recalculations on "risk". "Should I continue or should I return to the ground?" "Can I accomplish this myself, or do I need help?" "Am I able to keep myself safe, even when I feel intensely scared?"

If they execute this successfully, the participant will receive a sense of mastery, self-accomplishment, and their body will be flooded with hormones that motivate us to try again – our reward hormones have been designed to incentivise us to grow and to continue to discover! This "experiential learning" supports and leads to a "growth mindset" (Dweck, 2015). Furthermore, if we get it wrong, we learn what to do better next time, and we have the opportunity to manage our frustration and failure. In Megan McArdle's book *The Upside of Down: Why Failing Well Is the Key to Success,* she points out the critical need for permission to fail and how creating a safe space to fail allows individuals to learn from failure (McArdle, 2014). How, in our sessions, can we create safety to try, explore, succeed, fail, and therefore adapt?

The individual's ability to adaptively respond to the unique features of their environment is key to developing more sophisticated skills that support further development. As described above in the tree-climbing scenario, adaptive responses develop from active participation, not just thinking about climbing the tree. Only actually climbing the tree will allow for an adaptive response. During a forest session with a group of master's-level occupational therapy students, we found a relatively easy-to-climb oak tree. Many of the students who had grown up in major urban areas had never climbed a tree before. With some encouragement and support (knees being offered to step on), the students, after a few attempts, successfully climbed to the first branch for a group photo. It was fascinating to support both their actual development of praxis, figuring out the motor plan and executing it, and their understanding of the concept of praxis in real-time. Outdoor spaces provide the ideal opportunity for self-regulation, self-discovery, and self-organisation, all of which help build a greater sense of self physically and emotionally.

Benefit of Outdoor Spaces

There is growing evidence to show that children and adults today spend substantially less time outdoors than previous generations (Pretty et al., 2009). This trend is alarming because it limits access to the vast opportunities nature and outdoor environments offer for developing sensory modulation and discrimination skills, as well as praxis.

Playing in natural environments offers rich opportunities for climbing, balancing, swinging, and exploring, all of which support the development and engagement of the senses. Actively moving through natural environments, we need to maintain postural control against the forces of gravity, use our visual-perceptual skills, grade and plan our movements, build endurance, and so on. It is only through the interactions of our bodies with the environment and in relationships with others and ourselves that we can develop sensory integration in its most dynamic and integrative way.

Outdoor play that incorporates natural features has been shown to positively influence children's physical activity levels and motor development (Muñoz, 2009). Furthermore, Fjortoft (2001) notes that children engaging in outdoor play within natural spaces, especially forest environments, benefit more than those using traditional playgrounds. Nature is the ultimate sensory-rich environment; its constant change encourages more adaptive responses and praxis. Building the sand castle is different depending on whether the tide is high or low; climbing onto the log changes after rain; and walking through a meadow against the wind is different from walking with it.

The benefits are not just for children. Pretty et al. (2009) highlight how "participating in physical activity and experiencing nature both play an important role in positively influencing our health and wellbeing". They demonstrate that when physical activity levels drop dramatically, it significantly affects adult health and longevity. In the 2021 systematic review on nature-based outdoor activities and their benefits for mental and physical health, Coventry et al. found that nature-based activities were "consistently effective across all mental health outcomes" (p. 11).

We would do well to remember that we thrive by challenging our bodies, and we suffer physically, socially, and emotionally when we are not afforded these opportunities in the long term. Activities such as playing in muddy puddles may test a child's balance skills, but for adults, they help maintain balance and reduce the future risk of falls. Outdoor exercise, such as running in the natural environment, has been shown by the outdoor exercise research group at the University of Essex to benefit all (Gladwell et al., 2013). It's time to get on your wellies or running shoes and go outside to discover and benefit from the rich natural environment.

Scary-Funny

Humans will choose activities that are inherently risky. In the Adventure Experience Paradigm (Martin & Priest, 1986), they explore why people choose to participate in outdoor activities that could be deemed risky. They argue that individuals choose activities they believe will develop their competence, whether in skills, knowledge, or confidence.

Aldis (2013) argues that children also actively seek play that provides the "thrills of fearful situations" such as swinging or jumping from heights. Sandseter (2010), a Norwegian developmental educationist, researched what play activities young children enjoyed and why. She found that children particularly enjoyed activities that provided both an element of risk, mastery and challenge. Children reported that they liked the "*scary-funny*" emotions they experienced from this higher-arousal play, as they mastered the risks (Sandseter, 2010). In fact, these children would deliberately increase this arousal by increasing the risks, such as increasing the height or speed. It is the intense arousal that provides the pleasure, the "balance" between excitement and "the border of fear" (Sandseter & Kennair, 2011).

Children will gradually seek out risky play and thrills within their "zone of proximal development", which allows them to master the challenges involved (Aldis, 2013). For example, they start with stepping and balancing on the log before progressing to the tree. The child's perception of risk becomes more accurate and realistic. "Through risky play, children prepare for handling real risks and dangers; it is a serious risk-management exercise" (Harper, 2017, p. 320).

Risky play also has an important evolutionary function in reducing fear and phobias (Sandseter & Kennair, 2011). Certain fears, such as a fear of heights, water, or separation from a caregiver, emerge and resolve naturally at different developmental ages. This occurs as a child is given the opportunity to overcome these fears when they are developmentally ready to interact with their environment in appropriate ways.

Adults similarly seek out thrills. Michael Balint (2018) describes adults' desire for thrills, such as rollercoasters, as a loss of balance, stability and reliable contact with dependable earth. To be a "thrill" there must be fear and delight and confident hope. Balint suggests three criteria: (1) that there must be a certain amount of conscious fear, (2) the person must have decided to do it voluntarily, and (3) there must be a belief that the fear will be overcome and mastered and the danger will pass.

When our participants don't have a sense of the earth being reliable, such as those with praxis issues, or those who do not have a secure base to explore from, they are more likely to experience these activities as being in "the danger zone". Individuals without this sense of security often find change, novelty, and transitions difficult. As practitioners, we need to balance out this sense of safety and security with that of challenge and exploration.

As Balint suggests, something is thrilling rather than terrifying only if we know the danger will be overcome. This is where the ability to risk assess is essential. It is important to distinguish between what is a risk and what is a hazard.

Our desire for self-preservation drives the development of our risk assessment mastery. Generally, we do not want to take risks that provide no potential benefits and only hazards. For the most part, we don't actually want to get hurt. Sometimes our desire for self-preservation will prevent us from taking a risk. We are pushed into the "zone of anxiety", where our sympathetic system goes into overdrive.

For me, this was how I felt the first time I sat on a jet ski. Asked to go "very fast", I was petrified. Fear, self-preservation, and the preservation of my daughter (who sat behind, holding on) were too much. My partner, on the other hand, experienced this as exhilaration and was in "scary-funny".

In our EcoSensory sessions, we must always be aware of the fine balance and subtle art of supporting our participants as they navigate their "zone of curiosity" or "scary-funny", paying close attention and stepping in when this begins to shift into the "zone of anxiety". For different participants, these shift levels may vary widely. I am not scared of heights, so I would happily climb a tree, but for one of my clients with reduced motor skills, just stepping on a log was terrifying.

Porges' polyvagal theory suggests that we have an inhibitory neural mechanism that enables us to explore and take risks. The *vagal brake* can rapidly mobilise or calm an individual by inhibiting and disinhibiting the vagal tone to the heart. This enables the person climbing a tree to cope with the intensity and excitement of arousal without going into a survival response. There is currently a debate about the accuracy of the vagal brake and its neurophysiological underpinnings (Grossman et al., 2026). As facilitators, we might not need to understand the neurophysiology, but we might find it helpful to consider how we can support our participants' regulation, especially when exploring new and challenging activities. Are they tipping into a survival response, or are they able to manage the intensity of arousal? If positive risk-taking is maintained alongside feelings of safety, our clients will be able to explore, which will, in turn, allow more opportunities for the development of regulation.

Just as children start their exploration from their secure base and return to it when things go into the "danger/panic zone", the same principles apply to EcoSensory sessions, with individuals needing a visceral sense of safety, trusting that the practitioner leading the session is secure, reliable, and will work within their "zone of proximal development". For us as practitioners, we can also consider how we can step outside our comfort zone, supported by our secure base – from a nature perspective, the security of Mother Earth.

Risk–Benefit Analysis

Have we gone too far as a society in protecting ourselves from risk? Nevin Harper and colleagues, authors of *Nature-Based Therapy,* believe so. They argue that for many children, they are living in a "hyper-protective state", overprotected from both the risks and the many learning experiences that previous generations had. They advocate that practitioners and parents begin the dialogue on "the right to risk" as equally important to a child's right to play (Harper et al., 2019).

Discovery, exploration, and curiosity are intrinsically linked to risk. Csikszentmihalyi is categorical: risk is necessary for creativity, as curiosity requires risk and without curiosity, there is no creativity (Csíkszentmihályi, 1996). In EcoSensory Therapy, we understand that there is a fine balance between risk and exploration. As Harper (2017) suggests, a "hazard" (falling off the cliff) is harmful with no potential benefits, whereas a "risk", balancing as we walk along a log, also has potential benefits, especially to development. Everyone has their own perception of a particular risk or hazard.

Whether we find something too risky or not will be based on our own experiences, or lack of experience around an event. If we have experienced something before and our nervous system was overwhelmed, we are likely to experience fear the next time. Our brains are predictive. If our first experience of being out in a forest was frightening, our brains will tune in to the sensory experience of the forest and trigger fear responses the next time we go in. If our first experience is joyful, we will predict that the next forest experience will be pleasurable.

Kaplan's Attention Restoration Theory (ART) identifies compatibility as one of the four qualities a natural environment must have to be restorative. If there is a mismatch between what you want to do and the environment, it will require effort and not be restorative (Kaplan, 1995). In one of my sessions, a university student who was not able to take an invitation to lie on the ground and look up at the canopy came from a country where bugs can kill; although now in England, with limited life-threatening bugs, she still had a sympathetic response to lying down. Far from being restorative, the environment was incompatible with relaxation and instead threatening. To adapt this activity, we used a hammock with a net, which helped her feel safe and relaxed, and she was able to enjoy it. Slowly feeling safer, we removed the net. Her curiosity to see the canopy overrode her threat responses.

Using the discover element to identify our participants' compatibilities, preferences, and aversions in nature, and to assess their appetite for risk, can help us ensure that we can support exploration and growth without causing overarousal. A participant with anxiety may prefer a meadow or the beach to a forest.

Managing Risk in Sessions

So how do we manage risk in an EcoSensory Therapy session while promoting an individual's right to play, have fun, develop praxis and risk mastery? This was one of the key challenges that prevented me from taking my practice outside. "What did I need to do to strike this balance?"

Luckily, this balance has been considered and documented by many play, health, and safety organisations, including the Health and Safety Executive (HSE). In their statement on Children's Play and Leisure: Promoting a balanced approach (Joint HSE/Play Safety Forum, High Level Statement), they argue that allowing children to benefit from play while protecting them from serious risks requires striking the right balance. This is not achieved through eliminating all risks or by using complex risk/benefit calculation methods. Fundamentally, they argue that play is a safe and beneficial activity. Generally, sensible adult decisions are sufficient to ensure children derive the greatest benefits without being exposed to unnecessary risk.

Sensible risk management is not about creating a risk-free environment (HSE). Play England suggests that providers use a Risk–Benefit Assessment that considers both protecting the individual from serious harm and providing them with stimulating, adventurous opportunities.

Within our training opportunities at EcoSensory Therapy, we provide Risk–Benefit Assessment proformas, as well as more traditional, thorough Outdoor Risk Assessments that practitioners can use to assess the risk and compatibility of an environment. Before you go out, it is essential that you develop your own risk assessment, suitable for your local situation.

Summary

Humans are natural explorers; we have travelled the globe, from the highest mountains to the deepest trenches of the ocean, and out into space. Why have we done this? Partly, it is about finding new resources, but this exploitation–exploration dilemma is not the whole story. From birth, we have an innate inner drive to explore the world, pushing ourselves towards new skills, new knowledge and new challenges. Part of the drive behind this is the pleasure we inherently feel when we discover something new. It gives us a neurobiological buzz!

We are driven to take on challenges that push us gently outside our comfort zone and are "Just Right". If we get the challenges right, it will be in our "zone of curiosity" and development. If the challenge is too easy, we will struggle to find the motivation to complete it (we may need an external reward). If it is too hard, we may be in the danger, panic, fear zone, and our nervous systems may be overwhelmed.

Challenges that are "Just Right" will allow us to expand our skills, knowledge, and social connections. They help us develop our understanding of our bodies, feelings, others, and our environment. These discoveries will further expand our ability to know how to act in the world, or our "praxis". They also allow us to master risk assessment. Activities that are "Scary-Funny" will expand our "Window of Tolerance" and "vagal brake", allowing us to be slightly fearful or excited without being overwhelmed. As adults, we enjoy thrills that we know will stop, and we do so voluntarily. If we don't feel safe and are forced to do something, we may enter the panic, fear zone, where the ventral vagus system is switched off, and we are in either sympathetic fight/flight or parasympathetic flop.

Assessing the challenge will also help us develop our ability to assess risks. Life is not risk-free. However, we need to be able to assess whether a risk is potentially hazardous or not. Without experiencing smaller challenges, we will not learn what our bodies can do, and about the environment around us.

As practitioners, we often feel overwhelmed by the fear of taking our practice outside. This book and our training courses have been designed to give you a map on how you can do this safely. In our training resources, you will be provided with risk assessment pro formas that you can use to start to think about how you can assess and master the risks in your practice. Hopefully, this will help move this challenge from the panic zone to either the "scary-funny" zone or the "zone of curiosity". However, remember to take your compass, point it in the direction of travel and see what you discover on the way!

References

Aldis, O. (2013). *Play fighting*. Elsevier.

Balint, M. (2018). *Thrills and regressions*. Routledge.

Barrett, L. F. (2024, August 8). Simplistic "fight or flight" idea undervalues the Brain's predictive powers. *Scientific American*. https://www.scientificamerican.com/article/simplistic-fight-or-flight-idea-undervalues-the-brains-predictive-powers/

Berlyne, D. E. (1960). *Conflict, arousal, and curiosity*. https://psycnet.apa.org/record/2006-09643-000?doi=1

Chaiklin, S. (2003). The zone of proximal development in Vygotsky's analysis of learning and instruction. *Vygotsky's Educational Theory in Cultural Context*, *1*(2), 39–64.

Csíkszentmihályi, M. (1996). Creativity: Flow and the psychology of discovery and invention. Available at: https://www.semanticscholar.org/paper/52acfff7715d030abe11620b4d96f6435ba60dfa (Accessed: 27 April 2020).

Davis, W. (2009). The wayfinders: Why ancient wisdom matters in the modern world. House of Anansi

Day, H. I. (1971). *Intrinsic motivation: A new direction in education.*

Dobbs, D., & Nichols, M. (2013, January 1). Restless genes. *National Geographic*. https://www.nationalgeographic.com/magazine/2013/01/restless-genes/

Dweck, C. (2015). Carol Dweck revisits the growth mindset. *Education Week*, *35*(5), 20–24.

Ellis, M. J. (1973). Why People Play. Prentice-Hall.

Fisher, A. G., Murray, E. A. & Bundy, A. C. (1991). *Sensory integration: Theory and practice*. F.A. Davis.

Fjortoft, I. (2001). The natural environment as a playground for children: The impact of outdoor play activities in pre-primary school children, *Early Childhood Education Journal*, *29*(2), 111–117

Gill, T. (2014). The benefits of children's engagement with nature: A systematic literature review. *Children, Youth and Environments, 24*(2), 10.

Gladwell, V. F., Brown, D. K., Wood, C., Sandercock, G. R., & Barton, J. L. (2013). The great outdoors: How a green exercise environment can benefit all. *Extreme Physiology & Medicine*, *2*(1), 3.

Grossman, P., Ackland, G. L., Allen, A. M., Berntson, G. G., Booth, L. C., Buron, J., Dinets, V., Doody, J. S., Dutschmann, M., Farmer, D. G. S., Fisher, J. P., Gourine, A. V., Joyner, M. J., Karemaker, J. M., Khalsa, S. S., Lakatta, E. G., Leite, C. A. C., Macefield, V. G., … Zucker, I. H. (2026). Why the polyvagal theory is untenable: An international expert evaluation of the polyvagal theory and commentary upon Porges, SW (2025). Polyvagal theory: Current status, clinical applications, and future directions. *Clinical Neuropsychiatry*, *22*(3), 169–184, *23*(1), 100. https://doi.org/10.1016/j.biopsycho.2023.108589

Harlow, H. F. (1950). Learning and satiation of response in intrinsically motivated complex puzzle performance by monkeys. *Journal of Comparative and Physiological Psychology*, *43*(4), 289–294.

Harlow, H. F., Blazek, N. C., & McClearn, G. E. (1956). Manipulatory motivation in the infant rhesus monkey. *Journal of Comparative and Physiological Psychology*, *49*(5), 444–448.

Harlow, H. F., Harlow, M. K., & Meyer, D. R. (1950). Learning motivated by a manipulation drive. *Journal of Experimental Psychology*, *40*(2), 228–234.

Harper, N. J. (2017). Outdoor risky play and healthy child development in the shadow of the "risk society": A forest and nature school perspective. *Child & Youth Services*, *38*(4), 318–334.

Harper, N. J., Rose, K., & Segal, D. (2019). *Nature-based therapy: A practitioner's guide to working outdoors with children, youth, and families*. New Society Publishers.

James, W. (1910). *The principles of psychology / by William James*. https://doi.org/10.5962/bhl.title.47583

Jean Ayres, A., & Robbins, J. (2005). *Sensory integration and the child: Understanding hidden sensory challenges*. Western Psychological Services.

Kaplan, S. (1995). The restorative benefits of nature: Toward an integrative framework. *Journal of Environmental Psychology*, *15*(3), 169–182.

Krings, M., Stone, A., Schmitz, R. W., Krainitzki, H., Stoneking, M., & Pääbo, S. (1997). Neandertal DNA sequences and the origin of modern humans. *Cell*, *90*(1), 19–30.
Loewenstein, G. (1994). The psychology of curiosity: A review and reinterpretation. *Psychological Bulletin*, *116*(1), 75–98.
Martin, P., & Priest, S. (1986). Understanding the adventure experience. *Journal of Adventure Education, 3*(1), 18–21.
McArdle, M. (2014). *The up side of down: Bouncing Back in business and in life / Megan McArdle*. Head of Zeus. Print.
Muñoz, S.A. (2009). *Children in the outdoors*. Sustainable Development Research Centre [Preprint]. Available at: https://ltl.org.uk/wp-content/uploads/2025/09/children-in-the-outdoors.pdf.
Pretty, J., Angus, C., Bain, M., Barton, J., Gladwell, V., Hine, R., Pilgrim, S., Sandercock, G., & Sellens, M. (2009). Nature, childhood, health and life pathways. Interdisciplinary Centre for Environment and Society Occasional Paper 2009-02. University of Essex, UK. https://www.playaustralia.org.au/sites/default/files/LibraryDownloads/Nature%20Childhood%20and%20Health%20iCES%20Occ%20Paper%202009-2%20FINAL.pdf
Sandseter, E. B. H. (2010). *Scaryfunny: A qualitative study of risky play among preschool children* [NTNU]. https://hdl.handle.net/11250/270413
Sandseter, E. B. H., & Kennair, L. E. O. (2011). Children's risky play from an evolutionary perspective: The anti-phobic effects of thrilling experiences. *Evolutionary Psychology: An International Journal of Evolutionary Approaches to Psychology and Behavior*, *9*(2), 257–284.
Selhub, E. M., Logan, A. C., & Bested, A. C. (2014). Fermented foods, microbiota, and mental health: Ancient practice meets nutritional psychiatry. *Journal of Physiological Anthropology*, *33*, 2.
Siegel, D. J. (2020). *The developing mind: How relationships and the brain interact to shape who we are*. United Kingdom: Guilford Publications.
Stahl, A. E., & Feigenson, L. (2015). Cognitive development. Observing the unexpected enhances infants' learning and exploration. *Science (New York, N.Y.), 348*(6230), 91–94.
Wilson, R. C., Geana, A., White, J. M., Ludvig, E. A., & Cohen, J. D. (2014). Humans use directed and random exploration to solve the explore–exploit dilemma. *Journal of Experimental Psychology: General*, *143*(6), 2074–2081. https://doi.org/10.1037/a0038199
Yaffey, D. (1991). Outdoor pursuits and adventure experience. *Journal of Adventure Education and Outdoor Leadership*, *8*(2), 22–25.
Yaffey, D. (1992). Personal Growth and the Outdoor Experience: Some Empirical Evidence. *Journal of Adventure Education and Outdoor Leadership, 9*(1), 32–34.
Zeberg, H., Jakobsson, M., & Pääbo, S. (2024). The genetic changes that shaped Neandertals, Denisovans, and modern humans. *Cell*, *187*(5), 1047–1058.

Chapter 6

Attend

Claire Pemrick

Welcome to Attend

The *Attend* element is one of the most critical elements in the EcoSensory practitioner's toolkit, and we see "Attend" at the heart of the model. Consider how best you "attend" and what you may need to maintain your focus of attention for this chapter. Perhaps awaken your body with movement… move, stretch, or, better yet, do so outdoors. Perhaps take this book with you and find your "sit spot" to read from.

In the "Attend" chapter, we are going to look at the differing types of attention and how we use the senses to attend. To understand why attending to nature is so good for us, we are going to look at the evolution of the senses and the evidence behind attention restoration in nature. Towards the end, we will look at broader areas such as awareness and consciousness. Let us first start with the nature poet Mary Oliver. To be a good nature poet, you need to be at the top of your game when it comes to attending to nature, and it is always good to learn from the experts. In her last book of essays before she died, *Upstream*, Mary Oliver recounts the moment she feels she came into being, started noticing and paying attention. She describes being a little girl walking along the creek with her parents. Sometimes in the creek, sometimes along it. Somehow, amidst the ripples, she starts walking upstream, while her parents walk downstream, absorbed in the sensation of the cold water against her ankles. We bear witness to her private world and the attentiveness she achieves in a charged moment of aloneness. Also, her attention is drawn to the smallest visual details of the leaves, tactile sensations of the water, the smells, and the sounds. It is in noticing the sensations, the differences between one flower and another, that Oliver creates her poetry (Mary Oliver, 2019)

In the "Attend" element, it is this moment of attentiveness – that charged moment of connection with nature – that we aim to help our participants find. The tagline for EcoSensory Therapy is "working with nature to regulate through the senses", and it is through the senses that we start to attend and tune into nature.

DOI: 10.4324/9781003777465-8

What Is Attention?

There have been various propositions for categorising the different types of attention. It is helpful to think of some attentional tasks as *involuntary,* that we have no control over, and those that are *voluntary,* that require effort. Those that are involuntary, such as alerting attention (becoming aware of something) and orienting attention (taking actions to focus on a stimulus), happen lower in the brain (Fan et al., 2005), with the alerting network being processed mostly in the thalamus, and the orienting network in the parietal lobe and the frontal eye fields. These are thought of as "bottom-up" processes.

The "top-down" attentional networks require much more effort and are much more susceptible to fatigue. These executive attention networks, including focused, selective, and sustained attention, are higher-functioning networks that place a greater load on the brain. These processes require that we tune out irrelevant stimuli and use higher mental functions, such as working memory, to replay and manipulate information, which engages higher regions of the brain.

Stephen Kaplan (1995) suggests that modern life affects our attentional networks, especially the higher-functioning "top-down" voluntary attention. He described this as "attention fatigue" in 1995, with the modern, urban world tiring this key network. Just consider how different and more demanding of our attention the world is now, with the advent of the internet, AI, smartphones and social media. The internet and technological advancements have meant that we (as humankind) are rarely, if ever, switched off. Even when we are within the safety of our home, we are called into our workplaces through video conferencing platforms, pinged by work emails, social media notifications and news broadcasts.

Jon Kabat-Zinn (2005) quotes a Microsoft researcher, Linda Stone, describing our current state of mind as "Continual Partial Attention". We are writing an email, and the phone rings. We are on the phone, and we get a notification. We check out Facebook and message a friend, then remember the email; we start to write it, and the kids ask, "When is dinner?".

There is a continuous flow of interactions, which we are only partially engaged in. Kabat-Zinn (2005) highlights that in rarely being fully present, we may be losing our ability to give our "wholly undivided attention to one matter, or even that it might matter".

Attention requires the allocation of limited cognitive processing resources (Anderson & Autor Anderson, 1990). When our attention is bombarded with alerting and orienting involuntary stimuli, attentional bottlenecks arise; the brain can only process so much data per second. Human vision has a significant bottleneck: less than 1%, or about 1 megabyte per second, of visual input can pass through (Zhaoping & Li, 2014). This filtering keeps our brain from becoming overwhelmed; however, our attention will be on those distracting involuntary inputs, making it harder and harder to concentrate.

Our involuntary attention, the ability to be alert and oriented to danger, keeps us safe. First and foremost, attention is protective, and our attention to danger is always active. If you were suddenly to smell burning, no matter how much you were engrossed in this book, you would hopefully switch your attention to the potential threat of a fire.

All information the brain needs to attend comes through our senses. We could think of our attention system as being made up of our senses and their processing centres within the central nervous system.

One way of thinking about our senses is through Sherrington's model; at over a hundred years old (1900), this model is probably a little out of date; however, it is still commonly used in the literature. Sherrington breaks our senses into our exteroceptors (that tell us about the outside world), proprioceptors (that tell us about where our bodies are in that world), and our interoceptors (that tell us about the inner workings of our bodies). This is a simplistic categorisation, as our more developed understanding of the nervous system highlights that, neurologically, it is impossible to separate these functions; we integrate our senses. Given that the complexity of the nervous system is beyond the scope of this chapter, we will use Sherrington's model.

Each sensory system has a protective and discriminative function. Our "exteroceptors" or far senses have a protective role to warn us of oncoming danger from the environment. Porges describes these as our "neuroreceptors" – senses that tell us about danger (Porges, 2004, 2011). Our senses of smell, hearing, sight, touch, and taste are almost constantly alert to potential threats. In many cases, the protective senses have a different pathway to the discriminative pathways. For example, our sense of touch evolved as a reactive, even reflexive, response to noxious stimuli. The response to pain or anticipation of harm (e.g., the light touch of a mosquito) goes through the spinothalamic pathway, while the discriminative pathway, which provides information on pressure, texture and shape, goes through the Dorsal Column Medial Lemniscus. These protective senses are linked to heightened arousal, focused attention, orientation, and nervous system activation. When we sense danger, our bodies prepare, triggering our survival responses without thinking. It is our sense perception that enables this pathway to work so effectively, preparing us to fight, flight, freeze, or flop.

Our protective survival instincts were essential when we were prey. As prey, we need heightened awareness of our surroundings and the involuntary attentional networks that alert and orient us to danger. Our ancestors were in danger of being eaten by sabre-tooth tigers. Today, we create our own sabre-tooth tigers, whether that is work or relationship stress. The constant notifications trigger the same involuntary attentional networks and demand our immediate attention, even when they are mostly irrelevant to our survival.

In contrast, our discriminative senses are primed when we are the predator or gatherer. As predators or gatherers, we need the discriminative awareness to sense the deer in the field or the berries in the bush. The discriminative senses require voluntary attention. We must sustain attention on the bush to spot the berry, whilst not being entirely distracted by the bee.

While both attention systems can operate simultaneously, the brain's filtering allows only so much information to reach the thinking brain. We have an attentional bias. Protective information is higher up the attention hierarchy, and it works accordingly. There's no point looking for a berry in the bush when a sabre-tooth tiger is chasing you.

At the top of the food chain, mostly as humans, we have lost the sense of being prey. The only times we are likely to be eaten are during an unfortunate incident in a zoo, while surfing, or by mosquitoes or midges (hence the alerting properties of light touch). As a result, our species has thrived during periods of relative safety and when our "amygdala" (the brain's threat centre) is offline, allowing the brain's higher-functioning executive tasks to flourish. We can focus on our discriminative activities, remember them and manipulate this information. This deeper thinking and focused attention have benefited our species in bountiful ways.

When we are tuned in to our discriminative senses, our attention becomes sustained and focused, and we can learn, be curious and develop (and invent the internet!).

Generally, the fear of being preyed upon in 21st-century life comes only from our interactions with other humans: the shifty guy walking quickly behind us at night, the friend who has talked about us behind our backs, or the parent shouting at their child. Just like when we were preyed upon by predators, we will find our protective systems activated into overdrive, and we get ready to fight, run, or hide under the covers. Our attention and thoughts become fixed on this threat, and we find it hard to think about anything else. Children and adults who have experienced trauma and relational harm will be especially vigilant to danger around them, and may struggle to tune in to the learning expected in their classroom or job. Their involuntary attention systems are on overdrive, constantly alert to danger and scanning the environment.

Understanding these survival responses will help us understand how trauma survivors experience these survival situations. Trauma survivors often describe having symptoms instead of memories (Shapiro, 2014). In moments of extreme survival, we act on "auto-pilot", with our autonomic nervous system ensuring that we stay alive. While our systems are well designed to keep us alive, even in the face of the most extreme dangers, neuroscience also provides a window into why memory can be such an issue with experiences of trauma and adversity.

Neuroscience suggests that the hippocampus and amygdala are two important brain regions involved in memory formation. The hippocampus, a small part of the brain shaped like a seahorse, plays an important role in giving memories a "time" and "date" stamp. We experience the world through our senses. This information is encoded in our hippocampus and passed on to the appropriate "department" for long-term storage. During times of extreme danger, our amygdala becomes highly active and relays information to our autonomic nervous system, initiating the body's preparation for the threat. This, in turn, stimulates our hypothalamus (the relay system) to initiate our hypothalamic–pituitary–adrenal axis, releasing hormones, notably cortisol and adrenaline, to physically equip the body to navigate the stressful experience.

While our amygdala is fine-tuned to function even at the highest levels of arousal and stress, our hippocampus is not. When our stress levels get too high, when we are flooded with cortisol and adrenaline, then our hippocampus starts to fail in its everyday tasks and fails to stamp our memories with the "time" and "date" needed for processing.

That's why we speak of "unprocessed" memories within trauma (Shapiro, 2014). These unprocessed memories have some potentially serious implications. Without a stamp to place traumatic events in time and place, our brain remembers events in vivid detail, but without a when and where. Instead, we encode the information as if it were happening here and now, not there and then. As a result, our systems remain on high alert; "triggers", "reminders", and "cues" can take us to experience the event again, as if it were happening now. In a neurophysiological sense, *it is* happening now, or at least your body is reacting as if it were happening now. If you have read work by Bessel van der Kolk, you will understand these processes and why we colloquially say that the body remembers. Trauma is a bodily experience.

Furthermore, the additional stressors modern life places on us become *toxic stress* and have profound effects on our physical and mental health, contributing to heart disease, addictions, sleep disorders, and the constant stress associated with notification overload.

Rachel and Stephan Kaplan offered a theory on how we might restore attention fatigue, or "continual partial attention", through time in nature, and they coined the term *Attention Restoration Theory* (Kaplan, 1995). This theory postulates that time in *compatible* (see the "Discover" chapter) nature supports attention restoration as it:

1 Takes the individual away from the everyday stresses of modern life
2 Allows the individual to experience expansive spaces and contexts
3 Encourages the individual to engage in activities that are compatible with a reduction in stress
4 Provides "soft fascination"

However, we have to remember that "nature" is a broad context, and just like our emotional weather, the variety of weather conditions and natural environments means that for "time in nature" to be restorative, the environment and weather must be favourable to the task. Being in a small boat in a raging sea will increase attention, but this is likely to be the alerting involuntary attention! Researchers have looked at this theory and found that time in nature does indeed improve our "top-down" attention; however, it does not change our "bottom-up" attention (Ohly et al., 2016). We will still be alert to potential dangers.

Attending through Our Senses

We attend through our senses, which evolved in nature to adapt to it and are therefore *highly* attuned to the natural world. As sensory beings, it is important to consider what we attend to in our everyday lives. Increasingly, research into nature and psychology shows our preference as human beings for "green" and " " spaces, the natural world (Nichols, 2024; Pretty et al., 2017; Völker & Kistemann 2011; Wilson, 1984, White et al., 2010) (see Chapter 1).

Step into your garden, into your local park, or even experience nature through a TV screen, and you will notice the positive impact on our physiology that occurs when we place our attention on the here and now and within nature (Pretty et al., 2009). In their study exploring social media posts (31,534 posts) from 185 countries and life satisfaction, Chang et al. (2020) found that the proportion of photos with nature in the background correlated with national life satisfaction scores and concluded that "nature serves as a background to many of our positive memories".

We learned earlier about the autonomic nervous system, and increasing evidence suggests that the parasympathetic system may be dominantly involved in the restorative effects of being in green space (Brown et al., 2013; Farrow & Washburn, 2019; Laumann et al., 2003; Park et al., 2007; Tsunetsugu et al., 2009; Tyrväinen et al., 2014). In a review by Farrow and Washburn (2019) of studies on forest bathing and its impact on heart rate variability, they concluded that exposure to nature for as little as 15 minutes may benefit anxiety and stress. They linked these benefits to increased parasympathetic activation. Studies have also shown reduced sympathetic activity when having access to green space, with research showing that time in nature leads to decreased blood pressure, skin conductance, salivary cortisol levels and muscle tension, both whilst being in nature and as measured afterwards (Park et al., 2007; van den Berg et al., 2010).

Even simulated experiences of nature, such as listening to audio clips of bird song or watching videos of the forest and water, have shown to help slow down our heart rate and regulatory functions, effects consistent with parasympathetic and vagal responses (Ulrich et al., 1991).

Research also shows that simply viewing green spaces can lead to parasympathetic activation and stress reduction. Gladwell et al. (2012) demonstrated that parasympathetic activity was higher when viewing green spaces than when viewing built scenes, with no significant differences in sympathetic activity between the two conditions. Brown et al. (2013) found that viewing green spaces prior to a complex and stress-inducing task increased parasympathetic activation in the recovery period, as measured by "Vagal-Mediated Heart Rate Variability".

Development of the Senses

As we have already stated, all information the brain needs to attend to comes through our senses. We could think of our attention system as being made up of our senses and their processing centres within the central nervous system. Our senses developed within nature to process nature.

So why did we develop senses? We developed them to survive, avoid danger, find food, and reproduce. We co-evolved along with every other living thing on the planet from the first organisms. The very first organisms were floating around in a chemical soup. Over millions of years, they evolved an affinity for certain chemicals and an aversion to others, and developed a sense of position and direction, mechanisms for propelling themselves away from or towards these chemicals (the start of the *body* senses). Around the same time, some organisms became photosensitive (Gehring, 2014).

As organisms became more complex and refined, they developed specialist cells, which became nervous tissue, progressively concentrating towards one end, a process called Cephalisation, which eventually produced a head (Cozzi & Huggenberger, 2017). As other tactile receptors developed, we began to detect temperature, pressure, injury, texture, and contours, which the brain interpreted as pain, pleasure, heat, cold, shape, smoothness, numbness, etc. (Ackerman, 1991).

The sense of sight became acute as photoreceptors further developed into more sophisticated apparatuses (rods and cones in the mammalian retina), concentrating in specialised cells that became the eye. One of the last senses to develop was hearing.

Sensory integration theory suggests that we have eight sensory systems; sight, touch, taste, hearing, smell, and the extra ones: proprioception (body sense), interoception (visceral sense), and vestibular (balance) sense. Earlier, we introduced Sherrington's model categorising the senses as interoceptors (e.g., hunger and thirst) that tell us about the internal working of our bodies; proprioceptors that tell us about our bodies' relation to the world (proprioception, vestibular, and tactile); and exteroceptors (sight, sound, smell, and touch) that tell us about the external world. Cohen (2003) has suggested that we are not limited by eight senses; he suggests there are 54 natural senses and sensitivities that he grouped by their evolution:

- Chemical senses
- Radiation senses
- Feeling senses
- Vibration/Language sense
- Mental senses
- Sense of mind and consciousness

We will spend a little time looking at these, and how these senses developed, and how they are connected to nature, and how we can use them to attend to nature and regulate.

Chemical Senses

The senses developed as protective systems. Floating in a chemical soup, the first organisms developed an affinity for certain chemicals and avoided others. They developed chemoreceptors to distinguish safe from dangerous chemicals; these evolved into the senses of taste and smell (Erickson, 2000). Our sense of smell is still one of our most helpful danger detectors, sending threat-detection signals straight to our amygdala (Girgis, 1969; Zald & Pardo, 1997).

We can detect dangerous smells, such as those from a fire or toxic chemicals, and react quickly to them, bypassing conscious thought, through our involuntary attention system. We smell something rotten, and it makes us gag. Our disgust turns us away from it, keeping us safe from potentially harmful ingestion. We smell to check whether the food is good or past its best. Scent can be key to recognising whether a leaf is safe to eat in foraging. At the point in development when typically young children can walk off and try poisonous leaves, they helpfully develop an aversion to bitter tastes, such as those in leaves. This is protective, helping prevent them from eating poisonous plants, but, of course, it can be highly frustrating as a parent when, all of a sudden, it becomes an impossible task to get your child to eat their vegetables (Brown, 2012). Try to remember, they are fulfilling an important evolutionary survival period of development. Kids very typically will return to vegetables if you give them time!

We also tend to love the smell of things that are good for us. Scent hits the emotional centres and triggers memories like no other sense (Calvi et al., 2020; Mujica-Parodi et al., 2009). The olfactory bulb is situated right next to the hippocampus, our memory centre (Compston, 2010). We have all had the nostalgic experience of recognising a smell from our childhood. For me, the smell of roses takes me to my grandma's pink bathroom. The human nose can detect over a trillion different smells (Bushdid et al., 2014); however, we struggle to describe them or bring them to memory in the way we can with the sights we have seen. Try to recall the smellscape of your childhood home compared to the images of it (Konnikova, 2012).

While we still may smell fear, sadness, and sexiness, over half of our thousands of genes for nasal reception are inactive. As humans, we have lost many of our scent-detection skills; we rely much more heavily on other senses, such as vision. Just a walk with your puppy will illustrate that; they can tell so much more from a sniff of the gatepost than we can.

If we consider our immune system as a sensory system that perceives and responds to the "molecules of the living world" (Daëron, 2022), we can communicate bidirectionally with plants and use fragrances and terpenes to heal ourselves (Breitmaier, 2006). Our biochemistry has evolved to survive on this planet, with the rhythms and seasons to fit with nature. We have developed melatonin that is connected to our photoreceptors, so that we sleep when it is dark and too hard to find prey.

Radiation Senses

At the same time that organisms were developing sensitivity to chemicals in their environment, they were also evolving the ability to detect and orient to light. In plants, light is not just sensed; it is harvested. Chlorophyll, housed within chloroplasts, captures light to fuel the processes of life, while specialised photoreceptor proteins enable plants to orient, grow, and adapt to their surroundings. Leaves turn towards the light, drawn to the very energy they depend on for photosynthesis.

The sense of sight became acute as the photoreceptors soon further developed into more sophisticated apparatuses (rods and cones in the mammalian retina), concentrating in specialised cells that became the eye.

We have three cones (more than most animals) but not as many as butterflies and birds, which have five cones, and the Mantis Shrimp, which has 16 (Thoen et al., 2014).

Colours help us sense danger and find resources, especially food. Predators tend not to be green and blue, and we associate these colours with life-giving ecosystems. Colours and shades of red and orange tend to agitate and excite our nervous system, whereas colours and shades of blues and greens tend to calm us (Valtchanov, 2013).

Biological anthropologist and associate professor Amanda Melin, University of Calgary, argues that the indoor lifestyle of many people in cities and the use of computers pose problems for our eyes. She comments that all the time spent inside, in artificial lighting, we are not out in nature, in the "context in which our vision system evolved"; she goes on to argue that for our eyes to develop how they were designed to, we need to spend more time outside (Melin et al., 2019).

The research certainly suggests that looking at nature scenes is beneficial for us. Ulrich (1984) discovered that patients with rooms that had views of trees rather than a brick wall had fewer postoperative days, requested less pain medication, and had more positive attitudes towards health recovery.

Kuo and Sullivan (2001) studied violence/aggression and contended that individuals living with barren views are less likely to control impulsivity. Police reports revealed a strong link between the abundance of greenery and a reduction in various crimes, including assaults, homicides, vehicle thefts, burglary, and arson. Specifically, areas with more trees saw a significant decrease: 48% fewer property crimes and 56% fewer violent crimes.

Why are nature scenes beneficial, and why do we prefer them over urban scenes? The answer could be due to… fractals… "repeated patterns" that are found in our natural world.

The world that we live in is not naturally smooth-edged. Nature is characterised by non-uniform shapes and rough edges. The term "fractal" was coined in 1975 by Benoit Mandelbrot to describe shapes that are detailed at all scales, from the Latin word "fractus", meaning fragmented, broken, and discontinuous (Clarke et al., 2006).

Fractals are characterised by infinite detail, infinite length and the absence of smoothness. It turns out that humans naturally love fractals, and they are abundant in nature. One thing about fractals is that they are self-similar – that is, they have parts that resemble the whole. They look the same, no matter how big or small they may be. This is true of clouds, trees, rivers, lungs, shells, leaves, flowers, and seed heads. Your visual system is in some way hardwired to understand fractals. The fractal nature of your eye meets the fractal nature of the image. We are fractal, our eyes, our lungs, our circulatory system, our brains match the patterns we see in nature.

When we see fractals, we have positive physiological responses to viewing them, especially fractals that have a dimension in the mid-range. These mid-range fractals produce "feel good" alpha brain waves of a wake and relaxed state, and also engage the parahippocampus, which is involved with regulating emotions. We recover from stress 60% faster when looking at these mid-range fractals (Taylor et al., 2005a, 2005b; Hagerhall et al., 2006, 2015). Why mid-range fractals? Taylor et al. (2005a) argue that this is the exact range our bodies have developed (including our lungs, capillaries, neurons, and visual system). We also use a mid-range fractal pattern to search the environment, such as when searching for food or noticing differences between leaves. In one of my sessions, I noticed my participant's shift from a hypervigilant state to voluntary attention as she began to notice that the forest floor had no oak leaves. This was a significant indicator that she was moving away from a survival state and was more engaged and relaxed.

Furthermore, our visual cortex uses some kind of fractal algorithm to optimise sensitivity, allowing for visual closure. Seeing part of the bark can allow us to infer the rest of the tree (Barnsely et al., 1988). One engaging activity is using magnifying glasses or kaleidoscopes to look closely at a conifer cone or flower. Taylor and colleagues believe that our brains are hardwired to recognise kinship with the natural world and that a stress-reduction response occurs when there is physiological resonance with the fractal structure of the eye matching the fractal image the eye sees (Taylor et al., 2005b).

The Body Senses

Alongside developing our senses to tell us about the environment, what is safe and what is dangerous, we also developed senses to move towards or away from attractive or noxious stimuli. Our body senses developed a sense of position (proprioception) to tell us where we were in that environment, a sense of direction (vestibular), and the mechanisms to move towards or away. Our tactile sense probably first developed as a recoil reflex in response to noxious stimuli. Touch receptors later developed the ability to detect temperature, pressure, texture, shapes, and pain. Our sense of proprioception (where our body is in space) and our vestibular system (where our head is located) developed to allow us to flee from predators or move towards food. In fact, as Daniel Wolpert, Professor of Neuroscience, Columbia University, so eloquently explains in his TED talk, the only reason we have a brain is so we can move (*Daniel Wolpert: The Real Reason for Brains*, 2011).

He provides examples of species that have engulfed their own nervous system once they became stationary. Movement is so complex that it occupies most of the brain's functions. In therapy, we often find that movement, especially proprioception, is particularly regulating and calming for the nervous system. Furthermore, activities that move the head in a rhythmic, linear way, such as lying back in a hammock or swinging on a rope swing, can help us feel focused and relaxed. Our vestibular system is highly tuned to our existence on this planet. At its heart, it detects gravity.

Vibration Senses: Development of Sound

The last sense to develop was hearing. Some believe it developed from specialised tactile-sensitive cells (Ro et al., 2013). These cells (in the eardrum of humans) have become so specialised that they can detect tiny vibrations and pressure changes in the environment. Unlike light that can travel through a vacuum, sound cannot, since it requires a medium to propagate. In aquatic animals, it is the ability to detect these vibrations underwater; in land animals, it is the ability to detect them in the air.

Porges discusses the evolution of the ear and how, in mammals, the eardrum bone has detached from the skull. This has allowed mammals to communicate using mid-frequency sounds that are found in speech sounds. This is essential to our social engagement system, which we use to communicate safety (the discriminative sound system). Conversely, our protective sound system processes low-frequency danger sounds that signal predators, and high-frequency sounds that prey make when under attack (Porges, 1995). In the forest, sounds such as the scrunching of leaves, wind in the canopy, and bird song are all in the mid-range, and we typically find these sounds regulating.

Our senses developed in nature to understand nature. When we are in natural spaces, our sensory systems are more likely to be regulated and modulated by the environment around us.

The Attend Element in Practice

In our EcoSensory sessions, we consider the importance of "attention" and "awareness", as two distinct ways to be and to "take in" the positive effects of nature. With "attention" we highlight the use of activities that help our clients to enhance their ability to focus, concentrate and ignore distractions. In this way, "attention" refers to the deliberate placing of attention in the here and now, and "noticing". In the moment of noticing, we are reminded of roots of the word attend, the Latin word 'attendere' – 'ad' being towards and 'tendere' stretching. If you're stretching towards something, reaching for it, there's presumably a moment when you reach your destination, when you make connection. When we truly attend to something, we start to notice and connect to it. We notice how it changes, how it is formed, and we start to have a relationship and connection with it. We use active discrimination; we notice the difference between the tulips.

As we enhance our attentional capacity, we equip ourselves with more skills for self-regulation. As we feel increasingly regulated, the reverse is also true: that greater regulation will help with greater attentional capacity. When we begin to notice and connect with nature, we may ask, "When does nature end and I begin?" As Albert Einstein describes, we are all part of the *whole*, while we might only see our part of the spacetime continuum. When we see ourselves as separate, it is some kind of *delusion.* This imprisons us and traps us.

If we can notice, connect with, and be kind to the whole of nature, and, as we recognise ourselves as part of nature, we can learn the skills and state of being to be kind and non-judgemental of ourselves.

Awareness

The other side of *Attend* is "awareness" or, as it is spoken within mindfulness literature, "choiceless awareness", "clear awareness", an open focus of attention and "resting in the midst of experience" (Brown et al., 2007; Williams & Kabat-Zinn, 2011, p. 978). The poet, Jane Hirshfield, describes awareness as a deep form of consciousness, a moment of connection and harmony between oneself and everything (Hirshfield, 1997).

Rather than being task-oriented, or "doing" mindfulness right or wrong, we can offer invitations to just enjoy the experience of "being", just as they are, come as they may. Just as the seasons change, flowers blossom and leaves fall, our thoughts and feelings are transient and passing events too. We can encourage our clients to notice whatever catches their attention, with openness to whatever surrounds them.

Nature takes its time, charts its own course, and does not attempt to force its way forward. Just as nature practices, so we can encourage our clients to attend to and accept the present moment, the here and now, and whatever is happening in that moment, without trying to push things in any particular direction (Kabat-Zinn, 2005; Monshat et al., 2013).

Instead of learning to change the form or frequency of our private events, "don't think that", we can learn to relate to them differently. We can learn to "hold loosely" onto our thoughts. Like "leaves on a stream" or "clouds in the sky", we can learn to notice how thoughts come and go, and that we are observers of our experience. Like kids on a summer's day watching the white clouds pass on by, or the myriad of leaves pass down a brook or stream. For some, it can be revelatory to experience this shift in being.

Mary Oliver's essay concludes by encouraging the reader to teach the children and get them outside, in the stream, so they can learn to love nature. Attention, Oliver argues, is the beginning of Devotion.

What do we devote our time to? Is it the changing of the leaves, the setting of the sun, the water splashing at our ankles as we wade upstream, or is it the bleep of the WhatsApp notification or our ruminating thoughts?

What we notice becomes where we place our attention; where we place our attention – we place our devotion.

References

Ackerman, D. (1991). *A natural history of the senses*. Vintage.

Anderson, J. R., & Autor Anderson, J. R. (1990). *Cognitive Psychology and Its Implications*. W.H. Freeman.

Barnsely, M. F., Devaney, R. L., Mandelbrot, B. B., Petigen, H., Saupe, D., & Voss, R. F. (1988). *The science of fractal images*. Springer.

Breitmaier, E. (2006). *Terpenes: Flavors, fragrances, pharmaca, pheromones*. John Wiley & Sons.

Brown, D. K., Barton, J. L., & Gladwell, V. F. (2013). Viewing nature scenes positively affects recovery of autonomic function following acute-mental stress. *Environmental Science & Technology*, *47*(11), 5562–5569. https://doi.org/10.1021/es305019p

Brown, K. W., Ryan, R. M., & Creswell, J. D. (2007). Mindfulness: Theoretical foundations and evidence for its salutary effects. *Psychological Inquiry*, *18*(4), 211–237.

Brown, S. D. (2012). Rejection of known and previously accepted foods during early childhood: An extension of the neophobic response? *International Journal of Child Health and Nutrition*. https://doi.org/10.6000/1929-4247.2012.01.01.09

Bushdid, C., Magnasco, M. O., Vosshall, L. B., & Keller, A. (2014). Humans can discriminate more than 1 trillion olfactory stimuli. *Science*, *343*(6177), 1370–1372. https://doi.org/10.1126/science.1249168

Calvi, E. et al. (2020). The scent of emotions: A systematic review of human intra- and interspecific chemical communication of emotions, *Brain and Behavior*, *10*(5), e01585.

Chang, C. C., Cheng, G. J. Y., Nghiem, T. P. L., Song, X. P., Oh, R. R. Y., Richards, D. R., & Carrasco, L. R. (2020). Social media, nature, and life satisfaction: Global evidence of the biophilia hypothesis. *Scientific Reports*, *10*(1), 4125.

Clarke, A. C., Mandelbrot, B., & Stewart, I. (2006). *The colours of infinity*. Clear Book.

Cohen, M. J. (2003). *The web of life imperative: Regenerative ecopsychology techniques that help people think in balance with natural systems*. Trafford Publishing.

Compston, A. (2010). The hippocampus and the sense of smell. A review, by Alf Brodal. Brain 1947: 70; 179–222. *Brain: A Journal of Neurology*, *133*(9), 2509–2513. https://doi.org/10.1093/brain/awq242

Cozzi, B., & Huggenberger, S. (2017). Cephalization. In *Encyclopedia of animal cognition and behavior* (pp. 1–4). https://doi.org/10.1007/978-3-319-47829-6_1289-1

Daëron, M. (2022). The immune system as a system of relations. *Frontiers in Immunology*, *13*, 984678.

Erickson, R. P. (2000). The evolution of neural coding ideas in the chemical senses. *Physiology & Behavior*, *69*(1–2), 3–13. https://doi.org/10.1016/s0031-9384(00)00193-1

Fan, J., McCandliss, B. D., Fossella, J., Flombaum, J. I., & Posner, M. I. (2005). The activation of attentional networks. *NeuroImage*, *26*(2), 471–479. https://doi.org/10.1016/j.neuroimage.2005.02.004

Farrow, M.R., & Washburn, K. (2019). A review of field experiments on the effect of forest bathing on anxiety and heart rate variability. *Global Advances in Health and Medicine*, *8*, 2164956119848654

Gehring, W. J. (2014). The evolution of vision. *Wiley Interdisciplinary Reviews. Developmental Biology*, *3*(1), 1–40. https://doi.org/10.1002/wdev.96

Girgis, M. (1969). The amygdala and the sense of smell. *Cells Tissues Organs*, *72*(4), 502–519. https://doi.org/10.1159/000143266

Gladwell, V. F., Brown, D. K., Barton, J. L., Tarvainen, M. P., Kuoppa, P., Pretty, J., Suddaby, J. M., & Sandercock, G. R. H. (2012). The effects of views of nature on autonomic control. *European Journal of Applied Physiology*, *112*(9), 3379–3386. https://doi.org/10.1007/s00421-012-2318-8

Hagerhall, C., Laike, T., Taylor, R., Koller, M., Koller, R., & Martin, T. (2006). Semantic evaluations of silhouettes with different fractal dimension. *PsycEXTRA Dataset*. https://doi.org/10.1037/e666882007-001

Hagerhall, C. M., Laike, T., Küller, M., Marcheschi, E., Boydston, C., & Taylor, R. P. (2015). Human physiological benefits of viewing nature: EEG responses to exact and statistical fractal patterns. *Nonlinear Dynamics, Psychology, and Life Sciences*, *19*(1), 1–12. https://www.ncbi.nlm.nih.gov/pubmed/25575556

Hirshfield, J. (1997). *Nine gates: Entering the mind of poetry*. HarperCollins, Inc. ($22). https://eric.ed.gov/?id=ED418433

Kabat-Zinn, J. (2005). *Coming to our senses: Healing ourselves and the world through mindfulness*. Hachette UK.

Kaplan, S. (1995). The restorative benefits of nature: Toward an integrative framework. *Journal of Environmental Psychology*, *15*(3), 169–182.
Konnikova, M. (2012). Smells like old times. *Scientific American Mind*, *23*(1), 58–63. https://www.jstor.org/stable/24942111
Kuo, F. E., & Sullivan, W. C. (2001). Environment and crime in the inner city: Does vegetation reduce crime? *Environment and Behavior*, *33*(3), 343–367. https://doi.org/10.1177/0013916501333002
Laumann, K., Gärling, T., & Stormark, K. M. (2003). Selective attention and heart rate responses to natural and urban environments. *Journal of Environmental Psychology*, *23*(2), 125–134. https://doi.org/10.1016/S0272-4944(02)00110-X
Melin, A. D., Nevo, O., Shirasu, M., Williamson, R. E., Garrett, E. C., Endo, M., Sakurai, K., Matsushita, Y., Touhara, K., & Kawamura, S. (2019). Fruit scent and observer colour vision shape food-selection strategies in wild capuchin monkeys. *Nature Communications*, *10*(1), 2407. https://doi.org/10.1038/s41467-019-10250-9
Monshat, K. et al. (2013), "A conscious control over life and my emotions:" Mindfulness practice and healthy young people. A qualitative study. *The Journal of Adolescent Health: Official Publication of the Society for Adolescent Medicine*, *52*(5), 572–577.
Mujica-Parodi, L. R., Strey, H. H., Frederick, B., Savoy, R., Cox, D., Botanov, Y., Tolkunov, D., Rubin, D., & Weber, J. (2009). Chemosensory cues to conspecific emotional stress activate amygdala in humans. *PLoS One*, *4*(7), e6415. https://doi.org/10.1371/journal.pone.0006415
Nichols, W. J. (2024). *Blue mind*. Little, Brown Spark.
Ohly, H., White, M. P., Wheeler, B. W., Bethel, A., Ukoumunne, O. C., Nikolaou, V., & Garside, R. (2016). Attention restoration theory: A systematic review of the attention restoration potential of exposure to natural environments. *Journal of Toxicology and Environmental Health. Part B, Critical Reviews*, *19*(7), 305–343. https://www.tandfonline.com/doi/abs/10.1080/10937404.2016.1196155
Oliver, M. (2019). *Upstream: Selected essays*. Penguin Books.
Park, B. -J., Tsunetsugu, Y., Kasetani, T., Hirano, H., Kagawa, T., Sato, M., & Miyazaki, Y. (2007). Physiological effects of Shinrin-yoku (Taking in the atmosphere of the forest)—Using salivary cortisol and cerebral activity as indicators. *Journal of Physiological Anthropology*, *26*(2), 123–128. https://doi.org/10.2114/jpa2.26.123
Porges, S. W. (1995). Orienting in a defensive world: Mammalian modifications of our evolutionary heritage. A Polyvagal Theory. *Psychophysiology*, *32*(4), 301–318. https://doi.org/10.1111/j.1469-8986.1995.tb01213.x
Porges, S. W. (2004). Neuroception: A subconscious system for detecting threats and safety. *Zero to Three*, *24*(5), 19–24. https://www.zerotothree.org/resources/series/journal-archive
Porges, S. W. (2011). *The polyvagal theory: Neurophysiological foundations of emotions, attachment, communication, and self-regulation (Norton Series on Interpersonal Neurobiology)*. W. W. Norton & Company.
Pretty, J., Angus, C., Bain, M., Barton, J., Gladwell, V., Hine, R., Pilgrim, S., Sandercock, G., & Sellens, M. (2009). Nature, childhood, health and life pathways. *Occasional Paper*, *2*. https://www.playaustralia.org.au/sites/default/files/LibraryDownloads/Nature%20Childhood%20and%20Health%20iCES%20Occ%20Paper%202009-2%20FINAL.pdf
Pretty, J., Rogerson, M., & Barton, J. (2017). Green mind theory: How brain-body-behaviour links into natural and social environments for healthy habits, *International Journal of Environmental Research and Public Health*, *14*(7). https://doi.org/10.3390/ijerph14070706

Ro, T., Ellmore, T. M., & Beauchamp, M. S. (2013). A neural link between feeling and hearing. *Cerebral cortex*, *23*(7), 1724–1730. https://doi.org/10.1093/cercor/bhs166

Shapiro, F. (2014). The role of eye movement desensitization and reprocessing (EMDR) therapy in medicine: Addressing the psychological and physical symptoms stemming from adverse life experiences. *The Permanente Journal*, *18*(1), 71–77. https://doi.org/10.7812/TPP/13-098

Taylor, R., Newell, B., Spehar, B., & Clifford, C. (2005a). Fractals: A resonance between art and nature. In M. Emmer (Ed.), *Mathematics and culture II: Visual perfection: Mathematics and creativity* (pp. 53–63). Springer Berlin Heidelberg. https://doi.org/10.1007/3-540-26443-4_6

Taylor, R. P., Spehar, B., Wise, J. A., Clifford, C. W., Newell, B. R., Hagerhall, C. M., Purcell, T., & Martin, T. P. (2005b). Perceptual and physiological responses to the visual complexity of fractal patterns. *Nonlinear Dynamics, Psychology, and Life Sciences*, *9*, 89–114.

Thoen, H. H., How, M. J., Chiou, T.-H., & Marshall, J. (2014). A different form of color vision in mantis shrimp. *Science*, *343*(6169), 411–413. https://doi.org/10.1126/science.1245824

Tsunetsugu, Y., Park, B.-J., & Miyazaki, Y. (2009). Trends in research related to "Shinrin-yoku" (taking in the forest atmosphere or forest bathing) in Japan. *Environmental Health and Preventive Medicine*, *15*(1), 27. https://doi.org/10.1007/s12199-009-0091-z

Tyrväinen, L., Ojala, A., Korpela, K., Lanki, T., Tsunetsugu, Y., & Kagawa, T. (2014). The influence of urban green environments on stress relief measures: A field experiment. *Journal of Environmental Psychology*, *38*, 1–9. https://doi.org/10.1016/j.jenvp.2013.12.005

Ulrich, R. S. (1984). View through a window may influence recovery from surgery. *Science*, *224*(4647), 420–421.

Ulrich, R. S., Simons, R. F., Losito, B. D., Fiorito, E., Miles, M. A., & Zelson, M. (1991). Stress recovery during exposure to natural and urban environments. *Journal of Environmental Psychology*, *11*(3), 201–230. https://doi.org/10.1016/S0272-4944(05)80184-7

Valtchanov, D. (2013). *Exploring the restorative effects of nature: Testing a proposed visuospatial theory*. https://uwspace.uwaterloo.ca/handle/10012/7938

van den Berg, A. E., van Winsum-Westra, M., de Vries, S., & van Dillen, S. M. E. (2010). Allotment gardening and health: a comparative survey among allotment gardeners and their neighbors without an allotment. *Environmental Health: A Global Access Science Source*, *9*(1), 74. https://doi.org/10.1186/1476-069X-9-74

Völker, S., & Kistemann, T. (2011). The impact of blue space on human health and well-being–Salutogenetic health effects of inland surface waters: A review. *International Journal of Hygiene and Environmental Health*, *214*(6), 449–460. https://www.sciencedirect.com/science/article/pii/S1438463911000502

White, M., Smith, A., Humphryes, K., Pahl, S., Snelling, D., & Depledge, M. (2010). Blue space: The importance of water for preference, affect, and restorativeness ratings of natural and built scenes. *Journal of Environmental Psychology*, *30*(4), 482–493. https://doi.org/10.1016/j.jenvp.2010.04.004

Williams, J. M. G., & Kabat-Zinn, J. (2011). Mindfulness: Diverse perspectives on its meaning, origins, and multiple applications at the intersection of science and dharma. *Contemporary Buddhism*, *12*(1), 1–18.

Wilson, E. O. (1984). *Biophilia*. London, England: Harvard University Press.

Wolpert, D. (2011). *The real reason for bains*. [Dataset]. https://doi.org/10.1037/e521552012-001

Zald, D. H., & Pardo, J. V. (1997). Emotion, olfaction, and the human amygdala: amygdala activation during aversive olfactory stimulation. *Proceedings of the National Academy of Sciences of the United States of America*, *94*(8), 4119–4124. https://doi.org/10.1073/pnas.94.8.4119

Zhaoping, L., & Li, Z. (2014). *Understanding vision: Theory, models, and data*. Oxford University Press.

Chapter 7

Create

Claire Pemrick

Introduction

We have talked about human curiosity and how we have an inner drive to explore and discover new things. We believe that this natural curiosity, combined with the ability to focus our attention, leads to creativity (Csíkszentmihályi, 1996). Since we first used tools, humans have been driven to create, make, and "do" with the resources in the natural environment. Within earlier elements, we have focused on being, connecting, attending and discovering. We have also thought about time; if *Rhythm* was our temporal piece, *Create* can be considered our spatial piece, in which we make and create our place and space in the world. In the *Create* element, we consider what might be done. Create is our "doing" piece. It is where we move beyond supposition to creation.

In this element, we will consider why we create, the evolution of creativity, and how we evolved to be such a creative species and individuals. Alongside exploring models of creativity, we consider how to be creative outdoors and the affordances that nature provides for making and doing. Finally, we will look at the relevance of *Create* in relation to health, the links between creativity and mental health, and how "doing" and "creating" can be so healing.

Surviving through Doing

For most animal species, their "reason for being" is connected to their survival: hunting or gathering food, rearing young, avoiding predators and defending territory. They are naturally busy, occupied and doing. We see that when this is taken away from them in captivity, they show hallmarks of stress: stereotypic behaviours (Mason & Rushen, 2008), increased aggression and cortisol levels (Salas et al., 2016), and boredom (Meagher & Mason, 2012). Animals, like humans, like to be occupied and find pleasure in doing novel and adaptive activities. Many species of birds, mammals, and even octopuses have been discovered using tools. New Caledonian crows have been observed using their beaks to strip leaves from a twig and insert them into a decaying tree's crevice to search for beetle larvae (Bluff et al., 2010). Chimpanzees in Bossou, Guinea, were documented to grasp

DOI: 10.4324/9781003777465-9

stones and pound them against a nut to crack it open (Inoue-Nakamura & Matsuzawa, 1997). Octopuses have been observed building dens and making doors with shells (Anderson et al., 2013); carrying coconuts for future defence (Finn et al., 2009), and projecting objects in defence (Godfrey-Smith et al., 2022). A child fills a bucket with sand using a spade and decorates the tipped-out castle in shells. As a species, we are not the only ones to use tools, nor are we the only species to be creative. Anyone looking at a spider's web or a beaver's dam can appreciate the creativity other species have.

Evolution of Human Creativity

While it can be argued that some other species engage in novel adaptive behaviours, they pale into insignificance compared to *Homo sapiens*. When *Homo sapiens* first arrived in our ancestral home of Eastern Africa, we were like most other *Homo* species (and other creative species) in our tool use. *Homo habilis* provided the first evidence of creativity, with their Oldowan artefacts, mostly single-faced stone tools that would have been used to split fruit and nuts (Isaac et al., 1971; Leakey, 1971). However, these simple tools did not undergo any further development for hundreds of thousands of years. *Homo erectus*, with their larger brains, were the first humans to be in hunter-gatherer societies. They expanded on the simple tools and made symmetrical hand tools, tamed fire and learnt to cook meat. This increased their caloric intake, which in turn led to the growth of more neurons and a larger brain (Herculano-Houzel, 2016). When *Homo sapiens* emerged around 250,000 years ago in East Africa, we were equipped with a larger brain than our genetic cousins (other hominids); however, our creativity took another 210,000 years to catch up. Our "creative explosion" did not unfold until 40,000 years ago in the Upper Palaeolithic period, when we suddenly saw a vast expansion in the use of technology, from advanced hunting tools to art and music (Stringer & Gamble, 1993; Mithen, 1996).

Much of human creativity is linked to our survival: finding or making food, building shelters, defending territory, and attracting and keeping a mate. These could be described as core evolutionary occupations that, throughout our evolutionary history, we have valued and found pleasure and contentment in doing. Many of the popular nature-based leisure activities align with these core occupations, and people still find great pleasure in fishing, hunting, camping out, building a fire, weaving baskets to gather and forage food, and cooking over the campfire. Similarly, activities in an EcoSensory session may involve these core occupations. While we don't necessarily advocate hunting in your sessions, activities such as looking for animal tracks, building dens, gathering wood for a fire, weaving baskets, whittling wood, and foraging for food all lean into that evolutionary prior.

So what caused this explosion of new technologies? One theory is that the complexities of social living encouraged the development of higher intellectual faculties (Bateson & Hinde, 1976). Indeed, this "Creative Explosion" occurred in an area with an especially dense population of hunter-gatherers. Evolutionary anthropologists such as Joseph Henrich suggest the *Secret to Our Success* is this "collective brain", and that once *Homo sapiens* started swapping made objects and ideas, they created divisions of labour and they became specialists (Henrich, 2017). These specialisms exchanged within society are argued to have mutually benefited collective knowledge. By specialising, humans could focus on one area and innovate in it. On the other hand, self-sufficiency reduces the ability to pursue a specialism and master areas not tied to survival. In other words, by working collectively, you could have someone get really good at basket weaving and leave someone else to the hunting. Mastering skills, so that an individual had a narrow specialism, and then traded this with the rest of the community, allowed for prosperity, and the whole community to flourish (Shea et al., 2010).

Over the years, working with clients in nature, I have often been struck by participants' drive to improve and master a new skill, and by their tendency to repeat an activity frequently during sessions, whether it be creating a more elaborate fairy den or increasing the complexity of making cordage from nettles. The mastery and skill development has the evolutionary driver, "If I can get better and better at this task, I can specialise and find my place in the tribe".

This view is at the heart of occupational science. Wilcock wrote her "Reflections on doing, being, and becoming", contending that what we "do" is intrinsically linked to what we become, and how we belong in the world, and therefore our very being (Wilcock, 1988, 1999).

If we accept this theory for the evolution of creativity, then we can see that it is our instinct to connect and belong with others that has provided the means to create and specialise. The triad between bigger brains, society and skill led to this creativity. Wilcock also reflected that society itself will have a bidirectional impact on what we do. If we are nowhere near the sea, no need to make fishing rods.

Once settled in communities, we gave our children more time to play and build their imagination. Alison Gopnik (2020), a developmental psychologist at the University of California, Berkeley, explains that humans possess an unusually extended childhood compared to other primates. Unlike gorillas and chimpanzees, who nurse for three to five years, human infants are typically weaned around eighteen months, yet remain dependent for a much longer period. This prolonged phase of protection and play provides a unique window in which children can safely explore, experiment, and experience the rewards of curiosity and learning. Observing children at play or adults learning a new skill, we notice that much of play or "leisure" activities involve learning and practising skills, in my case, ever more complex knitting patterns.

Development of Creative Skills

Having a prolonged period to play, human children have time to build their creative skills. As young infants, we start to figure out what we can do, firstly with our bodies, and then with objects. As natural explorers, our curiosity and inner drive push us to figure out all the things we can do with something and its *affordances*.

The term affordance was coined by James Gibson, an American Psychologist, to describe what "the environment ... offers the animal, what it provides or furnishes, either for good or ill" (Gibson, 2001).

In other words, *affordances* are what you can do with the things around you. If we look at a stick, for example, we can see that the New Caledonian crow figured out it could use a stick as an extension of its beak to dig out beetle larvae. The chimp uses a stick to poke into a termite mound as an extension of their hands. A human may use a stick to toast a marshmallow on a fire as an extension of their body.

In their seminal work, *Children and Nature: Psychological, Theoretical, and Evolutionary Investigations,* Peter Kahn Jr. and Stephen Kellert explore the evolutionary drivers behind children's play in nature and the critical role of environmental affordances (Kahn & Kellert, 2002).

Anyone going into a forest with a child will notice this "affordance learning" with a stick. First, it transforms into a walking stick, and then it transforms anew, perhaps into a gun or a fairy's wand. The creative uses of the stick are endless. The stick becomes an extension of the individual, allowing them (whether a crow or a human child) to do things they could not do with their hands and limbs alone.

Piaget described how, in the first year of life, infants manipulate objects initially in an undiscriminating manner. They might throw, drop, bang, or shake objects regardless of the object's physical characteristics. If the result is interesting, they may try to repeat their action. As they develop more advanced motor skills, the number of ways they can use the object increases. They can do more with it. The stick starts to become a writing tool, a weapon, a walking aid and these ideas expand further with the development of lateral thinking and higher-level executive thinking. The child starts to pretend and use the stick in their imaginary world (Piaget & Cook, 1952).

These imaginative, creative play experiences use the same cognitive resources as adults when involved in creative thinking and problem-solving. These are the higher cognitive skills that Maslow puts at the top of his pyramid (Maslow, 1943). Similarly, when adults are working to build a new theory or are trying to find an original solution to a practical challenge, or creating a new work of art, they have to think: "Suppose I did it like this", or "Suppose I used this colour". "Creativity begins in one's mind in the form of insight" (Glăveanu & Kaufman, 2019).

However, to actually create, it is not enough just to have the idea. The insight needs additional support, the "knowledge and experience to nurture the idea ***and*** the actions required to implement and produce the idea" (Glăveanu & Kaufman, 2019).

Isaksen et al. (2023) have suggested a three-phase creative process that fits with the concepts of praxis that Ayres (1972) discussed in the Discover element: Ideas, Preparation, and Implementation. Finke and colleagues proposed a framework known as the "geneplore" model – a term derived from "generate" and "explore" – to explain universal cognitive creativity (Finke et al., 1992). According to this model, creative thinking unfolds in two main stages. The first involves generating an original or novel idea, and the second focuses on exploring that idea – developing, refining, and considering its implications – before deciding whether to apply or implement it (Finke et al., 1992; Smith et al., 1995; Ward et al., 1999).

This process reflects the human ability to ask hypothetical questions such as, "What would happen if I tried this?" or "What might that allow me to do next?" Such suppositional thinking lies at the core of both scientific discovery and technological innovation; without it, progress would rely solely on trial and error.

Within the creativity literature, the debate is between whether the ideas phase or the execution phase has a higher priority, "between head versus hands". The argument is over whether the "arts" (ideas, inspiration, and head) are superior to the "crafts" (execution, mastery, and hands). The composer versus the musician, the choreographer versus the dancer. In EcoSensory sessions, our goals are not to create masterpieces (though our clients might), the creative activities should allow both our clients to have ideas and develop their skills.

Development of Skills

For therapists and supporting professionals, the *Create* element can be key to supporting clients' skill and ideation development. Through feedback and discrimination, their creations will improve: the den will have more structural integrity, the leaves will have more consistency in the mandala, and the force will be more accurate in whittling the spoon. These adaptive skills are seen as early as infancy. In a study by Bourgeois et al. (2005), babies as young as six months old changed the way they handled objects depending on the object itself and the surface in front of them, which indicates they were already aware that how they hold objects creates new opportunities for action.

Adjusting behaviour in response to feedback is also observed in other animals. Capuchin Monkeys will particularly select stones, nuts, and anvils with certain properties that will make nut-cracking easier depending on the surface (Visalberghi et al., 2009). New Caledonian crows will select a perfect twig based on the length needed for the hole to be explored (Chappell & Kacelnik, 2002).

This exploration of the object's affordances, along with the exploration of the sensory qualities, helps the child develop their spatial perception and understanding of objects. As they mouth, touch, look at, bang, shake, and squeeze an object and relate it to a surface, they are fine-tuning their brains, including their somatosensory map, motor cortex, and visual-spatial areas. They start to understand what that texture feels like, what it looks like, and how it sounds (the basics of tactile discrimination, visual perception, spatial awareness, and auditory perception).

As the child develops, adapts and incorporates previously developed behaviours, they also expand their skills to create more affordances. This is where we humans have the edge. Our hands, with their opposable thumbs, can become increasingly skilled. The crow's beak doesn't have this variability. Our dexterous hands can interact with and manipulate objects in novel, more complex ways. As humans, once we have found one use for an object, we can think of and practise many more applications for it and imagine more goals it can help us accomplish. So, the feedback continues the cycle.

Research consistently demonstrates a strong relationship between hands-on interaction with objects and the development of spatial reasoning abilities (Frick & Wang, 2014; Johnson & Moore, 2020; Slone et al., 2018). Visual perception, spatial reasoning, and constructional praxis skills are often needed in areas related to science, technology, and the visual arts. They are also essential for daily living tasks such as cooking, dressing, and tidying your bedroom.

Studies indicate that children who demonstrate a greater interest in construction and build more complex structures achieve higher scores on standardised spatial intelligence tests (Jirout & Newcombe, 2015), including superior spatial visualisation, block building skills, and "mental rotation" – the cognitive ability to mentally rotate and analyse three-dimensional shapes (Casey, 2013).

Movement in the environment also helps us develop our spatial skills. Ayres (1972) states it is our relationship with the earth, in particular the gravitational pull, that is most fundamental to all living organisms on the planet, and core to space perception. "What is up and what is down" is the beginning of developing an *environmental scene*. As we crawl into our den, climb a tree, and step over a branch, we build an image of the world and our place in it. Whether it be a child building a bug house or an adult weaving a basket, EcoSensory sessions provide opportunities for new ways of seeing and perceiving the world.

Loose Parts Play

The more affordances an environment provides, the more opportunities for development it offers. Landscape architect Simon Nicholson (1972) proposed the *theory of loose parts*, which posits that children's creativity and inventiveness are directly linked to the variety, flexibility, and adaptability of materials present in their surroundings. According to Nicholson, the more adaptable a space is, the greater the potential for children's creative engagement.

Nature itself offers a rich example of a *loose parts* environment, offering materials such as branches, leaves, stones, moss, sand, soil, rocks, and water. Because these elements lack a pre-defined purpose, they invite children to impose their own rules, imagination, and meaning.

Research by Zamani and Moore (2013) highlights the profound difference between natural loose elements and fixed static objects (e.g., a slide or a bucket). They found that natural loose elements had "considerable potentiality" for affording constructive, dramatic, and exploratory play behaviours. In contrast, manufactured fixed elements mostly afforded only one type of cognitive play: functional play (Zamani & Moore, 2013).

The loose parts approach is crucial for promoting autonomy, adaptability, and a sense of agency in children. Brown (2002) noted that the flexibility of the environment directly influences a child's adaptability, confidence, independence, and sense of agency. Supporting this view, Duffy (2006) advocate for play spaces that offer children a degree of choice and control over their activities, reinforcing their autonomy and self-direction. Designers such as Laris have argued that children should act as the true *inventors* within their play (Laris, 2005). The natural world provides endless opportunities for children to view their surroundings in new ways, experiment, and develop emerging skills (Dahlberg et al., 2007), while also presenting manageable elements of risk and adventure that broaden experience and resilience (Garrick, 2009).

These creative affordances are also offered to adults. I am always amazed in my sessions with the inventive and creative ideas that my adolescent and adult clients have for creating in the natural world. We have made lotions and potions from foraged goods, dyes for cloth, and woven baskets and wreaths, made oyster shells into jewellery containers, cordage from daffodils, string from nettles, whittled spoons, and created mandalas and so much more.

Here, let's discuss how, as the facilitator, we can further increase the affordances for creation with the materials we bring to our sessions. Typically, I go into the forest or to the beach with a backpack of materials that may have multifunctional use. I bring tools for cutting, snipping, and whittling; a stove for cooking; water for drinking, dyeing, or rinsing; tarps and blankets; string and rope; and then some client favourite specifics: felting materials, wool, loom, oils … Bringing our own materials that we can remove at the end of our session from the natural environment can help protect that space. Repetitive use by groups can be quite impactful, even when recycling materials, such as branches. Knowledge of the specific environment and how we can protect it while "harvesting" for human use is important when we consider ourselves as part of an interconnected web of life (see Nourish for more on Honourable Harvesting).

Den Building

In a forest surrounded by the natural loose parts of branches and leaves, children (and adults!) seem to have an evolutionary urge to build a den. David Sobel suggests this is a "broad tendency, if not a universal experience" for children to find or make special places. These unique locations, referred to by children as everything from "robbers' dens" to "pirates' cabins" or "hidden rooms in the undergrowth", are vital, acting as a crucial proving ground for the developing self (Sobel, 2025). Michelle Langley, a childhood archaeologist, has explored the evolutionary drivers and the sociological and historical data behind the universal need for "secret" places amongst *Homo sapiens* children, places away from parental control (Langley, 2020). Langley quotes Elliot and Davies, that the universality of this behaviour may come from "an innate evolutionary drive for children to create hiding spaces or places – a vestigial survival strategy" (Elliot et al., 2010, p. 61). The ability to separate from their caregivers without going too far from the safe base (Kahn & Kellert, 2002).

Prospect–Refuge Theory

The ability to separate from the world and find a refuge is enjoyed by adults, too. The prospect–refuge theory suggests that we prefer environments where we can see out at the horizon, but it is hard for others to see us. An example of this is a den where we have a back, roof, and sides, and can be hidden (our refuge), but have an opening to view any prospective danger coming our way. Humans report greater comfort when they have trees or tall bushes around them, especially at their backs and sides (Appleton, 1996).

Our universal appreciation for certain natural landscapes is deeply rooted in evolutionary biology. A setting that offers a safe refuge, combined with a clear, long view over an open area, tends to be inherently calming. This preference echoes our ancestors' need for survival: the ability to spot potential predators without being exposed. Therefore, the environments we find aesthetically pleasing today are those that subconsciously satisfy a fundamental evolutionary drive, even though we no longer live as hunters and gatherers.

Well-Being Benefits of Creativity

We have discussed the evolutionary drivers for creativity and why we might want to create to survive and find our place within the tribe. Beyond this, we also enjoy creating, which itself brings significant well-being benefits. Let's go back to that New Caledonian crow. Research conducted by the University of Auckland found that not only did the crows make tools but they also enjoyed making them. They deduced this by measuring their optimism after using the tool. They found their optimism was highest, a feeling not linked to receiving the reward or the difficulty of the challenge itself. Is there something intrinsically motivating about solving problems and being creative? Csíkszentmihályi believes so – he described this state of pleasure from creative activities as *flow*.

Flow

Csíkszentmihályi (1996) conceptualised creative passion as "flow". Flow can be understood as a mental state when an individual is fully absorbed in an activity, time disappears, and the experience is exhilarating and pleasurable. The experience is in itself a reward. He called it flow after interviewing several "creatives" who used the metaphor of a water current carrying them along.

Flow states have six factors (Nakamura & Csikszentmihalyi, 2014):

- An intense and focused concentration on the here and now
- Action and awareness merge together
- There is no reflection on the self
- There is a sense of personal control or agency over the situation or activity
- The sense of time is distorted or altered.
- The experience is intrinsically rewarding

In *Attend*, we spoke of the state of awareness for Csíkszentmihályi; the state of flow has similar properties, allowing focus; a charged moment of connection is to an activity or a craft, such as playing a musical instrument or creating an artwork. The individual doesn't notice time; the activity itself is totally absorbing, there is no longer any ego, each action or thought is linked together (Csíkszentmihályi, 1996). Being in this "flow state" is reported to be a highly pleasurable experience. When in this state, people report that whatever they are doing feels highly self-rewarding (Stavrou et al., 2015).

Seligman argues that "flow" should be considered a significant factor in improving our human experience for its role in living a meaningful life. It connects us to "something much larger than we are, where we spend less time worrying about the inauthentic and the mundane". The activity hits the right spot between being too easy and boring and being too frustrating because the challenge is too hard (Seligman, 2002, p. 249).

Csíkszentmihályi developed a model to explain "flow" in relation to the balance between challenge and skill. Commenting that a challenge that is too simple will cause apathy, while one that is too high will cause anxiety. Furthermore, if the skill level is high and the activity is easy, it may be relaxing; however, to be meaningful and reach a state of "flow", the activity must challenge the highest skill level.

Arne Dietrich, a neurocognitive researcher, has furthered our understanding of the neuroscience behind "flow". Dietrich's findings suggest that the physicality of the creative activities gives the more "focused" pre-frontal cortex a "break". Other areas are allowed to take over, freeing us up temporarily from higher cognitive processes such as self-reflection, analytical thinking, and self-talk (Dietrich, 2004). There is no space for rumination, distracting thoughts, and painful thoughts or feelings. Indeed, being creative with our hands is a core tenet of occupational therapy, as Occupational Therapist, Mary Reilly, postulated as early as 1962, "man through the use of his hands, as they are energised by mind and will, can influence the state of his own health" (Reilly, 1962).

Csíkszentmihályi (1996) proposes that the "flow" state arises from complete absorption in an activity, which creates an "attentional bottleneck". This immersion leads the individual to lose awareness of everything else, including time, people, distractions, and even basic physical needs. He suggests that increasing the time spent in "flow" contributes to greater happiness and success in life. "Flow" experiences are expected to result in both enhanced performance and positive emotional states. For instance, studies have shown that antisocial and "delinquent" behaviour decreased in adolescents after two years of activities designed to enhance "flow" (Csikszentmihalyi & Nakamura, 2014).

In our sessions, it is the total immersion in an activity that will allow for a flow state. *Create* activities in particular allow for this focus; the temptation as facilitators is to move the session on, or change the activity, or feel driven to have a new activity each week. While offering a variety of Create activities, we also need to enable our participants to derive well-being from in-depth creative immersion. It is ok if making the wreath from foraged materials takes the whole session, or if even a few sessions. Creativity takes time, and we would do well to allow it.

Prosocial Creativity

Another interesting area of research into the "flow" experience, related to "social flow": how doing activities together increases the flow experience. Findings indicate that participants' joint coordination in activities heightened their task absorption, suggesting that "social flow" intensified the overall experience (Magyaródi & Oláh, 2017). Vygotsky (1978) suggests that children develop their creativity through their engagement with others. They acquire skills in interaction with others. Playing together, they can perform tasks they could not do alone. We find that group sessions, or those with family members such as a father and son, when engaged together in a shared endeavour, increase the well-being benefits. Communal den building, for example, has been researched to enhance prosocial benefits, with the process and the product providing participants with a focus for communication and building social relationships, praxis and ideation development, and exploration of "safety" and risk (Knight, 2009). Shared activities such as drumming in rhythm, putting up a tent, or collecting firewood for a communal fire build that sense of place and belonging within the tribe. Indeed, Eastern concepts of creativity link much more with society, the renewal of traditions, and the continuity of skills. Passing skills down from one generation to the next. In our sessions with families, it is wonderful to see parents sharing with their offspring how to build a fire or which berries are safe to pick. Have we in the Western world put too much value on individuality? Too much focus on novelty? By doing so, do we lose the connection between society and tradition, as demonstrated by Robert Macfarlane's beautiful *Lost Words*? Are we disconnected from our belonging in the world? In your sessions, is there a place to consider our rich craft traditions? Is there an opportunity to bring back the basket weaving (OTs!!), whittling, making tinctures, and building fires? We believe so! There is an abundance of nature-based "create" tasks that can provide healing and flow. Within our EcoSensory sessions, we work as a team with our clients and nature to enhance their abilities and increase engagement and satisfaction in shared tasks.

Social flow closely links with Forgeard and Mecklenburg's (2013) Reciprocal Mode of Creative Process, which suggests that our motivation to "create" is linked to both intrinsic motivators (such as flow) and social extrinsic factors. The four Gs:

- Gain: to create for yourself and for external reasons
- Growth: to create as the activity is meaningful and enjoyable
- Guidance: to create to mentor others
- Giving: to create to give to others

Thinking about these prosocial motivations in "create" may support our clients to "connect" more with themselves and with others, for example, making a basket for a friend, or creating a mandala that supports personal reflection and insight. We may also like to think that relationships in themselves are creative. Whether our connections are intimate or distant, we need to be creative in our interactions (Montuori & Purser, 1995).

Creativity for a Higher Life Purpose

According to Barron's research, creative people possess what he termed a "cosmological motive", a deep-seated need to find and communicate meaning in the world, which serves as their higher purpose. "Creativity is not a human invention or a human power isolated from the other powers of the universe... First came the universe's power of creativity" (Fox, 2004, p. 39). If we think of the universe as creative, ourselves as part of the universe, we must consider our interdependence and interrelatedness and the *"creativity of all phenomena"*. "We are surrounded by human creativity. We are human creativity" (Montuori & Purser, 1995).

Victor Frankl's Logotherapy has at its core the need to "do", to find life's meaning. Looking to the future, with a drive towards purpose and meaning, rather than delving into neuroses, is the central message of Frankl's *Man's Search for Meaning*. According to Frankl, existential frustration comes from a lack of purpose in life. He suggests that our health depends on the natural, productive tension that arises from measuring what we have already achieved against what we still aspire to accomplish. He argues that what we need is not a peaceful existence but a challenge we can strive to meet by applying all the skills at our disposal.

The Japanese have the concept of Ikigai, which can be translated roughly as "the happiness of being busy". The Japanese word Iki originates from the verb ikiru, which means "to live", and is connected to daily living.

Ikigai is best translated as "the value one finds in day-to-day living" – the reason to get up in the morning, our reason for being. Having your Ikigai brings satisfaction, happiness and meaning to life. Our sessions may focus on small creative activities or larger creative endeavours, such as life goals. Life itself can be seen as a creative project, and when we meet our clients at certain crossroads or transitions in their lives, we support them in shaping their future. Creating and sometimes remaking the life that, through circumstance or life weathering, needs rebuilding, so they can confidently travel forward (Barron, 2012; Simonton & Barron, 1992).

Summary

The Create element serves as the "doing" or "spatial" component of EcoSensory Therapy, driven by our inherent curiosity and attention to help individuals find and establish their place and space in the world. In our sessions, we think of "create" referring to the ideas and the execution, the head and the hands, the imagination, and the skills. Activities that explore ideas are equally welcome as those that explore skill. It is the "doing" that we believe holds value, rather than the product itself. We do not worry about where the product falls on the creativity spectrum, as we believe the creative process is inherently rewarding and good for our health.

There are significant well-being benefits derived from being creative, particularly the psychological state of flow. Flow is defined as a state of total, intrinsically rewarding absorption that provides a restorative "break" from higher cognitive functions such as self-reflection and rumination (Csikszentmihalyi, 2013). Beyond this individual benefit, we explored how social flow enhances task absorption when creating together and how creativity is connected to finding a higher life purpose.

Creativity is intrinsically linked to our existence and evolution. Exploring the evolutionary roots of creativity, from early tool use for survival in animals and hominids to the "creative explosion" in *Homo sapiens*, we have hoped to show how creativity is inherently linked to our place in the world. As part of our tribe and community, the "collective brain" allows us as a species to specialise and flourish. This mastery of skills is fundamentally linked to occupational science's contention that what we "do" is intrinsically connected to who we are, what we "become" and how we belong (Wilcock & Hocking, 2024).

During our sessions, we recognise that creativity is linked to the environment's affordances. Nature, as a rich "loose parts" environment, offers unparalleled opportunities for open-ended, exploratory, and constructive play that promotes praxis, autonomy, spatial perception, and skill development in both children and adults.

Working with nature's resources respectfully and for nature's benefit can also connect us to the creativity that abounds in it. If we understand this interdependence and learn about our world, we must take responsibility for our creations and ensure they are in tune with nature. We must acknowledge the impact our creations have on the universe and the interconnectedness of all things.

Creativity is not just in the objects we have created but, in the thoughts, we think and the words we say. We create in contexts, contexts of relationships, relationships with other humans and with the natural world. Our cultures, which we have created, also create us; they form our views, ideas, beliefs, and traditions. Have we grown so far from the land that we struggle to see how our creations impact the world that has created us?

In our sessions, we endeavour to create in harmony with the natural world, and connected to others, respectfully aware of the "doing" that nature is busy with.

References

Anderson, R. C., Mather, J. A., & Wood, J. B. (2013). *Octopus*. Timber Press.

Appleton, J. (1996). *The experience of landscape*. Wiley Chichester.

Ayres, A. J. (1972). *Sensory integration and learning disorders*. Western Psychological Services.

Barron, F. (2012). *Creativity and psychological health: Origins of personal vitality and creative freedom*. Literary Licensing, LLC.

Bateson, P. P. G., & Hinde, R. A. (1976). The social function of intellect. *Growing Points in Ethology*, 303–317. https://cogprints.org/1737/

Bluff, L. A. et al. (2010). Tool use by wild New Caledonian crows Corvus moneduloides at natural foraging sites. *Proceedings. Biological Sciences, 277*(1686), 1377–1385.

Bourgeois, K. S., Khawar, A. W., Neal, S. A., & Lockman, J. J. (2005). Infant manual exploration of objects, surfaces, and their interrelations. *Infancy, 8*, 233–252. https://doi.org/10.1207/s15327078in0803_3

Brown, F. (2002). *Playwork: Theory and practice*. McGraw-Hill Education, UK.

Chappell, J., & Kacelnik, A. (2002). Tool selectivity in a non-primate, the New Caledonian crow (*Corvus moneduloides*). *Animal Cognition 5*, 71–78 (2002). https://doi.org/10.1007/s10071-002-0130-2

Casey, B. M. (2013). Individual and group differences in spatial ability. In *Handbook of spatial cognition* (pp. 117–134). https://doi.org/10.1037/13936-007

Csíkszentmihályi, M. (1996). *Creativity: Flow and the psychology of discovery and invention.*

Csikszentmihalyi, M. (2013) *Flow: The psychology of happiness*. Random House.

Csikszentmihalyi, M., & Nakamura, J. (2014). The dynamics of intrinsic motivation: A study of adolescents. In M. Csikszentmihalyi (Ed.), *Flow and the foundations of positive psychology: The collected works of Mihaly Csikszentmihalyi* (pp. 175–197). Springer Netherlands. https://doi.org/10.1007/978-94-017-9088-8_12

Dietrich, A. (2004). Neurocognitive mechanisms underlying the experience of flow. *Consciousness and Cognition*, *13*(4), 746–761. https://doi.org/10.1016/j.concog.2004.07.002

Dahlberg, G., Moss, P., & Pence, A. (2007). *Beyond quality in early childhood education and care: Languages of evaluation*. Routledge.

Duffy, B. (2006). *Supporting creativity and imagination in the early years* (2nd ed.). Maidenhead: Open University Press.

Elliot, S. (2010). Children in the natural world. In Davis J. M. (Ed.), Young children and the environment. *Early education for sustainability* (pp. 43–75). Cambridge University Press.

Finke, R. A., Ward, T. B., & Smith, S. M. (1992). *Creative cognition: Theory, research, and applications*. Cambridge, MA: MIT Press.

Finn, J. K., Tregenza, T., & Norman, M. D. (2009). Defensive tool use in a coconut-carrying octopus. *Current Biology*, *19*(23), R1069–R1070. https://doi.org/10.1016/j.cub.2009.10.052

Forgeard, M. J. C., & Mecklenburg, A. C. (2013). The two dimensions of motivation and a reciprocal model of the creative process. *Review of General Psychology: Journal of Division 1, of the American Psychological Association*, *17*(3), 255–266. https://doi.org/10.1037/a0032104

Fox, M. (2004). *Creativity*. Penguin.

Frick, A., & Wang, S. H. (2014). Mental spatial transformations in 14-and 16-month-old infants: Effects of action and observational experience. *Child Development, 85*(1), 278-293.

Garrick, R. (2009). *Playing outdoors in the early years* (2nd ed.). London: Continuum International Publishing Group.

Gibson, E. J. (2001). *Perceiving the affordances*. https://doi.org/10.4324/9781410604248

Glăveanu, V. P., & Kaufman, J. C. (2019). *Creativity: A historical perspective*. The Cambridge Handbook of Creativity. Cambridge University Press.

Godfrey-Smith, P., Scheel, D., Chancellor, S., Linquist, S., & Lawrence, M. (2022). In the line of fire: Debris throwing by wild octopuses. *PLoS One*, *17*(11), e0276482. https://doi.org/10.1371/journal.pone.0276482

Gopnik, A. (2020). Childhood as a solution to explore-exploit tensions. *Philosophical Transactions of the Royal Society of London. Series B, Biological Sciences*, *375*(1803), 20190502. https://doi.org/10.1098/rstb.2019.0502

Henrich, J. (2017). *The secret of our success: How culture is driving human evolution, domesticating our species, and making us smarter*. Princeton University Press. https://press.princeton.edu/books/paperback/9780691178431/the-secret-of-our-success

Herculano-Houzel, S. (2016). *The human advantage: A new understanding of how our brain became remarkable*. MIT Press. https://play.google.com/store/books/details?id=DMqpCwAAQBAJ

Inoue-Nakamura N., & Matsuzawa T. (1997). Development of stone tool use by wild chimpanzees (Pan troglodytes). *Journal of Comparative Psychology*, *111*(2):159–173. https://doi.org/10.1037/0735-7036.111.2.159. PMID: 9170281.

Isaac, G. L., Leakey, R. E., & Behrensmeyer, A. K. (1971). Archeological traces of early hominid activities, East of lake Rudolf, kenya. *Science, 173*(4002), 1129–1134. https://doi.org/10.1126/science.173.4002.1129
Isaksen, S. G., Stead-Dorval, K. B., Treffinger D. J. (2023). Creative problem solving: An introduction Routledge.
Johnson, S. P., & Moore, D. S. (2020). Spatial thinking in infancy: Origins and development of mental rotation between 3 and 10 months of age. *Cognitive Research: Principles and Implications*, *5*(1), 10.
Jirout, J. J., & Newcombe, N. S. (2015). Building blocks for developing spatial skills: Evidence from a large, representative U.S. sample. *Psychological Science*, *26*(3), 302–310. https://doi.org/10.1177/0956797614563338
Kahn, P. H., & Kellert, S. R. (2002). *Children and nature: Psychological, sociocultural, and evolutionary investigations* (P. H. Kahn & S. R. Kellert, Eds.). MIT Press.
Knight, S. (2009). *Forest schools and outdoor learning in the early years*. SAGE Publications
Langley, M. C. (2020). Space to play: Identifying children's sites in the Pleistocene archaeological record. *Evolutionary Human Sciences*, *2*(e41), e41. https://doi.org/10.1017/ehs.2020.29
Laris, M. (2012). Designing for play. In Dudek, M. (2005). *Children's spaces* (pp. 14–29). Routledge
Leakey, M. D. (1971). *Olduvai Gorge, Volume 3: Excavations in Beds I and II, 1960–1963*. Cambridge University Press.
Magyaródi, T., & Oláh, A. (2017). The effect of social interaction on flow experience. *International Journal of Psychology & Behavior Analysis*, *2017*. https://www.graphyonline.com/archives/IJPBA/2017/IJPBA-126/
Maslow, A. H. (1943). Preface to motivation theory. *Psychosomatic Medicine*, *5*, 85–92. https://doi.org/10.1097/00006842-194301000-00012
Mason, G., & Rushen, J. (2008). *Stereotypic animal behaviour: Fundamentals and applications to welfare*. CABI. https://play.google.com/store/books/details?id=v3LgDwAAQBAJ
Meagher, R. K., & Mason, G. J. (2012). *Environmental enrichment reduces signs of boredom in caged mink, PloS One*, *7*(11), e49180
Mithen, S. (1996). On early Palaeolithic "concept-mediated marks," mental modularity, and the origins of art. *Current Anthropology, 37*(4), 666–670.
Montuori, A., & Purser, R. E. (1995). Deconstructing the lone genius myth: Toward a contextual view of creativity. *Journal of Humanistic Psychology*, *35*(3), 69–112. https://doi.org/10.1177/00221678950353005
Nakamura, J., & Csikszentmihalyi, M. (2014). The concept of flow. In M. Csikszentmihalyi (Ed.), *Flow and the foundations of positive psychology: The collected works of Mihaly Csikszentmihalyi* (pp. 239–263). Springer Netherlands. https://doi.org/10.1007/978-94-017-9088-8_16
Nicholson, S. (1972). The theory of loose parts, an important principle for design methodology. *Studies in Design Education Craft & Technology*, *4*(2).
Piaget, J. (1952). The Origins of Intelligence in Children. New York, NY: W.W. Norton & Co. https://doi.org/10.1037/11494-000
Reilly, M. (1962). Occupational therapy can be one of the great ideas of 20th century medicine. *The American Journal of Occupational Therapy: Official Publication of the American Occupational Therapy Association*, *16*, 1–9. https://www.ncbi.nlm.nih.gov/pubmed/14491211

Salas, M., Temple, D., Abáigar, T., Cuadrado, M., Delclaux, M., Enseñat, C., Almagro, V., Martínez-Nevado, E., Quevedo, M. Á., Carbajal, A., Tallo-Parra, O., Sabés-Alsina, M., Amat, M., Lopez-Bejar, M., Fernández-Bellon, H., & Manteca, X. (2016). Aggressive behavior and hair cortisol levels in captive Dorcas gazelles (Gazella dorcas) as animal-based welfare indicators. *Zoo Biology*, *35*(6), 467–473. https://onlinelibrary.wiley.com/doi/abs/10.1002/zoo.21323

Seligman, M. E. P. (2002). Authentic happiness: Using the new positive psychology to realize your potential for lasting fulfillment. New York: Free Press.

Shea, J. J., Adler, D., Barham, L., Conard, N. J., Eren, M. I., Lombard, M., Nowell, A., O'Connell, J. F., Potts, R., Tryon, C. A., et al. (2010). Homo sapiens is as Homo sapiens was: Behavioral variability versus "behavioral modernity" in Paleolithic archaeology. *Current Anthropology*, *52*(1). https://www.journals.uchicago.edu/doi/abs/10.1086/658067

Simonton, K., & Barron, F. (1992). Creativity and psychological health: Origins of personal vitality and creative freedom. *The American Journal of Psychology*, *105*(1), 119. https://doi.org/10.2307/1422985

Slone, L. K., Moore, D. S., & Johnson, S. P. (2018). Object exploration facilitates 4-month-olds' mental rotation performance. *PLoS One*, *13*(8), e0200468.

Smith, S. M., Ward, T. B., & Finke, R. A. (Eds.). (1995). *The creative cognition approach*. Cambridge, MA: MIT Press.

Sobel, D. (2025). *Childhood and nature: Design principles for educators*. https://books.google.co.uk/books?hl=en&lr=&id=4XM1EQAAQBAJ&oi=fnd&pg=PR7&dq=david+sobel+&ots=sq2bJPPcGC&sig=FK-i1bihXzBt4BSBLcUwU9aziLc

Stavrou, N. A. M., Psychountaki, M., Georgiadis, E., Karteroliotis, K., & Zervas, Y. (2015). Flow theory–goal orientation theory: Positive experience is related to athlete's goal orientation. *Frontiers in Psychology*, *6*, 1499. https://www.frontiersin.org/articles/10.3389/fpsyg.2015.01499/full

Stringer, C., & Gamble, C. (1993). *In search of the neanderthals: Solving the puzzle of human origins* (p. 247). https://eprints.soton.ac.uk/391482

Visalberghi, E., Addessi, E., Truppa, V., et al. (2009). Selection of effective stone tools by wild bearded capuchin monkeys. *Current Biology*, *19*, 213–217. https://doi.org/10.1016/j.cub.2008.11.064

Vygotsky, L. (1978). Interaction between learning and development. *Readings on the Development of Children*, *23*(3), 34–41.

Ward, T. B., Smith, S. M., & Finke, R. A. (1999). Creative cognition. In R. J. Sternberg (Ed.), *Handbook of creativity* (pp. 189–212). Cambridge University Press.

Wilcock, A. A. (1998). Occupation for health. *The British Journal of Occupational Therapy*, *61*(8), 340–345. https://doi.org/10.1177/030802269806100801

Wilcock, A. A. (1999). Reflections on doing, being and becoming. *Australian Occupational Therapy Journal*. https://onlinelibrary.wiley.com/doi/abs/10.1046/j.1440-1630.1999.00174.x

Wilcock, A. and Hocking, C. (2024). An occupational perspective of health (3rd edn.). London, England: Routledge.

Zamani, Z., & Moore, R. (2013). *The cognitive play behavior affordances of natural and manufactured elements within outdoor preschool settings*. https://www.academia.edu/download/33108251/Landscape_Research_Record_No.1.pdf#page=277

Chapter 8

Nourish

Chris West and Claire Pemrick

Introduction

To nourish: provide with the food or other substance necessary for growth, health, and good condition.

As we move from the element of Create to Nourish, we will be exploring the powerful and indisputable way in which nature nourishes us, physically, emotionally, and spiritually, feeding our bodies and souls in so many rich and powerful ways. Nature is the ultimate nourishing environment, offering opportunities to sense, move, feel, learn, explore, create, problem solve, and connect. These are the foundations that underlie our health and well-being. Many of these we have discussed in previous chapters and elements, and how they provide beneficial health-related outcomes for our participants and us. In this chapter, we want to expand our thinking beyond the ways *nature* is the environment, backdrop, or host to our activities, separate from us, to how we are *explicitly part of nature* and that there is no separation. Our bodies indeed host a multitude of more-than-human organisms; we are actually the natural backdrop that supports other organisms to live their lives. Just as we are nourished by nature, we ingest other natural products, whether it is food or smells, and we provide nourishment for others. It is this reciprocal, interconnected web of life that may, in itself, be pivotal to why being in nature promotes our health and well-being.

To explore this interwoven connection, we will consider research on how we can nourish ourselves, others, and the planet, and the mechanisms that support it. Considering our physiology, our immune system and endocrine system and how these are interwoven with the natural world. We will discuss the gut–brain axis and the powerful impact that our gut function has on so much of our lives. Furthermore, we will consider how we use our chemical senses (taste and smell) to support our well-being and regulation, which is crucial to our ability to connect and engage in our everyday lives.

This chapter will further consider how, as a species, we care for and nourish one another. We will consider how using food and nourishment can be a source of connection and a way to show love to those we hold dear. We will explore the impact of early adverse experiences and neurodiversity on gut health, as this affects many

DOI: 10.4324/9781003777465-10

of the individuals we work with. We will consider how, in our sessions, we can nourish our participants and help them nourish one another.

Finally, we will explore how we may also care for and nourish the planet, how reciprocal nourishment provides for future generations, and how we see ourselves as part of an interconnected, woven web, where we consider the other-than-human as kin, too. From there, we are going to look at the world of foraging for those young and old, the different ways we can think about the resources in nature to feed us, and how we can harvest ethically to support future generations and the planet. We will look at ways we can learn from indigenous communities about how to maintain the planet, such as the Honourable Harvest.

Nourish will mean different things to each of us. Some of us spend much of our time nurturing and caring for others, whether it be our children, parents, colleagues, pets, or gardens; the list is endless. We might be good at nourishing ourselves, or we might find it is at the bottom of a very long to-do list. We would like to encourage you to reflect on what *nourishment* means for you. How would you like to be nourished? How do you nourish yourself or others? This might influence both how you feel about it and how you use and apply this element when working with individuals.

Nourishing and Nurturing Ourselves and Others: Nourishing Our Bodies Through Sensory Experiences

There is a wealth of compelling evidence showing that our psychological health and well-being are intricately linked to our connection with the natural environment, and that these can be positively enhanced by spending more time in natural spaces. The ever-growing body of evidence reminds us of both the short- and long-term benefits to our physiological, physical, and psychological health (see Chapter 1 for an in-depth look at the health benefits). It is our pathway to wellness "one step, one breath, one leaf at a time" (Ożga et al., 2026, p. 12).

When we have our EcoSensory sessions in natural spaces free of human pollution, whether it is in the forest, by the beach, in the meadows, or by a river, we are inadvertently being nourished by the abundance of organisms, natural chemicals, microbes, and so on that we breathe, touch, eat, or somehow take into our bodies. Climbing a tree in the wild is not only different from climbing on a frame in the clinic in terms of its impact on how the body moves (see Discover) but also from the increase in healthy microbes that will end up on our hands, and the airborne natural chemicals we breathe.

Cast your mind back to Connect, where we looked at how nature communicates with us. Those very same communication tools, such as natural chemicals released by trees, also protect us. With each breath we take, we inhale all the chemicals (natural and non-natural) surrounding us. Lots of these chemicals we can detect with our olfactory receptors; some we can't. Take a moment now and notice what you can smell. As I write this, I have the lovely scent of narcissus flowers I have picked from the garden this morning, a faint whiff of tea, a rather putrid smell of old dog breath (the seaweed supplement to stop this only works so far) and the smell of my favourite perfume on my jumper.

Mostly, these smells provide some form of information. The flowers are telling insects where they are to encourage pollination, the dog's breath is telling you he might have an infection, and the perfume is telling any potential suitors that I am a good catch! When we are out in nature, we are also sending out and picking up these communication chemicals (see our "Connect" chapter).

Plants communicate directly with our immune system, healing us through biological signals that our unconscious understands, even without our needing to touch or ingest them. The foundation of this language lies in terpenes, abundant bioactive substances that give plants and essential oils their fragrances, such as Limonene (citrus smell), Pinene (pine), and Linalool (lavender). They serve many functions for the plant, including acting as a sunscreen, attracting insects, warning others, producing toxins to deter predators, and even helping it find a mate (well, for … mushrooms). Scientists have encoded 2,000 fragrance words from 900 plant families, but an estimated 40,000 terpenes remain uncoded (Koechlin, 2012). The concentration of terpenes is highest in the densest part of a forest, nearest to the floor, and rapidly increases in April, peaking in July and August in the Northern Hemisphere. Some terpenes also have a protective function; these airborne chemicals are called phytoncides and are released by trees, mushrooms, mosses, and ferns to protect them from decay and insects (Breitmaier, 2006). Phytoncide comes from the Greek "phyton", meaning plant, and the Latin "-cide", meaning kill, so they are literally plant killers! They don't just smell good; they prevent other plants from growing nearby. Conifers such as pine and spruce, as well as herbs (rosemary and geranium), have high levels of these phytoncides.

Our immune system has been described as a sensory system – our "nature connection system" (Dozmorov & Dresser, 2010), with an inherent ability to receive and process information from the outside world for defence and self-maintenance. When we enter the forest, our immune system communicates directly with the communication systems of the trees and plants, absorbing terpenes and phytoncides through our skin and by breathing. It decodes these messages and reacts similarly to other plants by increasing our internal defences. As Avary expresses, the "forest air is like a healing elixir we inhale" (Avary, 2018, p. 84)

What we know from the extensive research of Dr. Q Li and other Shinrin Yoku practitioners is that these terpenes are generally good for us, with Avary (2018) describing them as "anticancer terpenes". They have been shown to:

- Increase the number of natural killer (NK) cells in our immune system
- Make the NK cells more active, increasing the level of anticancer proteins
- Lower our stress hormones

NK cells are specialised white blood cells responsible for identifying and destroying harmful cells, such as those infected by viruses or showing cancerous changes. They achieve this by releasing potent anticancer proteins, including perforin, granulysin, and granzymes, which lead to the destruction of target cells. Research has consistently shown that higher NK cell activity is associated with a reduced risk of developing illnesses such as cancer.

After just three days and two nights in a forest, Dr. Li found significant increases:

- NK cell activity went up from 17.3% to 26.5% (an increase of 53.2%)
- NK cell numbers went up from 440 to 661 (50% increase)
- The presence of anticancer protein granulysin was up by 48%; granzyme A by 39%; granzyme B by 33%; and perforin by 28%

This enhanced NK activity and cell count can persist for up to 30 days following a forest bathing experience. Furthermore, studies found that walking in a forest decreased cortisol levels by 12%, sympathetic nervous system activity by 7%, heart rate by 6%, and blood pressure by 1.4% (Song et al., 2016). Naturalistic spaces are the only environments where we connect and engage with all our senses, becoming fully and physically alive (Williams, 2017).

Dr. Li also found that people living in areas with fewer trees have significantly higher stress levels and mortality rates than those living in areas with high tree density (Li et al., 2009). There is clear and compelling evidence that being in forest spaces positively impacts the health of humans by boosting and supporting the psycho-neuro-endocrino-immune network (Kotte et al., 2019).

Ming Kuo, from the University of Illinois, argues that this immune system response is the *central pathway* through which being in nature supports our health. While 21 pathways link nature to beneficial health outcomes (including environmental factors, psychological states, and physical activity), many of which we have discussed in previous chapters, Kuo concludes that it is the immune system pathway that takes the "lion's share". The effect sizes for nature affecting the immune system are large, and enhanced immune function can wholly or partially explain 18 specific health outcomes. Other nature-related pathways, such as improved sleep, social ties, physical activity, and stress reduction, will also improve immune function (Kuo, 2015).

The nourishing effects of nature are not limited to the forest. Similarly, when we are by the sea, the beach's immune benefits are driven by sea spray aerosols and negative air ions. Sea spray aerosols are microscopic droplets, formed by bursting bubbles in the surf, that carry marine bacteria, salt ions, and biogenic molecules. Low-level exposure to *endotoxins* in these aerosols has been shown to dampen the immune system's inflammatory response. Negative air ions are generated by moving water, particularly breaking waves or waterfalls. These ions enter the bloodstream and trigger biochemical reactions that increase serotonin levels, alleviate depressive symptoms, and regulate sleep patterns.

I know that whenever I (Claire) take my clients to my beach hut, come rain or shine, they comment that just smelling the sea makes them feel better. After an hour, they are almost always relaxed. Dose is important; the longer we breathe in these chemicals, the greater the chance of a beneficial effect. It's not surprising that so many of us want to live by the sea.

We also know that interacting with the elements of nature, including the soil, is beneficial. Research shows that soil contains antidepressant microbes, *Mycobacterium vaccae*, which have the same effect on our brain as antidepressants, but without the side effects (Douglas, 2020). Our immune systems have been exquisitely fine-tuned over millions of years of evolution to enable us to live in balance with the many dangerous microorganisms that exist. It's important that we are exposed to these and don't live in a sterile environment, so that we can respond quickly and build up a natural immunity to them. The best way to train your immune system ... give in to dirt! (Ruebush, 2009). In your sessions, get muddy, build mud pies, sandcastles, dig for treasure, sniff the earth, and get down in the soil.

There can be no doubt that we are designed to be in nature. This understanding has led to social prescribing, which is becoming widely used in primary care to support mental and physical health, with 95% of doctors reporting that it brought well-being to their patients and to them too (Hardman, 2020). Connecting with nature can be free, nearby, or at home, and is one of the most powerful ways we have to support our physical and mental well-being. To strengthen your immune system, spending at least two hours in forest spaces, or three days if you can, is recommended. Pick spaces that meet your own physical needs and abilities, where you can take a break to rest, perhaps having a drink and something to eat, or quietly meditate, soaking in the rich atmosphere.

Regulating Properties of Smell

From an evolutionary perspective, our sense of smell was the first to develop (see *Attend* for a detailed look at the evolution of the senses). Diane Ackerman, in her wonderful poetic exploration of the senses (1990), explains that our thinking and our ability to smell are intrinsically linked, as our cerebral hemispheres evolved from the olfactory centres.

Professor Kara Hoover spoke at the American Association for the Advancement of Science conference in 2017, exploring how our environments have changed in relation to smell, and how humans' noses appear to be misaligned with the modern world. She talks about how our sense of smell originally evolved in odour-rich landscapes, where we actively interacted in these environments. However, we now interact less with natural environments and live in heavily polluted environments, which disrupt our sense of smell. This disconnection with our natural scent-scape places us at greater risk of mental health difficulties, such as depression and anxiety, greater risk for physical health problems, such as obesity, as well as greater risk for our social health. A disrupted sense of smell may also lead to overeating because people get less enjoyment from their food. She goes on to state that greener cities would be better for our sense of smell and might also help us to come away from our computers, go out to the parks, and play in the warm sunshine.

We are so sensitive to certain smells that we can detect the equivalent of seven drops of Geosmin (a chemical compound released by soil after it rains) in a swimming pool. Douglas (2020) describes how, as humans, we are programmed to find the smell of rain attractive, linking it to our early ancestors' reliance on it for survival, such as finding fresh water to drink. This is the smell of survival. It would have told thirsty prehistoric humans where the water was. Like the chemicals released by trees or the waves crashing, geosmin has antibacterial properties (Neff, 2018). The earthy scent that rain gives off is known as petrichor and is caused by a number of chemical reactions that occur when rain hits the ground, interacts with bacteria, and releases a scent. Also, when it rains, terpenes on plant leaves are released into the air.

One of the key activities we may do in an EcoSensory session is to lie on the forest floor, in the woods, or even in a field and *smell the earth*. In the children's home where I (Chris) work, I often take children out to smell the earth, and I am reminded of one young person in particular who was finding it so hard to nourish herself and I said "come on let's grab a blanket, we're gonna go out and smell the earth!" and she looked at me with a "what on earth are we doing Chris" look, and we went outside and we lay on the ground and smelt the earth together. I watched the amazement on her face. She couldn't quite believe that something seemingly so crazy and simple could be so nourishing. This led us on a journey to explore more ways for her to nourish herself, culminating in our final session together, where we put up hammocks in the forest and drank hot chocolate. We even had different flavours of hot chocolate! Nourishing herself in a way that she hadn't been able to be nourished by her mother was a really important part of the work we did together.

Remembering the powerful impact of scents can be a powerful tool in our sessions. Research suggests that certain smells have a strong stress-suppressing effect, while others can induce stress. Masuo et al. (2021), in their review of the connection between smells and the stress response, found that essential oils such as rosemary, bergamot, grapefruit, lavender, cedar, or cypress can reduce stress. Scented plants have been shown to play an important part in rehabilitation programmes in Sweden, where the citrus-scented pelargonium evoked emotions and promoted sensory awareness and memories (Pálsdóttir et al., 2021). Floral scents such as plum blossom could also improve mood, memory, speech, and movement, with impacts on emotional health, depression, and memory disorders.

The very essence of EcoSensory Therapy is how being in nature supports our regulation and well-being, in so many rich and diverse ways, feeding our bodies, minds, and souls. Our sense of smell can have a significant impact on our arousal levels and sense of well-being, such as the familiar smell of another person or one that reminds us of our childhood (Breitmaier, 2006). A mother can recognise her infant by their scent alone (Vaglio, 2009). Similarly, we can detect emotional distress in others by chemosensory cues. We can actually *smell* fear. In an experiment, volunteers were asked to smell shirts of people who had either skydived or stayed on terra firma. The "smellers" were able to accurately detect stress hormones from the scent of skydivers' shirts (Mujica-Parodi et al., 2009). We can even detect the odour in "sad tears" (Calvi et al., 2020).

Our emotions are also deeply linked to our hormone levels and the immune functions in the body. It is the early experiences of the child tasting, smelling, and exploring that support immunity, by allowing the immune system to explore its environment, becoming stronger and more robust when exposed to these kinds of experiences, immunologist Ruebush tells us (2009).

There are so many ways that nature shares its scents with us that support our regulation and well-being, such as plants in our homes, the use of essential oils, which we can use to make things to nurture ourselves, such as lip balms, and of course things we can eat. One of the favourite activities to do in my sessions (Claire) is to make a hand balm. Recently, I made one with a teenage girl who had significant mental health challenges; we used my camping stove to boil some water and make a "bain-marie" in which we melted equal parts of coconut oil, shea butter, and beeswax, then added a few drops of essential oil. She was able to take this away from the session, in a little pot that she can use whenever she is feeling a return of her negative thought patterns, as a way to break this cycle and evoke the sensations of being by the beach making balms.

Nourishing Our Bodies through Sensory Experience of Eating

Our sense of taste plays a powerful and essential role in our lives. Remarkably, our sense of taste is 90% smell. Taste and smell are closely linked, and although the sense of taste is very primitive, the sense of smell is much more sophisticated.

Paul Breslin, Professor of Nutritional Science and expert on taste, has written on the evolutionary foundations of taste. He states that there is a "mismatch" between the way our senses evolved and the modern world, which is making us "ill", and goes on to say that one reason for the obesity crisis is our taste for sugary foods, which stems from our origins as apes. He suggests that our love of sugar may be tied to the fact that we are primates who share a common ancestor with other apes on the planet, dating back millions of years. In the forests, the fruits come and go as the trees come into fruit. Animals go up into the trees and eat sugary foods until there is nothing left to eat; however, we live in a world where sugary treats are available all the time (Breslin, 2013).

Breslin discusses our other food preferences in his book *Chemical Senses in Feeding, Belonging and Surviving: Or Are You Going to Eat That?* He suggests that our preference for sour tastes is linked to our evolutionary preference for fruit that may have a sour or citrus flavour (Breslin, 2013). Breslin discusses how the sour taste allows for the detection of acids, which although not necessarily considered nutrients, let us know about vitamin C. Interestingly, while infants have an aversion, children have a higher tolerance for sour flavours than adults, maybe they need more vitamin C! Which also explains those crazy playground challenges to eat the most sour sweet!

Umami flavours, on the other hand, allows for the detection of amino acids (proteins), particularly glutamate and aspartate, which are typically found in fermented foods. They are also found in cooked foods. Both cooked and fermented foods have the breakdown of macronutrients; Breslin suggests that our preference for fermented foods may have predisposed us to like cooked foods. Salty tastes allow for the detection of certain minerals, which we need to survive. It is also thought to prepare the body for the nutrients that the body is going to absorb (Breslin, 2019).

The experiences of tasting, eating, and smelling offer a multitude of opportunities to regulate our arousal, uplifting us when we need to be in this state, such as through the taste of a sour citrus orange, or downregulating us by drinking silky-smooth hot chocolate. We can think of food, its flavour, and its texture as regulating tools that can shift our arousal. After checking for any contraindications such as allergies, as practitioners we can think about how we might use food in our sessions to calm or increase alertness. In my sessions (Claire), I often take a variety of chewy, crunchy, sour, sweet, umami, and salty snacks to share with my clients. Often I find that hot chocolate is the number one choice at the end of a session.

Using mindfulness when eating and drinking is a powerful way to feel more grounded, connected, and centred, becoming fully conscious of what we eat and how we eat, and truly tasting it. Approaches that have mindful eating at the core of their model and support a greater sense of self include the Just Right State Programme, part of the Sensory Attachment Intervention approach pioneered by Occupational Therapist Éadaoin Bhreathnach, which recognises the powerful effect that food can have on our arousal states.

Doing these things in the forest, whether it is drinking in the warm air into our lungs, or a warm cup of tea from a flask, eating wild strawberries, or the taste of food cooked out in the open, all these experiences provide rich opportunities to feed and nourish all of our senses, and so much more. Somehow our sense of taste and smell is more intense when we are outside, perhaps because it feels more unusual, more novel, when we do it in the outdoor environment. Doing these things with others offers opportunities for co-regulation and connection that, in turn, can lead to higher levels of regulation and emotional well-being.

In one final session with a young man, I (Chris) asked, "What should we do for our last session in the forest?" and he said, "I want bacon sandwiches". I spoke to his mum in the morning, and she said: "I'm going to bring some tomato ketchup because he loves tomato ketchup with his bacon sandwiches". So we cooked the bacon on the stove in the forest, and his mother brought out this tomato ketchup in a little pot, and he looked at his mum with such surprise and love as she remembered the ketchup he loves with his bacon sandwiches. They were some of the best bacon sandwiches I have eaten!

Even when we are not outside, it can be powerful to connect what we eat with where it has come from. While some food is hothoused, the majority of the food we eat has some connection to the earth and the sun. It is a gift from nature. If we can be mindful of that connection, that gift, we can be reminded of the interconnectedness of all life. In each mouthful, we are connected to the cosmos, as Buddhist Monk, Thich Nhat Hanh (2014) reminds us in his book on mindful eating, "*How to Eat*". This reciprocity is in us nourishing ourselves and remembering that the universe is providing us with that nourishment and that to continue to do so requires our support. How can we care for the universe so the soil is rich to put nutrients in our food, the sun not too hot to scorch it, and the water not polluted to damage it?

We Are Multitudes

So, along with the regulating properties of eating that nourish us, we are also nourishing all the other organisms living inside us. There is a common misconception that we are outnumbered 10 to 1. Although it is often claimed that there are 10 organisms living inside us for every human cell, Ed Yong, in his book *I Contain Multitudes*, suggests that a more rigorous estimate is a ratio of one human cell to one microbe; however, that still suggests we are host to about 39 trillion microbes (Yong, 2023). This fact often blows my mind!

The Gut–Brain Axis Theory

If we go back to the idea that there is a *central pathway* that supports the well-being impacts of nature, it is our immune responses (Kuo, 2015). While inhaling beneficial chemicals supports this mechanism, what we eat and ingest is also critical. Seventy percent of our immune system is in our gut. Researchers have identified a powerful connection between the gut and the brain. Like the brain, the gut is full of nerves. It contains the largest area of nerves outside the brain, with the digestive tract and the brain sharing many of the same nerve connections (Dawson et al., 2025).

The gut–brain axis refers to the communication network connecting our gut and brain, which are closely linked, both physically and biochemically, and that governs the function of our gastrointestinal (GI) tract. Our gut, or enteric nervous system, is often called our *second brain* (Gershon, 1999). It does not work in isolation; its activity is directed by the brain and the central nervous system. Communication between the brain and the digestive tract occurs through the autonomic nervous system (ANS), specifically its sympathetic and parasympathetic divisions. This system operates automatically and regulates vital functions such as heart rate, respiration, and digestion. The vagus nerve, a primary component of our ANS, is the fastest route from the gut to the brain, and it sends bidirectional signals between these two organs (Enders, 2017). It is our ANS, along with homeostatic functions, that mediates social engagement, trust, and intimacy with others. It is an open system and is influenced by our interactions with others.

The gut sends signals to the insula, the limbic system, the prefrontal cortex, the amygdala, the hippocampus, and the anterior cingulate cortex; these regions influence self-awareness, emotion, morality, fear, motivation, and memory. The insula is where the self originates. It receives information about feelings from the entire body and represents a map of our feelings (Craig, 2020).

Cooperation between the gut and the brain begins early in life; both are responsible for our emotional world and play important roles in stress responses. The

ANS also plays a key role in digestive function by controlling how quickly food moves through the GI tract, how much stomach acid is released, and how much protective mucus is produced along the intestinal lining. In addition, the brain communicates with the gut through the hypothalamic–pituitary–adrenal (HPA) axis, a hormone-based pathway that further helps regulate digestive processes.

Emerging research shows that the brain is not only responsive to the microbes living in our gut but that these microorganisms can also shape how we experience the world and influence our behaviour. Scientists are increasingly recognising that the effects of the gut microbiome extend well beyond digestion, reaching into areas of human biology once thought unrelated – including mental processes. For instance, gut bacteria help regulate serotonin levels, a powerful neurotransmitter involved in our well-being and sense of happiness. We previously thought that neurotransmitters were only produced in the brain; some, such as serotonin and dopamine, are produced in the gut (Yong, 2023). Many commonly prescribed medications for anxiety and depression function by adjusting serotonin activity. These are probably just one of many chemical messengers linked to mood and behaviour that are affected by the gut microbiota. Other transmitters produced in the gut help us to control our feelings of anxiety and fear.

The ever-growing body of research in this field is helping us to understand that the gut microbiota is a key regulator of the gut–brain axis. Summarising the findings from the 2016 Neurobiology of Stress Workshop, symposium "The Microbiome: Development, Stress, and Disease" Foster and colleagues remind us that we have *co-evolved* with the microbiota, that we are host to and that we are *"mutually dependent for survival"*. There never has been a time that we have existed without this reciprocal relationship (2017, p. 125). The gut microbes play a crucial role in our stress-related behaviours, regulating changes in physiology, behaviour, and brain function. Your gut–brain axis is also connected through the immune system, and your gut and its microbes play important roles in this connection (Yong, 2023).

Dysregulation of the microbiota influences anxiety and stress behaviours, and in many of these disorders, this dysregulation (also known as dysbiosis) affects the gut, the central nervous system, the immune system, and the HPA axis. It is also important to note that the relationship between the gut and these systems is not unidirectional; stress and emotional states can, in turn, influence the makeup of the gut microbiome. Hormones released during stress may affect bacterial growth and weaken the gut's protective lining, allowing bacteria and toxins to enter the bloodstream, thereby altering the gut microbiota and immunoregulation (Malan-Muller et al., 2017). This can trigger inflammation, which has been linked to a range of psychiatric conditions. Therefore, a person's stomach or intestinal distress can be the cause *or* the product of anxiety, stress, or depression. That's because the brain and the GI system are intimately connected. The job of our stress hormones is to help us to become alert and produce a fight/flight/freeze response. This takes precedence over all other bodily functions, subduing the gut and immune system, lowering your "guard" in respect of these, thus allowing damaging pathogens to be produced. So, when we are stressed, our defences are down, and we become more susceptible to infection and inflammation, leading to greater stress, and a vicious cycle ensues (Anderson et al., 2017).

For us supporting our participants, the important takeaway is that breaking the cycle of stress and gut health will hopefully change the spiral downwards to an upward one, where we can reduce stress and improve gut health. Being out in nature, as we have demonstrated, is researched to do both.

Early Life, Trauma, and the Gut Microbiome

The framework for the enteric nervous system of the gut is laid down in the first and second trimester of pregnancy, but this network has significant modifications in the postnatal period (Green & Ratcliffe, 2024). The birth experience provides the baby with a healthy dose of bacteria; however, the route of delivery will influence the baby's lifelong microbial signature (Foster et al., 2017), while the bacterial signature associated with the route of delivery may influence the newborn's health (Coelho et al., 2021). While caesarean sections have saved many lives and are used routinely and safely, there is growing evidence that the mother's vaginal microbiome in a vaginal delivery sets up the infant with favourable gut flora, which helps to promote the infant's developing immune system (Korpela et al., 2020; Mitchell et al., 2020). When they are squeezed down the birth canal, they are baptised in this bacterial layer even before birth (Anderson et al., 2017, p. 179). The developing infant and toddler further develop their gut biome by crawling on the floor, putting things in their mouths, picking their nose, and playing with their pets. Yong points out that our move to homes away from mud and fields, smaller families, chlorinated water, and sanitised food and a reduction in animals, both pets and livestock, has all impacted our gut biome and the link to allergic and inflammatory diseases (Yong, 2023).

For those of you working with animals, especially animals that are outside or go outside and bring in dirt, use this as encouragement.

The Impact of Adverse Early Experiences in Development

Many of the children we work with have experienced early adverse experiences; in truth, many of the adults using our services have. Interestingly, research is starting to show how children, young people, and adults who have experienced early challenges, or have neurodevelopmental difficulties, may indeed have poorer gut health (Callaghan et al., 2020; O'Mahony et al., 2017). In their review of the literature on early-life adversity, brain development, and microbiome, O'Mahony and colleagues summarised that adversity in both prenatal and postnatal periods significantly impacts the establishment and integrity of the gut microbiota, which in turn influences brain development through the brain–gut–microbiome axis. Prenatal stressors, such as maternal stress, infection, malnutrition, or obesity, can alter the maternal microbiome and potentially impact the baby's gut microbiota

(Mayer, 2016). This, in turn, can lead to long-lasting effects on how the child and later adult deals with stress and increases the risk for anxiety and autism spectrum disorder. They pointed out that it is not just the prenatal impact, but postnatal factors further impact the gut flora, including early-life nutrition (breastfed vs. formula-fed), and maternal separation (O'Mahony et al., 2017).

Researchers have long recognised the close relationship between the digestive system and the brain. Earlier studies have found that for adults diagnosed with irritable bowel syndrome (IBS), a key factor is past experiences of trauma or abuse (Moloney et al., 2016). While the link between trauma and increased risk for both digestive and mental health difficulties is well documented in adults, it has received far less attention in studies involving children (Callaghan et al., 2020).

In their research using data from 344 youth (3–18 years olds) who were raised with their biological parents or were exposed to early adverse caregiving experiences (i.e., institutional or foster care followed by international adoption), Callaghan and colleagues explored the connection between early adversity, anxiety, and GI associations. Young people who experienced disruptions in early caregiving showed clear differences in their gut microbiome compared with those who were raised by their biological parents from birth. Brain imaging further revealed that patterns of neural activity were associated with the presence of specific types of gut bacteria. For instance, children raised in stable parental environments tended to have greater microbial diversity in their digestive systems, which was connected to activity in the prefrontal cortex – an area of the brain involved in emotional regulation. The investigators propose that the brain–gut–microbiome axis is a critical mechanistic pathway through which early adversity affects emotional neurobiology and mental health. The findings suggest that early stress exposure coincides with a sensitive period for the maturation of the brain, the digestive system, and the microbiome, and these differences may persist (Callaghan et al., 2020).

People who experience trauma in childhood have a greater likelihood of developing post-traumatic stress disorder later in life, and the alterations in their gut microbiome may begin early, as a response to that childhood trauma (Labus et al., 2017).

Some researchers suggest that individuals with autism have GI issues (Anderson et al., 2017). Gershon has suggested that serotonin seeping from the second brain might even play some part in autism. He discovered that the same genes involved in synapse formation between neurons in the brain are involved in alimentary synapse formation. "If these genes are affected in autism", he says, "it could explain why so many kids with autism have GI motor abnormalities" in addition to elevated levels of gut-produced serotonin in their blood (Gershon, 1999). A small study of 18 children with autism who also had severe digestive problems found that a faecal transplant to rebalance their gut microbiome reduced both their digestive symptoms and their autism expressions. The improvements persisted during the two-year study follow-up period (Zhang et al., 2023).

Some researchers suggest that up to 60% of individuals with IBS report experiencing significant adverse childhood experiences (ACEs). This figure is consistently supported across different cultural contexts, indicating a universal link between early-life trauma and adult functional GI health, such as inflammatory bowel disease (Alsubaie et al., 2022; Bonaz et al., 2024; Moloney et al., 2016).

Malan-Muller and colleagues, in their 2017 review of the gut microbiome and mental health, conclude that the research into the microbiome and especially gut microbiota is "emerging critical players in mental illness and maintenance of mental health" (p. 76). In depression, they suggest that part of the GI tract becomes compromised due to either psychological or organic stress. A translocation of bacteria occurs and enters the immune system, as well as the enteric nervous system, and increases HPA axis responsivity.

Exposure to stress early in life, for a whole variety of reasons, can change our microbiota compositions, and the microbial populations can change our responsiveness to this stress. With this in mind, we can therefore think about what we can do, both for ourselves and for those we work with, to think about how we can support a different microbiota, and the changes that will support a more healthy gut–brain axis and microbiota to develop.

So how does being out in nature improve gut health and support the multitudes that live within us? Given what we now understand about how indoor environments affect our microbial health (Gilbert & Hartmann, 2024), along with the strong evidence showing how time spent in nature environments benefits our emotional, physical, and overall well-being, it's clear that we need to spend more time outside to build resilience and support healthy regulation.

The Need for a Gut Health Approach

How can we have a gut health approach in our sessions? Our busy lives today mean we often reach for convenience foods that offer fast ways to feel satiated. The problem with these is that they take no account of your gut bacteria and often lead to us being trapped in a cycle of eating "bad mood food", leading to depressive-like behaviours such as despair and anxiety, elevated HPA activity, and increased response to stress (Howard, 2010). Our physiological state dictates the range of behaviour and psychological experience. So where does this take us to…?

Firstly, we can provide our participants with education around the links between gut health and well-being. Anderson et al. (2017) propose the Psychobiotic Food Pyramid, along with other recommendations from The Medicine Doctor, which also offers really helpful advice on simple, healthy ways to look after ourselves. Good mood foods include protein, vegetables, fat, liquids, fruit, and wholegrains. The amounts required depend on age, health, and other factors.

A key part of the Nourish element is us thinking about how we as practitioners can nourish our participants. If we are bringing food and have the training to handle it, can we be thinking about whether it is nutrient-rich food, such as raw and fermented foods, or does it include pre- and probiotics, which are more dense and more filling? For individuals who have had adverse early experiences, neurodevelopmental differences, and sensory processing difficulties such as poor interoceptive awareness, eating these kinds of foods can enhance gut–brain axis function, improve awareness and feedback to this sensory system, and positively impact regulation at a physiological level. Never was it truer that we really are what we eat, a favourite saying of my Dad!

Ways to support better gut health:

- Bacteria are essential to life. Eating pro/prebiotic healing, nutrient-rich foods improves digestion, immune function, mental health, and well-being.
- Fermented foods are a powerful aid to digestion/protection against disease. They are also a powerful source of nourishment for the microbiota.
- Coffee and chocolate are also fermented (beans), and lots of people swear by the psychobiotic effects that these provide!
- The following are fun and satisfying to prepare: milk kefir, sauerkraut, kimchi, sourdough, and kombucha, and they help us use our bodies at the same time, pushing, kneading, and pressing down.

Prebiotics – these are non-digestible food ingredients that promote the growth of certain bacteria. Foods such as artichokes, lentils, beans, onions, garlic, leeks, bananas, and broccoli are all rich in prebiotics.

Probiotics – yoghurt, kefir, kombucha, sourdough bread, and some cheeses. Research indicates that the effects of stress can be reversed by eating foods from this group.

Note: Always seek appropriate advice regarding dietary intake to ensure this is best for your/others' needs.

Nurturing Nature

Planting, tending and growing things can bring such a sense of joy, excitement, and pleasure to our lives. In his essay on why we need gardens, neurologist Oliver Sacks reflects on how in his patients he could notice the restorative effects of being in nature, even for the most neurologically disabled. He suggests that being outside in these environments is more impactful than pharmaceutical interventions (Sacks, 2019).

Growing things that can be eaten, such as tomatoes, herbs, lettuce, and carrots, engages use and development of the senses, through activities such as digging and picking fruit, eating healthily, encourages healthy eating, greater interactions with the environment around them, introduces scientific concepts, supports taking responsibility, and highlights how we can take care of ourselves, others, and the environment.

When we grow things, we have to tend to them, look after them, and water them. This supports our clients to develop a sense of how what they do can have a positive and lasting impact, as well as lead to eating something delicious! Evidence shows that children who grow things tend to eat more healthily. The people you work alongside may also want to grow flowers with beautiful colours and smells, such as chocolate cosmos, plants that are soft to touch, such as lamb's ears, or grand plants such as sunflowers!

Gardening can be a powerful stress reliever for children and adults, as it teaches them to relax, calm down, and manage their emotions. Spending time in nature, amongst flowers and trees, has been proven to support both children and adults to feel happier, emotionally stronger, and more resilient.

We also know that it helps develop patience, improves focus, and enhances memory. In his book, *Last Child in the Woods*, Louv (2008) tells of how parents of children with (attention deficit hyperactivity disorder) ADHD notice significant changes in the stress levels and hyperactivity of their children after being in nature. He coined the phrase "Nature's Ritalin", some definite food for thought here.

According to a Dutch study, working in the garden for just 30 minutes a day significantly reduces cortisol levels (Van Den Berg & Custers, 2011). Lampert et al. (2021) describe how "community gardeners had significantly better health outcomes than their neighbours not engaged in gardening activities in terms of life satisfaction, happiness, general health, mental health, and social cohesion". Therefore, gardening is a perfect activity to introduce to those with whom you work, as it helps keep stress away. Engaging them by asking them what they would like to grow will support their motivation and interest in this incredible opportunity to ground, connect, discover, create, and nourish themselves. A word on children and vegetables … children who grow their own vegetables are more likely to eat them; for many parents, that's definitely something that they would like to happen!

Being engaged in nature, watching things grow, seeing the bugs scuttle about, provides an opportunity to share with children the interconnectedness of life. Sampson (2015) talks about how this connection to nature helps individuals to see how all forms of life are subjects, not objects, things to be admired, cared for, and inspired by. He suggests a lovely activity where we ask the individual to picture every plant and animal in its own sensory bubble, and then imagine its world in this way, for instance, "what do spiders see"? Inviting individuals into the world of nature and all that is in it invites them to be curious, imaginative, and to see how everything in our world is interwoven.

At the secure children's home where I work (Chris), we have developed a regulating garden in partnership with Éadaoin Bhreathnach. I often find I am bringing together EcoSensory Therapy and regulating gardens.

With one young woman who was so hard to reach, so self-protective in her responses, who struggled to let people come near her and feel safe, we went out into the regulating garden space in the secure children's home that I work in. We put up some hammocks and she said to me, Chris why do you love this space so much and I said, because I think it's really nourishing for people in different ways, and she climbed into the hammock and she said "I feel like I've been *sensoried* Chris" with such a level of peace in her voice. And all of these moments in nature, with young people, and with adults, I think really bring that sense of why we nourish those who find it so hard to nourish themselves or to feel nourished by others. How the seemingly simple but complex way that nature does this can enable people to do more of that for themselves.

Foraging in Nature

Many individuals, regardless of age, love the experience of being outside, searching for hidden treasures, whether it's bugs, summer berries, or herbs to make tea tinctures. Things picked can make delicious jellies, leaves for salads, hazelnuts for chocolate spread, or be added to a curry as a superfood, in the case of nettles! Foraging provides so many opportunities to Connect, Discover, Attend, Create, as well as, of course, Nourish.

The Woodland Trust has a really helpful website (www.woodlandtrust.org.uk), giving details about different things to forage for each month of the year, including responsible foraging guidelines.

Always ensure that you are confident that what you have picked is edible. The foragers' rule is to have 100% identification before eating. This means if in doubt, don't eat it! There are some fantastic courses across the United Kingdom and around the world where you can enhance your foraging knowledge and skills.

Foraging Journal

You could encourage clients to keep a journal of things that they have seen. This could be in the form of writing, drawings, or photos. It could include:

- Where they were;
- Who they were with;
- The weather conditions; and
- What they saw.

Humans as Part of Nature

Humans and plants have evolved together, living side by side from the very beginning. Plants create an environment in which we can live, regulating our planet's water and air supply. Nevin Harper et al. (2019) remind us of the importance of accepting our inextricable place within the web of life, and how essential this is for the "preservation and protection of life on this planet" (p. 126). We must recognise the impact of our way of living on the environment around us, and continue to explore how we can nourish it and enable it to continue to flourish. Research shows that when we spend more time out in nature, we show an increase in pro-environmental attitudes and compassion for our environment, shifting us to a more "ecological world view, and increasing our ability to partner with nature in deeper and more complex ways" (Harper et al., 2019, p. 127).

Our Changing World

In our ever-changing world, we also need to support children and adults to be a part of taking responsibility for preserving our unique and special world, to have a sense that we can do something to support environmental preservation. Green education and supporting this concept to protect our planet are developing areas of practice and include supporting individuals in engaging in activities such as allotments, gardens, and woodlands. This is becoming increasingly important worldwide, as climate-related issues grow more pressing and high-profile. Supporting children and adults in understanding this and how they can contribute is an exciting and growing area in our ever-changing world. It is clear from extensive evidence that spending time in green outdoor environments helps both children and adults nurture lifelong positive attitudes about nature and the wider environment (Louv, 2017).

Sampson (2015) helps us to understand that supporting others to engage positively with the natural environment in these ways creates a bond with it, a sense of connection. Creating a sense of caring, rather than fear, about climate change and vanishing environments is suggested as a way to support and encourage protection. Place-based learning is a powerful way to support this by encouraging children and all ages of individuals to spend time in nature. Along with being key to development, the experience of being out in nature is irreplaceable; it can't be simulated on a computer screen, and as Kellert reminds us, "nothing less than the future of our species is at stake in maintaining and, when compromised, restoring this relationship" (Kellert, 2009, p. 101).

How can we as practitioners be mindful of the impact we have on the natural environments we find ourselves in? Especially when we are doing activities such as foraging or any kind of harvesting. Robin Wall Kimmerer (2020), in her popular *Braiding Sweetgrass,* talks of *the Honourable Harvest*, an Indigenous-rooted ethical framework for taking from the land that sees nature's affordances as kin rather than as a commodity. In a world where we humans are extracting and using ever more of the earth's resources, there is an ethical necessity to ensure that, in our EcoSensory sessions, we are mindful of how we use them. The key principles in the Honourable Harvest are: to ask permission before taking; take only what you need (leaving the first and last to ensure regeneration); minimise harm (harvest in a way that allows the plant to thrive); reciprocity (use everything that you take, and give back to the land in gratitude); and share what you have. All guiding principles that could be used in all our resource gathering, whether doing the weekly shop or building our homes.

Nourishing Relationships

Perhaps this chapter has opened your eyes to the hidden and powerful ways that spending time in nature "nourishes" our mind, body, and soul. In holding the EcoSensory Model of Practice in mind, we are reminded that no "element" exists in isolation and no one exists in isolation. We are all connected – to the natural world and to each other. We encourage you to hold on to the simple but transformative power in offering "nourishment" in your sessions with others.

Perhaps you are meeting with someone who finds it hard to look after themselves or has had few experiences of being "nourished" by others. Perhaps they have great skills in nourishing others, but how well do they nourish themselves and accept nourishment from others?

Within your EcoSensory sessions, consider how you might offer "tolerable" nurture and nourishment for those that you support who are within their window of tolerance. Can you be fully present with them, with whatever they bring and wherever they are in their life journey? "Containment" is the process in a therapeutic relationship where the practitioner receives, holds and "makes bearable" the person's raw experiences. Sometimes, just "being together" in nature, without looking to change anything, can be the true agent of change. Perhaps you can facilitate a space for your client where all parts are welcome, and all emotions are allowed?

Summary

Nourishing ourselves, through our relationships with others, immersing ourselves in nature experiences, food, and the spaces around us, is crucial for our physical and emotional well-being. How often do we allow ourselves to just sit, take time with our food, sniff the earth, watch the leaves blow in the trees and be quiet with ourselves? Kabat-Zinn reminds us what an act of self-love it is to find that precious time (2005, p. 86).

It is within the context of a sensory-rich environment, one which feeds all of our senses with rich and diverse information, that we can truly create and develop strong, solid foundations that support our health, regulation, and well-being. Nature is a place to immerse ourselves in and experience all of our senses in such rich and powerful ways. It enhances our sense of self, gives us a sense of mastery, builds our relationships with others, and the world around us. Connecting with the sensory world offers the potential for inexhaustible new discoveries about ourselves and the world around us that provide the richest opportunities to feed our mind, body, and soul.

References

Ackerman, D. (1990). *A natural history of the senses*. Vintage.

Alsubaie, M. A., Alkhalifah, H. A., Ali, A. H., Bahabri, M. A., Alharbi, B. A., & Alfakeh, S. A. (2022). Adverse childhood experiences and their effect on irritable bowel syndrome among Saudi Arabian adults. *Cureus*, *14*(6). https://doi.org/10.7759/cureus.25791

Anderson, S. C., Cryan, J. F., & Dinan, T. (2017). *The psychobiotic revolution: mood, food, and the new science of the gut-brain connection*. National Geographic Books.

Avary, C. G. (2018). *The biophilia effect*. Sounds True.

Bonaz, B., Sinniger, V., & Pellissier, S. (2024). Role of stress and early-life stress in the pathogeny of inflammatory bowel disease. *Frontiers in Neuroscience*, *18*, 1458918. https://doi.org/10.3389/fnins.2024.1458918

Breitmaier, E. (2006). *Terpenes: Flavors, fragrances, pharmaca, pheromones*. John Wiley & Sons. https://play.google.com/store/books/details?id=9HF5JccSn_0C

Breslin, P. A. (2019). *Chemical senses in feeding, belonging, and surviving: Or, are you going to eat that?* https://www.cambridge.org/core/elements/are-you-going-to-eat-that/6DA172022D3D7A78CED8C6EE2F4F4D8F

Breslin, P. A. S. (2013). An evolutionary perspective on food and human taste. *Current Biology*, *23*(9), R409–R418. https://doi.org/10.1016/j.cub.2013.04.010

Callaghan, B. L., Fields, A., Gee, D. G., Gabard-Durnam, L., Caldera, C., Humphreys, K. L., Goff, B., Flannery, J., Telzer, E. H., Shapiro, M., & Tottenham, N. (2020). Mind and gut: Associations between mood and gastrointestinal distress in children exposed to adversity. *Development and Psychopathology*, *32*(1), 309–328. https://doi.org/10.1017/S0954579419000087

Calvi, E., Quassolo, U., Massaia, M., Scandurra, A., D'Aniello, B., & D'Amelio, P. (2020). The scent of emotions: A systematic review of human intra-and interspecific chemical communication of emotions. *Brain and behavior*, *10*(5), e01585.

Coelho, G. D. P., Ayres, L. F. A., & Barreto, D. S. (2021). Acquisition of microbiota according to the type of birth: An integrative review. *Latino-Americana de...* https://www.scielo.br/j/rlae/a/r959F4dwG98qnXMgf3Y8wBb/abstract/?lang=en

Craig, A. D. (2020). *How do You Feel?: An Interoceptive Moment with Your Neurobiological Self*. Princeton University Press. https://play.google.com/store/books/details?id=qvrDDwAAQBAJ

Dawson, S. L., Todd, E., & Ward, A. C. (2025). The interplay of nutrition, the gut microbiota and immunity and its contribution to human disease. *Biomedicines*, *13*(2), 329. https://doi.org/10.3390/biomedicines13020329

Douglas, F. (2020). *The nature remedy*. Harper Collins Publishers Ltd.

Dozmorov, I. M., & Dresser, D. (2010). Immune system as a sensory system. *International Journal of Biomedical Science: IJBS*, *6*(3), 167–175.

Enders, G (2017). *Gut*. Scribe Publications.

Foster, J. A., Rinaman, L., & Cryan, J. F. (2017). Stress and the gut-brain axis: Regulation by the microbiome. *Neurobiology of Stress*, *7*, 124–136.

Gershon, M. D. (1999). The enteric nervous system: A second brain. *Hospital Practice (1995)*, *34*(7), 31–32, 35–38, 41–42 passim. https://doi.org/10.3810/hp.1999.07.153

Gilbert, J. A., & Hartmann, E. M. (2024). The indoors microbiome and human health. *Nature Reviews Microbiology*, *22*, 742–755. https://doi.org/10.1038/s41579-024-01077-3

Green, M., & Ratcliffe, E. M. (2024). Influence of the microbiota on the development and function of the "second brain"—the Enteric nervous system. In *The gut-brain axis* (pp. 95–116). Elsevier. https://doi.org/10.1016/b978-0-323-99971-7.00004-7

Hardman, I. (2020). *The natural health service*. Atlantic Books.

Harper, N., Rose, K., & Segal, D. (2019). *Nature-based therapy. A practitioners guide to working outdoors*. New Society Publishers.

Howard, C. (2010, June 2). Bad-mood foods: Researchers studying importance of diet, mental health. *The State Journal-Register*. https://www.sj-r.com/story/news/2010/06/02/bad-mood-foods-researchers-studying/46193290007/

Kabat-Zinn, J. (2005). *Coming to our senses: Healing ourselves and the world through mindfulness*. Hachette UK.

Kellert, R. (2009). *Reflections on children's experiences of nature* (Vol. 1, No. 2). Children and Nature Network.

Kimmerer, R. W. (2020). *Braiding sweetgrass: Indigenous wisdom, scientific knowledge and the teachings of plants*. Penguin.

Koechlin, F. (2012). Interview mit Florianne Koechlin: Pflazen bilden alllianzen und kommunizieren. In H. Willer (Ed.), *Okologie und Landau 4* (pp. 36–37). Stiftung Ökologie & Landbau (SÖL).

Korpela, K., Helve, O., Kolho, K.-L., Saisto, T., Skogberg, K., Dikareva, E., Stefanovic, V., Salonen, A., Andersson, S., & de Vos, W. M. (2020). Maternal fecal microbiota transplantation in cesarean-born infants rapidly restores normal gut microbial development: A proof-of-concept study. *Cell*, *183*(2), 324–334.e5. https://doi.org/10.1016/j.cell.2020.08.047

Kotte, D., Li, Q., & Shin, W. S. (2019). *International handbook of forest therapy*. Cambridge Scholars Publishing. https://play.google.com/store/books/details?id=a1K3DwAAQBAJ

Kuo, M. (2015). How might contact with nature promote human health? Promising mechanisms and a possible central pathway. *Frontiers in Psychology*, *6*, 1093. https://doi.org/10.3389/fpsyg.2015.01093

Labus, J. S., Hollister, E. B., Jacobs, J., Kirbach, K., Oezguen, N., Gupta, A., Acosta, J., Luna, R. A., Aagaard, K., Versalovic, J., Savidge, T., Hsiao, E., Tillisch, K., & Mayer, E. A. (2017). Differences in gut microbial composition correlate with regional brain volumes in irritable bowel syndrome. *Microbiome*, *5*(49). https://doi.org/10.1186/s40168-017-0260-z

Lampert, T., Costa, J., Santos, O., Sousa, J., Ribeiro, T., & Freire, E. (2021). Evidence on the contribution of community gardens to promote physical and mental health and well-being of non-institutionalized individuals: A systematic review. *PLoS One*. https://doi.org/10.1371/journal.pone.0255621

Li, Q., Kobayashi, M., Wakayama, Y., Inagaki, H., Katsumata, M., Hirata, Y., Hirata, K., Shimizu, T., Kawada, T., Park, B. J., Ohira, T., Kagawa, T., & Miyazaki, Y. (2009). Effect of phytoncide from trees on human natural killer cell function. *International Journal of Immunopathology and Pharmacology, 22*(4), 951–959.

Louv, R. (2008). *Last child in the woods: Saving our children from nature-deficit disorder*. Algonquin books.

Louv, R. (2017). *Vitamin N. The essential guide to a nature rich life*. Atlantic Books.

Malan-Muller, S., Valles-Colomer, M., Raes, J., Lowry, C. A., Seedat, S., & Hemmings, S. M. J. (2017). The gut microbiome and mental health: Implications for anxiety- and trauma-related disorders. *Journal of Integrative Biology*, *21*, 90–101.

Masuo, Y., Satou, T., Takemoto, H., & Koike, K. (2021). Smell and stress response in the brain: Review of the connection between chemistry and neuropharmacology. *Molecules*, *26*(9), 2571.

Mayer, E. (2016). *The mind-gut connection. How the hidden conversation within our bodies impacts our mood*. Harper Wave.

Mitchell, C. M., Mazzoni, C., Hogstrom, L., Bryant, A., Bergerat, A., Cher, A., Pochan, S., Herman, P., Carrigan, M., Sharp, K., Huttenhower, C., Lander, E. S., Vlamakis, H., Xavier, R. J., & Yassour, M. (2020). Delivery mode affects stability of early infant gut microbiota. *Cell Reports. Medicine*, *1*(9), 100156. https://doi.org/10.1016/j.xcrm.2020.100156

Moloney, R. D., Johnson, A. C., O'Mahony, S. M., Dinan, T. G., Greenwood-Van Meerveld, B., & Cryan, J. F. (2016). Stress and the microbiota-gut-brain axis in visceral pain: Relevance to irritable bowel syndrome. *CNS Neuroscience & Therapeutics*, *22*(2), 102–117. https://doi.org/10.1111/cns.12490

Mujica-Parodi, L. R., Strey, H. H., Frederick, B., Savoy, R., Cox, D., Botanov, Y., Tolkunov, D., Rubin, D., & Weber, J. (2009). Chemosensory cues to conspecific emotional stress activate amygdala in humans. *PLoS One*, *4*(7), e6415. https://doi.org/10.1371/journal.pone.0006415

Neff, E. P. (2018). Stop and smell the geosmin. *Lab Animal*, *47*(10), 270–270. https://doi.org/10.1038/s41684-018-0161-1

Nhat Hanh, T. (2014). *How to eat*. Parallax Press.

O'Mahony, S. M., Clarke, G., Dinan, T. G., & Cryan, J. F. (2017). Early-life adversity and brain development: Is the microbiome a missing piece of the puzzle? *Neuroscience*, *342*, 37–54. https://doi.org/10.1016/j.neuroscience.2015.09.068

Ożga, A., Chojacka, B., Bryksy, S., Boba, B., Kolano, P., Przybyłowska, A., Krzeszowiak, J. W., & Podolska. A. (2026). The impact of forest bathing on psychological and physical well-being – Review of current literature. *Annales Academiae Medicae Silesiensis*, *80*, 7–13. https://doi.org/10.18794/aams/211873

Pálsdóttir, A. M., Spendrup, S., Mårtensson, L., & Wendin, K. (2021). Garden smellscape–experiences of plant scents in a nature-based intervention. *Frontiers in psychology*, *12*, 667957.

Ruebush, M. (2009). *Why dirt is good*. Kaplan Trace.

Sacks, O. (2019). *Everything in its place: First loves and last tales*. Picador.

Sampson, S. D. (2015). *How to raise a wild child: The art and science of falling in love with nature*. Houghton Mifflin Harcourt.

Song, C., Ikei, H., & Miyazaki, Y. (2016). Physiological effects of nature therapy: A review of the research in Japan. *International Journal of Environmental Research and Public Health*, *13*(8). https://doi.org/10.3390/ijerph13080781

Vaglio, S. (2009). Chemical communication and mother-infant recognition. *Communicative & Integrative Biology*, *2*(3), 279–281. https://doi.org/10.4161/cib.2.3.8227

Van Den Berg, A. E., & Custers, M. H. G. (2011). Gardening promotes neuroendocrine and affective restoration from stress. *Journal of Health Psychology*, *16*(1), 3–11. https://doi.org/10.1177/1359105310365577

Williams, G. (2017). *Natural space and the human experience*. Routledge.

Yong, E. (2023). *I contain multitudes: The microbes within us and a grander view of life*. Lian Pu Wen Hua/Tsai Fong Books.

Zhang, J., Zhu, G., Wan, L., Liang, Y., Liu, X., Yan, H., Zhang, B., & Yang, G. (2023). Effect of fecal microbiota transplantation in children with autism spectrum disorder: A systematic review. *Frontiers in Psychiatry*, *14*, 1123658. https://doi.org/10.3389/fpsyt.2023.1123658

Chapter 9

Reflect

Chris West

Introduction

In this final EcoSensory Therapy element, we explore the concept of "Reflect". We consider how nature offers us a myriad of opportunities to reflect, the powerful ways in which we might use metaphors in nature, explore spiritual connections, and how we might use these concepts to support greater awareness.

We recognise that we are part of the complex web of life, and that as sentient beings we are connected to everything in the world. We are nature. Throughout all our EcoSensory elements, we have reflected on our interconnectedness with nature, recognising the incredibly powerful impact of this on our very being on this EcoSensory. We are but just one part of a very complex, interrelated organism.

When we were developing and writing EcoSensory Therapy, we recognised the importance and undeniable significance of this, which inspired our model's continuous circle, starting and ending with Ground. Of course, the world is round, with no beginning and no ending, existing in the universe, which is infinite. Think about how the rain waters the tree, the leaves fall and nourish the soil, and the water goes back into the soil, a continuous circle with no beginning and no ending.

Humans as Meaning-Making Beings

To reflect is, in many ways, to be human.

We are not simply organisms moving through the world, reacting to what is around us. We are sentient, meaning-making beings, living not only in the external world but also within an ongoing internal landscape of thought, memory, anticipation, and imagination. Much of our life is not just lived through action, but through interpretation, through the stories we form about what is happening, what has happened, and what might come next.

It is often suggested that we have tens of thousands of thoughts each day. The precise number is less important than what it points to: our inner world is rarely still. A continuous stream of images, sensations, words, and predictions moves through us, shaping how we experience ourselves, others, and the world. From a neuroscientific perspective, the brain is not a passive receiver of reality, but an

DOI: 10.4324/9781003777465-11

active organiser of it, constantly generating models based on prior experience (Clark, 2013). In this sense, we are always, to some degree, living within the interpretations our minds create.

Across human history, storytelling has been one of our primary ways of making sense of this inner and outer world. Long before written language, we gathered around fires, sharing stories to explain the land, the seasons, the stars, and our place within them. Myths, folklore, and cultural narratives, from ancient Greek mythology to the stories passed between generations, have always helped us organise experience into something meaningful. And in many ways, this has not changed. We continue to understand our lives through narrative.

As White and Epston (1990), founders of Narrative Therapy, proposed, people do not simply live their lives; they live through the stories they construct about them. We all do this. We construct stories about who we are, what has shaped us, what things mean, and what lies ahead. These stories shape what we notice, how we feel, what we remember, and how we act (McAdams, 2001). Two people may walk the same woodland path, yet inhabit entirely different worlds within it, shaped by the narratives they carry.

In therapeutic work, this becomes particularly visible. At times, I find myself wondering with clients about the difference between fear and excitement. Physiologically, the body responds in remarkably similar ways: the heart rate increases, breathing quickens, and the body becomes more alert. Yet the meaning attributed to these sensations can differ profoundly. One may say, *"I'm anxious, I'm scared"*, while another might say, *"I'm excited, this is awesome!"* The difference matters, and this difference is about interpretation, and about story.

Working with children and groups in woodland spaces, I often invite curiosity about the "story in the moment", the story being told about themselves, about the task, or about what might happen next. A tree climb or barefoot walk becomes either something to fear or something to explore. A challenge becomes either evidence of failure or an opportunity to grow. Through "reflect", we gain access to notice these narratives, to question them, and, at times, to support our clients to reshape them.

From an evolutionary perspective, this capacity has been essential. The human mind did not evolve simply to register the present moment, but to anticipate, plan, and make sense of complexity. Our ability to step back and reflect on our own thoughts and experiences has supported learning, adaptation, and survival. This capacity is closely associated with what is often referred to as the brain's "default mode network", which is active during self-reflection, autobiographical thinking, and the construction of personal meaning (Raichle et al., 2001).

Yet this same capacity can also become a source of distress.

In my work with young people, I am often struck by how the mind can become a place that feels difficult to escape, a space of repetitive loops of worry, self-criticism, and imagined futures. One young person described this vividly as feeling *"trapped in my own head"*. As we walked together through the woods, their attention began to shift, first to the sound of leaves underfoot, then to the movement of branches overhead, and finally to the task at hand of cooking on the stove. My sense was feeling less trapped, less in their heads, with greater access to "reflect" on internal and external experience rather than being overwhelmed by it.

Reflection, we should say here, is not simply thinking more. It is the capacity to step into awareness of our thoughts, rather than being carried by them. It allows us to notice the narratives we are constructing, to become curious about them, and, where needed, to reshape them. It is the movement from being immersed in experience to being able to observe and make sense of it, a process closely linked to reflective functioning, or mentalising (Fonagy et al., 2002).

And for that, to see what we take for granted, to see our view of the world, we so often need a guide and external support. That can be our role in EcoSensory sessions, to ask questions, to be curious and to bring attention to what we notice with our clients. But nature as co-therapist can also offer this. More on this in a moment when we get to the use and power of metaphors.

One of the things I have consistently noticed in outdoor therapeutic work is the presence of more pauses. More shared silence. Less pressure to speak, to perform, or to fill the space. And within these pauses, I've often found that clients start to notice more, not only what is around them but also what is within them.

Reflective Functioning

To access thinking, reflection, and higher-order cognition, we need to begin with our foundations. In EcoSensory terms, this means Ground, Connect, and Rhythm. From a neurosequential perspective (Perry, 2006), regulation and safety come first. This is why Reflect sits at the top of our model: it depends on what comes before.

In practical terms, this means supporting individuals to remain within their "window of tolerance" (Siegel, 2012), where they are neither overwhelmed nor shut down, but able to engage, think, and reflect. Within EcoSensory work, this is supported through grounding in the present moment, through sensory awareness, movement, rhythm, and connection to the natural environment.

Reflective functioning, or mentalising, refers to our capacity to understand our own and others' mental states, including thoughts, feelings, intentions, and desires (Fonagy et al., 2002). It allows us to make sense of behaviour in terms of underlying experience and is central to how we navigate relationships and the social world. However, this capacity is not constant; it is state-dependent. When individuals move outside of their window of tolerance, the ability to reflect and mentalise reduces. Under threat, we tend to shift away from curiosity and into certainty, reactivity, and more fixed interpretations of ourselves and others.

This is particularly relevant for many of the individuals we work with. For those with experiences of stress, trauma, or relational disruption, reflective functioning may be harder to access, especially in moments of high stress and relational difficulty. What can appear as resistance, avoidance, or rigidity is often better understood as a temporary reduction in the capacity to mentalise, rather than a lack of willingness.

Within EcoSensory work, nature supports the conditions in which reflection can emerge. Natural environments offer regulating, less demanding contexts where attention can settle and broaden. Through sensory engagement, movement, rhythm, and shared presence, individuals are supported to return to a state in which thinking, noticing, and meaning-making become more accessible.

From here, reflection can begin through our support and nature's support. Through gentle curiosity, shared attention, and simple invitations to notice, individuals are able to step alongside their experience rather than be caught within it. One of the most effective ways we support this process within EcoSensory practice is through the use of metaphor. Being able to do this in calming, regulating nature spaces has the potential to support the development of this, so that they might further enhance this skill and the ability to use it in other areas of their life.

Natural Metaphors

Nature is abundant with metaphors, things that help us to reflect and think about the meaning of life, of our place here on earth, and the different possible meanings of our life experiences. We can use them to explore and reflect on the struggles being experienced, and how it helps the individual, enabling them to think "if I can do this, I can do that".

Think back to our very first element, "Ground" (which possibly feels a long time ago now!), and the analogy of a journey. We start all our journeys, walk all our paths and return to earth, all from our own place in the world.

Other metaphors we might use when we are in an EcoSensory session could include crossing a bridge or threshold, and consider how this relates to transitions, such as life transitions, providing a crossing over into a new way of thinking and seeing something, and the possibilities that this affords.

Think back to the research we explored in "Connect" with the fathers and sons, and the little boy's comment on the video about how if they can cope with the challenges they experienced together in the forest, they can cope with the everyday challenges they are experiencing in their relationship when they are away from the forest. Metaphors give a different language, a representation of life's challenges, managing change, and how they can be overcome.

Nature's metaphors can be powerful vehicles to support change, enabling individuals to reflect on how something might resonate with them, how this can facilitate change, and to think about how they might develop, transform, and adapt to different situations and life events.

Metaphors such as growth, decay, and the interconnectedness of this cycle provide new ways for people to think about their lives and new ways to see things. Rivers, as the sustenance of life, forever renew the fertility of land. Like a river, a professional trajectory might have exciting, exhilarating parts and slow more sedate parts.

The majestic oak tree, and its roots under the earth that ground you. The trunk standing tall and strong. The branches that represent different areas of your life, for instance, your relationships, and then the leaves, which could represent different possibilities, or maybe abundance. They soak up the sunshine and feed your soul.

And then there are pathways, pathways in the forest and woods, and the different paths that we might choose to take in life, and where they might take us.

The natural world, and its unpredictable nature, invites clients to "discover their natural selves, to see, hear, and touch the natural world with wonder and intimacy" (Siddons-Heginworth & Nash, 2020, p. 123).

Metaphors can be seen as one of the principal tools and vehicles of change in Reflect. Through metaphorical association, clients are able to transfer insights and accomplishments gained within EcoSensory sessions to their everyday life. Through "mastery and performance-based success" within nature-based settings, this form of therapy uses metaphors to help transfer accomplishments and insights to wider psychosocial challenges in everyday life (Norton et al., 2014; Stevens et al., 2004, p. 279). As Elad et al. (2003, p. 202) recognise in their research of a nature-based expedition with teenagers, "the key to applying coping strategies on the participants' returning home lies in visualizing and finding meaning in the parallels between the adventures and real life".

Another analogy is a spiral staircase. Life is not a running circuit, but a spiral staircase. We're never back at the same spot; every time we complete the circle, we're one level advanced in the cycle of life. We may be looking out at the same terrain, but our vantage point is far higher.

The lotus flower can serve as a meaningful metaphor. In many cultures, particularly in Eastern spiritual traditions, it represents purity, enlightenment, renewal, and the ability to regenerate. The flower is seen as a symbol of rebirth because it emerges from murky waters and unfolds into a striking bloom with soft white and pink petals. Similarly, humans begin from nothing and gradually develop into something graceful and remarkable. This concept of beginnings leads us to thinking about beginnings in life, and how we might use the analogy of nature's beginnings to support those we are working with to think about this, and what it might mean for them.

And so often in sessions, we might share a story as we walk, and offer an analogy from which our client may draw meaning. So let me share a story with you now, an ancient one from ancient times…

Within a field once stood a mighty oak and a willow tree. Each morning, the willow looked on enviously at the power and strength that the oak tree possessed. "How strong you are Mighty Oak and how weak I am to bend to every passing wind", cried the Willow Tree.

One day, a storm like no other passed through the field, whipping winds and torrential rain. The Oak leaned into the wind, pushing against the storm with all its strength and might. The Willow, unable to stand firm, was moved by the winds all night as it was thrown this way and that.

The next morning, the storm had passed, and the Willow shook out its leaves, thankful to be out of the rain. It looked towards the Oak and was overcome with confusion to see it split, lying on the ground before him.

An old Owl, who had seen many storms and lived for many years in the forest, called over to the Willow Tree and offered his wisdom. "The mighty Oak Tree was strong, solid and mighty, of course. It was also rigid and inflexible … It was your flexibility and adaptability that enabled you to bend with the wind and weather the storm". Aesop's moral to this fable is, "It is better to bend than break. There is great strength in flexibility".

In *Rhythm*, we used the metaphor of seasons, considering what season the individual might be in, how this might impact them, what it might mean for them, and how our understanding of this can be used in supporting them through the use of EcoSensory principles and approaches. In Discover, we used the analogy of a compass, considering what direction they might be travelling in, and how understanding this might help us to think about how we might use nature to facilitate this further.

Metaphors serve not just to help conceptualise ideas but also act as a "scaffold" in discussions of change, guiding the exploration of complex therapeutic issues and supporting the restoration of a sense of control. By incorporating an experiential aspect, they allow intense bodily sensations to be processed and integrated, with the metaphor providing a framework for organising personal experiences and rebuilding a sense of agency (Tay & Jordan, 2015).

Within Acceptance and Commitment Therapy (ACT), metaphors are not simply illustrative tools, but central mechanisms of change. Rooted in Relational Frame Theory, ACT proposes that human suffering is often maintained by rigid patterns of language and meaning, the ways in which we relate thoughts, feelings, and experiences to one another (Hayes et al., 2012). Metaphors work by gently loosening these patterns. Rather than arguing with a thought or attempting to replace it, a metaphor shifts the context in which it is held.

For example, when a person describes themselves as "stuck", this can feel absolute and defining. Yet when this experience is explored through a metaphor – such as being caught in thick mud, or standing at a fork in a forest path – there is room for reflection, and in turn, manoeuvre. The experience becomes something that can be observed and responded to, rather than something that simply is. The metaphor introduces flexibility.

Crucially, metaphors are not only cognitive, but they are also embodied and experiential. When working in natural environments, this becomes even more apparent. A client balancing on a fallen log, navigating uneven ground, or pausing at the edge of a river is not just talking about challenge, uncertainty, or transition; they are experiencing it in real time. The metaphor is lived as well as spoken. This integration of bodily sensation and symbolic meaning allows experiences to be processed more deeply, supporting the organisation of personal narratives and the rebuilding of a sense of agency.

In this way, metaphors do more than describe experience; they reshape our relationship to it. They open up space for new meanings to emerge, for alternative perspectives to be considered, and for movement where previously there may have been a sense of being stuck.

Metaphors drawn from nature, as well as the natural elements themselves, provide a broad framework for self-exploration and the integration of bodily experiences linked to past trauma. When incorporated into various therapeutic or personal growth practices, these nature-inspired metaphors can gently highlight unresolved issues or unmet needs, while also suggesting potential ways to address them, ultimately supporting an individual's overall well-being (Răban-Motounu, 2015).

Metaphors also help us to recognise that everything is in flux, developing, transforming, and becoming.

Think of the caterpillar that transforms into a beautiful butterfly that we talked about in Create. This metaphor is often used to help us think about the process of transforming states of consciousness and understanding, from knowing something on the surface, then going through a deeper experience that leads to a whole new perception and way of thinking, and how our awareness and our consciousness change and grow.

Spiritual Connections with Nature

There is a long human tradition of experiencing nature not simply as an environment, but as something alive with meaning, something that we are part of, rather than separate from. Across cultures and throughout history, this sense of connection has often been described in spiritual terms. Whether expressed through Indigenous worldviews, Eastern philosophy, or contemplative traditions, there is a recurring recognition that there is a less clear boundary between the self and the world we inhabit.

In modern therapeutic practice or care settings, spirituality can sometimes feel like a difficult terrain to navigate, uncertain, subjective, and at times avoided altogether. Yet when approached with care, humility, and respect for individual belief systems, it can offer a powerful dimension to therapeutic work. What matters is not imposing a particular worldview, but creating space for individuals to explore their own sense of connection, meaning, and place in the world.

Within EcoSensory Therapy, nature provides an accessible pathway into this exploration.

Spending time in natural environments, whether walking through woodland, sitting in a park, or pausing beside water, often evokes a shift in perspective. The primacy of the self can feel less, and there is, at times, access to a sense of being part of something larger, something ongoing.

In practice, this might be as simple as inviting someone to notice more deeply. Not just to look at a tree, but to take a moment to consider its age, its rootedness, its relationship to the soil, the light, and the seasons. To imagine, briefly, what it might be like to be that tree, steady, enduring, shaped by time. Or to observe a bird moving through the space, attuned to its environment in ways we have long since lost.

In Eastern contemplative traditions, there is often an emphasis on dissolving the rigid boundaries of the self, recognising that what we experience as a separate "I" is, in many ways, part of a wider, interconnected system. Similarly, in psychological terms, we might understand this as a shift away from rigid self-referential processing towards a more expansive, less self-centred awareness. Contemporary research on awe and self-transcendent experience suggests that encounters with vastness, often found in nature, can reduce self-focused attention and increase a sense of connection to something larger than oneself (Keltner & Haidt, 2003; Monroy & Keltner, 2023). Experiences of awe, connection, and perspective can reduce the intensity of self-focused distress, allowing individuals to step outside of habitual patterns of thought and emotion.

This connects closely with contemporary psychological frameworks such as the Power Threat Meaning model (Johnstone & Boyle, 2018), which invites us to understand distress not as disorder, but as a meaningful response to life experiences. From this perspective, reconnecting with nature can support individuals in re-evaluating the meanings they have constructed, not by removing difficulty, but by situating it within a broader context. A problem that once felt all-consuming may, in the presence of something vast or enduring, begin to shift in scale.

Ethically, it is important that this space remains invitational. Not everyone will resonate with spiritual language, and it is not necessary that they do. The role of the practitioner is not to lead someone towards a particular belief, but to remain open, curious, and responsive to what emerges for them. For some, this may be a deeply spiritual experience. For others, it may simply be a sense of calm, connection, or perspective. Both are equally valid.

What is consistent, however, is that nature offers a context in which these experiences *can* arise, if that should be helpful for the needs of the individual or group you're working with.

So, we encourage you to find moments to pause, moments to connect with the natural world, and to allow the possibilities of reflection.

In practice, this can be uncomplicated. It might look like sitting together in the woods, allowing space for quiet, and noticing what comes. It may be walking side by side, where conversation ebbs and flows, and moments of reflection arise naturally when we're short of breath. It might be taking time to pause at a tree, a path, or lying suspended in a tree hammock, and offering a wondering, *"What are you noticing right now?"*, *"What does this bring up for you?"*, *"Does this connect to anything in your life?"* At times, it may be saying very little at all, trusting that the environment and the experience itself are already doing much of the work.

Developing a Sense of Self: Awareness

The concept of "dwelling within awareness" is hard to grasp, and certainly took me a while to comprehend. Awareness itself becomes an entity, something that, if only momentarily, we can reside in. A place with no centre and no boundary, as boundless as space itself. We have spoken of awareness in the *Attend* chapter and again about flow in the *Create* chapter. Awareness itself has its own special *atmosphere*, as David Abram states in *Becoming Animal*; he speaks of how it expands and shrinks, inside us, and surrounding us (2010). We find ourselves unable to get any distance from awareness, to examine it objectively, for wherever we step, it is already there. Another interesting way to think about dissociation might be to consider how it functions to enable us to fall out of awareness, maybe.

It is this concept of awareness that is the cornerstone of many eco therapies and mindfulness training. That to be able to "dwell in awareness" will in some way help us and support healing. In a study by Pischel et al. (2025), they invited psychotherapists to support the development of awareness in those they were working with by working to reflect on where they see those they are working with, and to integrate therapy into outdoor spaces. The results indicated how those they were working with felt a greater sense of connection, which has the potential to enhance awareness and a greater capacity for reflective functioning.

The senses, as we have already learned, developed to protect and nourish the organism. By their very evolution, our senses developed to be self-centred to allow us to survive. For each organism, they developed differently, specifically for that species. Humans learned to rely on vision and sound, dogs on smell, and bats on echolocation. Even within a species, each individual will process sensory information differently. To some of us, that smell is too strong; to others it is attractive. If the processing of our senses differs, then so must our perception of the world. What one person sees as safe, another may see as dangerous.

Is our awareness the reality? We know the planet spins around the sun; however, we are happy to refer to the sun rising in the East and setting in the West. We cannot see the Earth spinning, but we do see the sun rising. In our view, the information from our senses becomes our truth, and our awareness radiates from our viewing.

When we look at the world from our preoccupied point of view, we lack the capacity to see how it could seem different to others. We are blindsided by our subjective viewpoint, unable to see the full scope of reality, even when it is impacting our lives. Our viewpoint is personal; we are the seer, the feeler, the knower, the thinker, and we cannot help but take things personally.

There are moments, glimmers, when we suddenly see the world from someone else's perspective; we feel their emotions, we have empathy, and we suspend our point of view for a moment. It is in those moments that we "dwell in awareness".

While much of our awareness is focused on the human world, our interactions with others of our species, David Abram in his book *The Spell of the Sensuous* (2012), reminds us that our mind, our sentience and awareness have also been shaped by the other "earthly powers" (p. 158). That our ability to stop, ponder, and reflect has arisen out of our interplay with nature. Abram describes how thought develops from our curiosity, which leads on from our need to survive – arriving at a dried-out river bed, when we are thirsty, drives us to think – how else can we quench our thirst? It is our drive to protect and nourish ourselves and our offspring that tuned our awareness to the potential for food, or danger, and further developed our ability to think and mentalise. In our modern world, we lack awareness of these rhythms; we rarely hunt or go hungry, and this further pushes us to a self-centric view of the universe.

Natural spaces offer individuals the opportunity to explore what Selhub and Logan (2012) refer to as the liminal phase. This is known as a suspended state of partial knowing, which is activated in natural spaces. During this phase, a person integrates, discards, and experiences an ontological shift, and then experiences transformation, known as a post-liminal phase. Once the individual is in the liminal space, they experience a sense of calm and mastery. Immersion in nature can lead to a transformative way of knowing and understanding the self.

Reflecting on the EcoSensory Therapy Elements

In our Introduction, we explored where we came from, our journey into the world millions of years ago, and how we have evolved and adapted in an ever-changing world.

Think back to our Ground element, and the importance of being present in order to support others to do this, and how grounding ourselves helps us, and those we are working with, to do this.

Connect where we explored self-regulation, co-regulation, and connection with ourselves, others, and nature, and the ways that we have explored this, throughout many of our elements.

It may be that you have reflected on your EcoSensory journey, physically, spiritually, emotionally, and on those you have perhaps been on the journey with, colleagues, and clients. I know I have reflected on the journey of creating and developing this with Claire and Matt, the time we have spent together exploring, discussing, and reflecting. It has been such a rich experience; we have connected through our love and passion for nature, and all that this means to each of us.

In *Attend,* we considered the concept of attention, how our senses developed, how we attend with our different senses, and how this links to our awareness of ourselves, of others, and of consciousness.

Create provided an opportunity to look at creating and how we evolved to be such a creative species. We considered why we create, the evolution of creativity, and how we develop to be creative as individuals. We looked at models of creativity, and in particular looked at the triad of creativity: Cognition, Skill, and Motivation. Finally, we looked at creating in relation to health, the links between creativity and mental health, and how "doing" and "creating" can be so healing.

Nourish gave the opportunity to explore the powerful way in which nature nourishes us, physically, emotionally, and spiritually, feeding our bodies and souls in so many rich and powerful ways.

And now to *Reflect*, and an exploration of what this may mean for you, and for the individuals you are working with. Taking time to reflect on this will be important as you go forward in your EcoSensory journey, and the journey of those you walk alongside, considering where it might take you, and where you will take those who walk alongside you.

References

Abram, D. (2010). *Becoming animal: An earthly cosmology*. Pantheon Books.

Abram, D. (2012). *The spell of the sensuous: Perception and language in a more-than-human world*. Vintage.

Clark, A. (2013). Whatever next? Predictive brains, situated agents, and the future of cognitive science. *Behavioral and Brain Sciences, 36*(3), 181–204.

Elad, P., Yagil, Y., Cohen, L., & Meller, I. (2003). Jeep trip with young adult cancer survivors: Lessons to be learned. *Supportive Care in Cancer*, *11*, 201–206. https://doi.org/10.1007/S00520-002-0426-4

Fonagy, P., Gergely, G., & Jurist, E. L. (2002). *Affect regulation, mentalization, and the development of the self*. Other Press.

Hayes, S. C., Strosahl, K. D., & Wilson, K. G. (2012). *Acceptance and commitment therapy: The process and practice of mindful Change*. American Psychological Association.

Johnstone, L., Boyle, M., Cromby, J., Dillon, J., Harper, D., Kinderman, P., ... & Read, J. (2018, March). The power threat meaning framework: Overview. Leicester: British Psychological Society.

Keltner, D., & Haidt, J. (2003). Approaching awe, a moral, spiritual, and aesthetic emotion. *Cognition and Emotion, 17*(2), 297–314.

McAdams, D. P. (2001). The psychology of life stories. *Review of General Psychology, 5*(2), 100–122. https://doi.org/10.1037/1089-2680.5.2.100

Monroy, M., & Keltner, D. (2023). Awe as a pathway to mental and physical health. *Perspectives on Psychological Science, 18*(2), 309-320.

Norton, C. L., Tucker, A. R., Russell, K., Norton, C. L., Tucker, A. R., Russell, K., Bettmann, J. E., Gass, M. A., Hillis, H. L., & Behrens, E. (2014). Adventure therapy with youth. *Journal of Experiential Education*, *37*(1), 46–59. https://doi.org/10.1177/1053825913518895

Perry, B. D., & Szalavitz, M. (2006). *The boy who was raised as a dog*. Basic Books.

Pischel, M., Wüster, A. L., Metz, K., Wulf, H., Lahmann, C., & Pfeifer, E. (2025). They talk the talk and walk the walk: Psychotherapists' experiences of psychotherapy while walking in nature. *Counselling and Psychotherapy Research*, *25*(3), e70035.

Răban-Motounu, N. (2015). Metaphors inspired from nature use for self-exploration and personal development. *Current Trends in Natural Sciences*, *4*(8), 106–109.

Raichle, M. E., MacLeod, A. M., Snyder, A. Z., Powers, W. J., Gusnard, D. A., & Shulman, G. L. (2001). A default mode of brain function. *PNAS, 98*, 676–682.

Selhub, E. M., & Logan, A. C. (2012). *Your brain on nature*. John Wiley & Sons Canada.

Siddons-Heginworth, I., & Nash, G. (Eds.). (2020). *Environmental arts therapy. The wild frontiers of the heart*. Routledge.

Siegel, D. J. (2012). *The developing mind: How relationships and the brain interact to shape who we are* (2nd ed.). Guilford Press.

Stevens, B., Kagan, S., Yamada, J., Epstein, I., Beamer, M., Bilodeau, M., & Baruchel, S. (2004). Adventure therapy for adolescents with cancer. *Pediatric Blood & Cancer*, *43*, 278–284. https://doi.org/10.1002/pbc.20060

Tay, D., & Jordan, J. (2015). Metaphor and the notion of control in trauma talk. *Text & Talk*, *35*(4), 553–573. https://doi.org/10.1515/text-2015–0009

White, M., & Epston, D. (1990). *Narrative means to therapeutic ends*. W. W. Norton.

Closing Reflections

Matt Slavin

As we reach the end of this book, we would like to pause for a moment and return to the spirit in which it began. When Claire first welcomed you into these pages, our intention was to share something of the thinking, experience, and practice that has grown into what we now call EcoSensory Therapy. Throughout these chapters, we have explored our evolutionary relationship with the natural world. We have travelled through the elements of Ground, Connect, Rhythm, Discover, Attend, Create, Nourish, and Reflect, each one offering a different lens through which to understand how people regulate, learn, relate, and grow.

Our hope is that as you have moved through these chapters you have begun to see how nature can support thoughtful practice in many ways: how grounding begins with the body and the present moment, and how readily this becomes possible in the natural world where we can quite literally touch the ground beneath our feet; how connection grows through shared attention and relationship, with ourselves, with others, and with the natural world around us; how rhythm emerges through movement, time, and the seasons, and how spending time with someone outdoors allows us to notice and work with their rhythms of energy, regulation, and engagement; how curiosity and discovery are sparked through exploration and the presence of risk; why attending on purpose in the world we evolved within is so important; how creativity unfolds through making, building, and working with the affordances of nature; how we can nourish ourselves, others, and the natural world we inhabit; and how reflection arises through shared experiences outdoors.

If there is one thing we hope this book offers, it is confidence. You do not need elaborate equipment or complicated programmes to begin working in nature. Often the most meaningful moments come through the simplest experiences: walking slowly through woodland, noticing sounds carried on the air, feeling the ground beneath bare feet, building something together from branches, or sharing food beside a fire. What matters most is the thoughtfulness and intention we bring to these moments.

As we send this book out into the world and into your hands, we are reminded of one of our favourite things to do in nature: to pick up a small stone and cast it into the stillness of a pond. We watch it touch the water and see the ripples

DOI: 10.4324/9781003777465-12

spread outward, travelling far beyond where the stone first fell. Each time, we are reminded how far even a small impact can reach.

In many ways, we see this book as such a small stone. If the ideas within these pages encourage even a small shift – a practitioner stepping outdoors with greater confidence, a therapist noticing the sensory foundations of regulation, a teacher or support worker recognising the power of nature in development – then we will find ourselves staring in awe at the beauty of those ripples.

And if even one person reconnects with the natural world, feels inspired to step outside, or begins to work with the sensory richness of nature, then we will feel a profound sense of wonder, knowing that something small we have placed into the water has travelled further than we could have ever imagined.

And if, as you close this book, you find that those ripples lead you to want to explore this approach more deeply, then our EcoSensory training pathway is there to support you on that journey. We will be waiting with open arms, ready to welcome you into the next chapter of the work, and eager to see where the ripples take you.

Index

For Product Safety Concerns and Information please contact our
EU representative GPSR@taylorandfrancis.com Taylor & Francis
Verlag GmbH, Kaufingerstraße 24, 80331 München, Germany